More advance praise for
Investment Mistakes Even Smart Investors Make and How to Avoid Them

The truism that investments perform better than investors has long since been fully confirmed. Part of the reason is that the costs of investing over the long term are confiscatory—Wall Street wins; investors lose. The other part is that the behavior of investors—notably investors in mutual funds—is so counterproductive. They are too often their own worst enemies, making foolish mistake after foolish mistake. Larry Swedroe's wonderful new book lists fully 77 of the worst of these commonplace errors. (I agree with nearly all of the author's warnings; in fact, I might even add a few of those on my own list!) Using *Investment Mistakes* . . . as your checklist, you cannot help but improve your share of the financial market returns to which you are entitled.

—John C. Bogle, Founder, The Vanguard Group

While always spot on, most of Larry's books to date have been about the overwhelming evidence that investors shoot themselves in the foot. In this book he and RC Balaban delve much deeper into why the shots are fired to begin with. Together the body of work forms a nearly complete picture of how and why investors avoid passive investing and cost themselves trillions. As a money manager who hopes they continue in these erroneous practices, I can only beg Larry and RC to halt publication immediately.

—Cliff Asness, Ph.D, Founding and Managing
Principal, AQR Capital Management

Swedroe and Balaban use their unique ability to demystify what it is that so often makes "smart" people do dumb things as investors. Unfortunately for these investors, the authors have isolated 77 types of common investing mistakes. Thus, the odds of these investors being successful are indeed small. But, the authors come to the rescue by providing the simpler path for successful investing that avoids the common types of investing mistakes.

—John A. Haslem, Professor Emeritus of Finance at the
University of Maryland, and editor of *Mutual Funds: Portfolio
Structures, Analysis, Management, and Stewardship*

In this, his eleventh book, Larry and coauthor RC identify and discuss 77 investing mistakes and provide guidance to help you avoid them. Knowledge is power, and this book is filled with helpful information. Read it and reap!

—Mel Lindauer, *Forbes* columnist and coauthor of
The Bogleheads' Guide to Investing and
The Bogleheads' Guide to Retirement Planning

Swedroe and RC Balaban have identified 77 common mistakes that investors make. In clear and concise language readers learn details of each mistake and why it is a mistake. In my opinion, this book deserves a place on every investor's bookshelf.

—Taylor Larimore, coauthor of
The Bogleheads' Guide to Investing

Many people don't know what they don't know, which is why they are often their own worst enemies when it comes to investing. The authors show all investors—both smart and not so smart—in a series of short lessons how to avoid 77 investment mistakes commonly made by them. These lessons have particular relevance and value now with world financial markets in turmoil. All investors—yes, even those who think they know it all—will benefit enormously from reading this absorbing and timely book.

—W. Scott Simon, JD, CFP, AIFA, author of
The Prudent Investor Act: A Guide to Understanding,
and columnist, *Morningstar's Fiduciary Focus*

Swedroe and Balaban provide sage advice through a series of simple stories. As an endowed professor of investments, my investment philosophy is based on four decades of academic and professional research, both my own and others. My philosophy mirrors their advice because they both embody this research. I encourage you to buy and read this book and follow its advice. It will make you a better investor.

—Dr. William Reichenstein, CFA,
Pat and Thomas R. Powers Chair in Investment Management,
Baylor University, Hankamer School of Business

Compelling logic, practical wisdom, and memorable quotes. A sound strategy for finding and adhering to your sweet spot on the efficient frontier between risk and expected return.

So much of what goes wrong with our investment choices is self-inflicted through ill-conceived investment ideas and practices. Not only is this a valuable resource for both novice and experienced investors, it is also highly readable and even entertaining.

The most "sure fire" way to improve investment results is to sidestep the multitude of ways to destroy value. Swedroe and Balaban take the reader on a journey well informed by behavioral finance, the developing field of financial planning, evidence- based investing, and stories of actual investors to give the reader a road map to confident wealth building.

It is unlikely that any investor will make all 77 mistakes outlined in this book. But almost everyone is guilty of making at least a few of them, and it takes only a handful of uninformed or irrational decisions to do serious damage to a retirement nest egg. By showing us the dozens of ways investors can penalize themselves, Swedroe and Balaban reveal why so many investors without a simple and sustainable investment plan meet with disappointment.

Investment Mistakes Even Smart Investors Make and How to Avoid Them

Investment Mistakes Even Smart Investors Make and How to Avoid Them

Larry E. Swedroe

RC Balaban

New York   Chicago   San Francisco   Lisbon   London
Madrid   Mexico City   Milan   New Delhi
San Juan   Seoul   Singapore
Sydney   Toronto

1 2 3 4 5 6 7 8 9 0   DOC/DOC   1 6 5 4 3 2 1

ISBN   978-0-07-178682-9
MHID   0-07-178682-1

e-ISBN   978-0-07-178683-6
e-MHID   0-07-178683-X

This publication is designed to provide accurate and authoritative information in regard to the subject matter covered. It is sold with the understanding that neither the author nor the publisher is engaged in rendering legal, accounting, securities trading, or other professional service. If legal advice or other expert assistance is required, the services of a competent professional person should be sought.

—*From a Declaration of Principles Jointly Adopted*
by a Committee of the American Bar Association
and a Committee of Publishers and Associations

Library of Congress Cataloging-in-Publication Data
Swedroe, Larry E.
  Investment mistakes even smart investors make and how to avoid them by
/ Larry Swedroe.
     p. cm.
  Includes bibliographical references and index.
  ISBN-13: 978-0-07-178682-9 (alk. paper)
  ISBN-10: 0-07-178682-1 (alk. paper)
  1. Investments. 2. Investments—Psychological aspects. 3. Investment
analysis. I. Title.
  HG4521.S898   2012
  332.6—dc23

                                                        2011033678

McGraw-Hill books are available at special quantity discounts to use as premiums and sales promotions or for use in corporate training programs. To contact a representative, please e-mail us at bulksales@mcgraw-hill.com.

This book is printed on acid-free paper.

CONTENTS

FOREWORD

I n investing, it simply isn't enough to understand how markets work, how to properly allocate a portfolio, and how to choose proper investment vehicles. We must also understand how our natural human tendencies and behaviors affect our investment decisions. The field of behavioral finance helps us to understand this relationship, which in turn helps investors become better investors, better able to carry out their plans.

Larry Swedroe and RC Balaban provide a list of 77 investment mistakes our behaviors cause—directly or indirectly. For instance, they teach us to beware of overconfidence that tempts us into misguided attempts to beat the market. Much of over-confidence comes from faulty framing. When I am tempted to beat the market by buying particular stocks touted by men and women on television programs, I ask myself, "Who is the idiot on the other side of the trade? If I'm buying because the stocks are sure to go up, who is the idiot who is selling?" In every trade there is an idiot, and the idiots are likely to be individual investors who are hard pressed to bear the cost of their idiocy.

Our behaviors also cause us to tend to frame trading as tennis games played against practice walls, when in reality trading is tennis played against opponents on the other side of the net, perhaps insiders or hedge fund managers, or those lightning-speed computer systems that return the tennis ball to our side of the court faster than we can hit it back. These opponents aren't just regular opponents, but might as well be opponents who combine the top skills of other top tennis players.

Well, you might say, if hedge fund managers beat the market, why not hire them to manage our money? This would be a good idea if hedge fund managers were our generous uncles, willing to manage our money at no cost. Alas, in reality, we bear management costs and are likely to carry less than nothing once hedge fund managers take their 2 percent plus 20 percent of profits. Swedroe and Balaban teach us to consider trading costs before we trade and consider management costs before we place our money in the hands of managers who promise to beat the market by more than the cost they impose on us.

The debate about the efficiency of investment markets will persist long after you read this book. The ambitious definition of efficient markets is their definition as rational markets, where security prices always equal intrinsic values. The modest definition of efficient markets is their definition as unbeatable markets. Bubbles cannot occur in rational markets, but they can occur in unbeatable markets. There is much evidence that markets are not rational. The prices of houses are sometimes in bubbles, deviating from their intrinsic values, and the prices of stocks are often in bubbles. But the fact that markets are not rational does not imply that they are easily beatable any more than the fact that markets are crazy implies that we are all psychiatrists. The dot-com market was crazy, but investors who attempted to beat it by selling short dot-com stocks lost money unless their liquidity lasted longer than the craziness of the dot-com market. And bubbles are seen much more clearly in hindsight than in foresight. Some investors did see the 2008 crisis in foresight, mostly those who were intimately involved in mortgage and banking markets. But did all investors who sold their stocks in October 2007 remember to buy them back in March 2009? Hindsight opens the door to regret. We kick ourselves for being so stupid as not to sell our stocks in October 2007 or buy them back in March 2009.

Lessons are easier to teach than to learn, but we are intelligent people, able to learn. After all, we have learned that the earth is round even though it still looks pretty flat in our eyes. Still, we have to combat our cognitive errors and misleading emotions every day. I highly recommend this book for helping with those combative efforts when it comes to investing. I hope that readers of this book would thank Swedroe and Balaban for teaching us 77 good lessons about avoiding 77 mistakes. And I hope that they would not have to wait years for the gratitude they deserve today.

—Meir Statman

PREFACE

> If you want to see the greatest threat to your financial
> future, go home and take a look in the mirror.
> —Jonathan Clements
> *Wall Street Journal*, April 27, 1998

One of the great tragedies is that despite its obvious importance to every individual, our education system almost totally ignores the field of finance and investments. This is true unless you go to an undergraduate business school or pursue an MBA in finance. Eighteenth-century English poet Thomas Gray wrote, "Where ignorance is bliss, 'tis folly to be wise." When it comes to investing, ignorance is not bliss—it pays to be wise. Just ask the investors who lost an estimated $50 billion in the Bernard Madoff scandal. Without the basic understanding of how capital markets work, there is no way that individuals can make prudent investment decisions.

While the massive losses suffered by those caught in the Madoff scandal were a tragedy, perhaps an even greater tragedy is that there are so many investors who think they know how markets work—but the reality is quite different. As humorist Josh Billings noted, "It ain't what a man don't know as makes him a fool, but what he does know as ain't so." The result is that individuals are making investments without the basic knowledge required to understand the implications of their decisions. It is as if they took a trip to a place they had never been with neither a road map nor directions.

Lacking a formal education in finance, most investors make decisions based on the accepted *conventional wisdom*—ideas that have become so ingrained that few individuals question them. Unfortunately, much of what is conventional wisdom on investing is wrong. The result is that investors make many mistakes, often with disastrous results.

During Larry's roughly 15 years as a principal and director of research at the Buckingham Family of Financial Services, he has witnessed investors make many costly mistakes. These mistakes were made for a variety of reasons. Some were made simply because investors are human beings, prone to behavioral errors. For example, individuals have a strong tendency to be overconfident of their skills. And overconfidence can lead to many errors, including excessive risk taking.

Some investors also made mistakes because they were ignorant of the facts. You can be ignorant about lots of things (such as nuclear physics) and get through life quite well. However, it is much harder to successfully get through life being ignorant about investing.

We hope that by providing you with the knowledge contained in this work, you will avoid the most common mistakes investors make, learn the winning investment strategy, and reach your financial and life goals. This book is about making you an informed investor. Your investment performance should improve as you become aware of how vulnerable you are to your own psychology and as you come to understand how behavioral mistakes can cause you to stray from proven investment principles. Understanding just how powerful psychological forces can be may help you to control them. At the very least, being armed with as much information as possible should improve your odds of success. If we are successful, the time and money you spent on this book will be the best investment you ever made.

One of our favorite expressions is: "If you think education is expensive, try ignorance." We hope this book will whet your appetite for a deeper understanding of the issues raised and create a desire to broaden your knowledge. If you find this book both entertaining and educational and wish to learn more, Larry has authored a quartet of the "Only Investment Guides You'll Ever Need." The first, *The Only Guide to a Winning Investment Strategy You'll Ever Need*, focuses on equities. The second, on bonds, is *The Only Guide to a Winning Bond Strategy You'll Ever Need* (coauthored with Joe Hempen). The third is *The Only Guide to Alternative*

Investments You'll Ever Need (coauthored with Jared Kizer). And the fourth is *The Only Guide You'll Ever Need for the Right Financial Plan* (coauthored with Kevin Grogan and Tiya Lim).

Larry's other books include *What Wall Street Doesn't Want You to Know, The Successful Investor Today, Rational Investing in Irrational Times, Wise Investing Made Simple, Wise Investing Made Simpler,* and *The Quest for Alpha.*

As you read this book, keep the following in mind: Even smart people make mistakes. That is what makes us human. However, once smart people learn that a behavior is a mistake, they neither repeat nor perpetuate that mistake. That is the behavior of fools. Einstein put it this way: "The definition of insanity is doing the same thing over and over and expecting different results."

In this business there are 50 ways to screw up.
If you're a genius, you can think of 25 of
them, and you ain't no genius.
—*Body Heat* (the movie)

Only two things are infinite, the universe and human
stupidity, and I'm not sure about the former.
—Albert Einstein

Investment Mistakes Even Smart Investors Make and How to Avoid Them

PART 1

Understanding and Controlling Human Behavior Is Important for Investment Success

We have met the enemy and he is us.
—Pogo

MISTAKE 1

Are You Overconfident of Your Skills?

People exaggerate their own skills. They are optimistic
about their prospects and overconfident about their
guesses, including which managers to pick.
—Richard Thaler

Jonathan Burton, in his book *Investment Titans*, invited his
readers to ask themselves the following questions:

› Am I better than average in getting along with people?
› Am I a better-than-average driver?

Burton noted that if you are like the average person, you probably answered yes to both questions. In fact, studies typically
find that about 90 percent of respondents answer positively to
those types of questions. Obviously, 90 percent of the population cannot be better than average in getting along with others,
and 90 percent of the population cannot be better-than-average
drivers.

While, by definition, only half the people can be better than
average at getting along with people, and only half the people
can be better-than-average drivers, most people believe they are
above average. Overconfidence in our abilities may in some ways
be a healthy attribute. It makes us feel good about ourselves,
creating a positive framework with which to get through life's
experiences. Unfortunately, being overconfident of our investment skills can lead to investment mistakes.

The following illustrates this effect. A survey of investors
about expectations of returns found they persistently forecasted
that their portfolios would outperform the market.[1]

Forecasts of Market Returns versus Forecasts of Investor Returns

	MARKET	INVESTOR'S PORTFOLIO
June 1998	13.4%	15.2%
February 2000	15.2%	16.7%
September 2001	6.3%	7.9%

Another great example is a February 1998 survey by Montgomery Asset Management. It found that 74 percent of investors interviewed expected their funds to consistently outperform the market.[2] It is simply impossible for the average investor to beat the market since investors collectively are the market. The logic is inescapable: the average investor must, by definition, earn market rates of return, less the expenses of his or her efforts.

In a *New York Times* article, Professors Richard Thaler and Robert J. Shiller noted that individual investors and money managers persist in their belief that they are endowed with more and better information than others and that they can profit by picking stocks.[3] This insight helps explain why individual investors believe they can

> Pick stocks that will outperform the market
> Time the market so they're in when it is rising and out when it is falling
> Identify the few active managers who will beat their respective benchmarks

Even when individuals think that it is hard to beat the market, they are confident they themselves can be successful. Here is what the noted economist Peter Bernstein had to say: "Active management is extraordinarily difficult, because there are so many knowledgeable investors and information does move so fast. The market is hard to beat. There are a lot of smart people trying to do the same thing. Nobody's saying that it's easy. But possible? Yes."[4] That slim possibility keeps hope alive. Overconfidence leads investors to believe they will be one of the few who succeed.

Remember that to profit from the market's mistakes, either you must have information the market doesn't have (and remember, if it is inside information, you cannot legally trade on it), or you must interpret the information better than the collective wisdom of the market. Obviously, not everyone can be above average in doing so. And to beat the market, you must be well above average since you incur expenses in the effort.

Let's take a look at some further evidence on investor overconfidence. Brad Barber and Terrance Odean have done a series of studies on investor behavior and performance. The following is a list of their main findings:

> Individual investors underperform appropriate benchmarks.[5]
> Though the stock selections of women do not outperform those of men, women produce higher net returns due to lower turnover (lower trading costs). Also, married men outperform single men.[6] The obvious explanation is that single men do not have the benefit of the spouse's sage counsel to temper their overconfidence. It appears that a common characteristic of human behavior is that, on average, men have confidence in skills they don't have, while women simply know better.
> Individuals who traded the most (presumably due to misplaced confidence) produced the lowest net returns.[7]

Overconfidence causes investors to see other people's decisions as the result of mood, feelings, intuition, and emotion. Of course, they see their own decisions resulting from objective and rational thought. Overconfidence also causes investors to seek only evidence confirming their own views and ignore contradicting evidence. The late John Liscio, respected veteran bond reporter and founder of the Liscio Report, put it this way:

Forecasters, by definition, are biased and untrustworthy recorders of current economic events. In other words, they tend to uncover evidence that supports their forecasts, and they ignore or analytically dismiss anything that challenges it. And, even if the headline data appear to contradict their disclosure of the universe, they will undoubtedly uncover some statistic or extenuating circumstance that dovetails neatly with their worldview.[8]

Examining the results of the Mensa (a high-IQ society) investment club provides an amusing bit of evidence on overconfidence. If any people deserve to be confident of their skills, it seems logical to believe that it should be the members of this group. Yet the June 2001 issue of *SmartMoney* reported that the Mensa investment club returned just 2.5 percent over the previous 15 years, underperforming the S&P 500 Index by almost 13 percent per year. Warren Smith, an investor for 35 years, reported that his original investment of $5,300 had turned into $9,300. A similar investment in the S&P 500 Index would have produced almost $300,000. One investor described his strategy as buy low, sell lower.[9] The Mensa members were overconfident that their superior intellectual skills could be translated into superior investment returns.

Wall Street Journal columnist Jonathan Clements made the following observation: "Beat the market? The idea is ludicrous. Very few investors manage to beat the market. But in an astonishing triumph of hope over experience, millions of investors keep trying."[10] Overconfidence helps explain this triumph of hope over experience. Investors may even recognize the difficulty of the task, and yet they still believe they can succeed with a high degree of probability. As author and personal finance journalist James Smalhout put it, "Psychologists have long documented the tendency of Homo sapiens to overrate his own abilities and prospects for success. This is particularly true of the subspecies that invests in stocks and, accordingly, tends to overtrade."[11]

Recognizing our limited ability to predict the future is an important ingredient of the winning investment strategy. Being aware of the tendency toward overconfidence, you can avoid the mistake of trying to outperform the market. Meir Statman, a finance professor at Santa Clara University, provided the following advice on how to avoid the mistake of overconfidence: "Start keeping a diary. Write down every time you are convinced the market is going to go up or down. After a few years, you will realize that your insights are worth nothing. Once you realize that, it becomes much easier to float on that ocean we call the market."[12]

Do You Project Recent Trends Indefinitely into the Future?

We've found people tend to buy what has done well recently. But, in fact, studies have shown that they cost themselves money with poorly timed purchases and sales.

—Scott Cooley
Analyst at Morningstar, *St. Louis Post-Dispatch*, February 11, 1999

As we age, our long-term memory skills tend to remain strong, while our short-term memory skills erode. Unfortunately, individuals don't benefit from that tendency when it comes to investing. It seems to be a simple human failing to fall prey to *recency*—the tendency to give too much weight to recent experience and ignore long-term historical evidence. This leads to being overconfident (a mistake we have already identified) and to treating the unlikely as impossible (a mistake we will discuss later).

Consider the following example. From 1990 through 2002, the S&P 500 Index outperformed the MSCI EAFE (Europe, Australasia, and Far East) Index by 8.5 percent per year (9.7 versus 1.2). Why would you invest internationally when you can invest all your money safely in the United States? This led many investors to avoid international stocks. Then from 2003 through 2009, the MSCI EAFE outperformed the S&P 500 by 3.7 percent per year (10.4 versus 6.7).

More recent examples of this phenomenon are the rushes by investors into commodities and into emerging market (especially China) funds *after* the spectacular returns from 2003 through 2007. In 2008, investors fled as quickly as they entered.

Perhaps the best examples of the dangers of recency are provided by the following studies. Morningstar tracked the performance of the least popular fund categories from 1987 through 2000. It defined popularity by the amount of cash flowing into or out (redemptions) of funds. The least popular funds are those receiving the least amount of inflow or experiencing the most amount of outflow. As it turns out, the three least popular categories of funds have beaten the average fund 75 percent of the time, and more amazingly, they have beaten the most popular funds 90 percent of the time.[1]

The Financial Research Corporation looked at fund flows following the best and the worst four quarters for each of Morningstar's 48 investment categories. What Financial Research found is that investors follow a consistent pattern of buying high and selling low—not exactly a prescription for investment success. In the quarters following high returns, an average of $91 billion in net new cash flowed into funds—investors bought high. On the other hand, after the worst-performing quarters, cash inflows dropped to just $6.5 billion—investors missed out on the opportunity to buy when investments were on sale.[2]

Also consider that during the great bull market of 2009 and through almost all of 2010, investors were pulling money out of U.S. equity funds.

The Cost of Performance Chasing

The returns reported by mutual funds are called *time-weighted returns* (TWRs), which assume a single investment at the beginning of a period and measure the growth or loss of market value to the end of that period. This is what we can call investment returns. Investors, however, earn *dollar-weighted returns* (DWRs) that are impacted by the timing of additions and withdrawals. This is what we can call *investor* returns. And as you will see, the DWRs can differ greatly from the reported TWRs.

Morningstar analysts studied the performance of mutual funds and their investors and found that the returns earned by investors were below the returns of the funds themselves in all 17 fund categories they examined. For example, among large-cap growth funds, the 10-year annualized DWR was 3.4 percent less than the TWR. For mid-cap growth and small-cap growth funds, the underperformance was 2.5 and 3.0 percent, respectively. Even value investors fared poorly, though their underperformance was not as severe. Large-cap value investors underperformed the funds they invested in by 0.4 percent per year, and small-cap value investors underperformed by 2.0 percent per year.[3]

We also have evidence from a study done by the Bogle Financial Markets Center. The sample consisted of the 200 funds with the largest cash inflows for the five-year period 1996 through 2000. The TWRs of the funds and the DWRs of investors in those funds were compared for the 10-year period 1996 through 2005. The average TWR for the 200 mutual funds was 8.9 percent per year. However, the actual DWR earned by investors was just 2.4 percent per year, a gap of 6.5 percent per year. The study also found the TWR exceeded the DWR in all but two of the 200 funds—and there was not a single case where the DWR exceeded the TWR by more than 0.5 percent. Even more shocking was that in the case of 76 funds, the cumulative shortfall ranged from –50 percent to –95 percent.[4]

Even index fund investors are subject to recency. We can see the evidence of this from a Morningstar study that covered the 10-year period ending in 2005. The TWR of no-load index funds was 8.9 percent, 1.8 percent greater than the 7.1 percent DWR earned by investors in these funds.[5]

Summary

Falling prey to recency means trying to buy yesterday's returns. You have to keep in mind that you can only buy tomorrow's returns. This problem can be avoided by ignoring the media, the financial press, and "expert" advice from Wall Street urging you to act on the mistaken assumption that somehow this time it's different. Before jumping on any bandwagon, check the long-term historical evidence and the logic of the conclusions (and watch out for overconfidence). Those who do jump on the bandwagon are likely to be found abandoning it in the near future.

MISTAKE 3

Do You Believe Events Are More Predictable After the Fact Than Before?

There is an old saying that on Monday morning we all make great quarterbacks. With the benefit of hindsight, the right play to call and the winning strategy are always obvious. Unfortunately, it seems to be a human failing that we are either unable or unwilling to recall what our beliefs were before the events actually occurred. We have a tendency to exaggerate our pre-event estimate of the probability of an event occurring. This *hindsight bias* may lead us to believe that events even the "experts" failed to foresee were not only painfully obvious but also possibly inevitable. Every day we hear after-the-fact analysis explaining market moves in a way that sounds as if an event were predictable. To demonstrate that this phenomenon is a result of hindsight bias, consider the following:

In the 21 years from 1990 through 2010, the S&P 500 Index outperformed an index of Japanese large-cap stocks by 10 percent per year (8.5 versus –1.5). Although many investors may believe that it was easy to foresee this occurring, let's see just how obvious it actually was.

It's 1989. Japanese asset prices are rising rapidly. The Nikkei is at 40,000, having risen almost 500 percent for the decade, and no top is in sight. Land values have risen so high, the land under the Imperial Palace is worth more than all the real estate in California. The Japanese "managed capitalism" model, with a few government officials deciding how capital will be allocated, is the envy of the world, a model other countries should adopt. Japan is running huge budget and trade surpluses. On the other hand, the United States is running huge budget deficits, the economy is growing slowly, and the market is about to fall again in 1990. Sony's cofounder Akio Morita states:

America no longer makes things; it only takes pleasure in making profits from moving money around. America is by no means lacking in technology. But it does lack the creativity to apply new technologies commercially. This, I believe, is America's biggest problem. On the other hand, it is Japan's strongest point. America assuredly faces gradual decline.[1]

Of course, the world turned out to be quite a different place from what most experts were predicting. At the start of 2011, the Nikkei Index was still down almost 75 percent.

Summary

Hindsight bias is dangerous. It causes investors to recall their successes but not their failures. It also causes investors to believe that investment outcomes are far more predicable than they actually are. Meir Statman put it this way: "Hindsight bias makes it easy to believe not only the future is preordained, but that anyone with half a brain could have seen it."[2]

Hindsight bias promotes both overconfidence and a perception that investing entails less risk than it actually does. This mistake can be avoided by remembering that stock market returns are unpredictable. The best solution to the unpredictability of the market is to build a globally diversified portfolio of index and passive asset class funds that reflects your unique ability, willingness, and need to take risk. Finally, take the advice of columnist Jason Zweig: "Whenever some analyst seems to know what he's talking about, remember that pigs will fly before he'll ever release a full list of his past forecasts, including the bloopers."[3]

MISTAKE 4

Do You Extrapolate from Small Samples and Trust Your Intuition?

People often draw faulty conclusions from information. One reason is that they mistakenly trust their intuition. Another reason is that the information may be complicated. When information involves investment decisions, mistakes in judgment can be costly. A Hebrew University psychologist, Amos Tversky, tried the following experiment in human behavior:

> Imagine that two bags are filled—out of sight—with the same number of poker chips. Bag A has two-thirds chips that are white and one-third that are red. In bag B the proportions are reversed. Your task is to guess which is the bag with mostly red chips. From bag A you are allowed to withdraw only 5 chips, 4 of which turn out to be red. From bag B you are allowed to withdraw 30 chips, 20 of which turn out to be red. Which bag would you guess has the most red chips?[1]

If you are like most people, you would probably guess bag A, since 80 percent of the chips you withdrew were red, versus just 67 percent from bag B. However, statistics tell us that you are more likely to be right if you chose bag B. The reason is that because the sample size from bag B is much larger, you have more confidence in the result. Statistical theory tells us that the 20-out-of-30 bag is more likely to be the bag with more red chips than the 4-out-of-5 bag.

What does this have to do with investing? Like those guessing bag A, investors often make decisions based on small samples. For example, from 1996 through 1998, growth stocks outperformed value stocks, and large-cap stocks outperformed small-cap stocks. The S&P 500 Index rose 28.3 percent per year and outperformed the DFA Micro Cap Fund, the DFA Small Value Fund, and the DFA Large Value Fund by 18.1 percent, 12.8 percent, and 8.5

percent per year, respectively. The press and airwaves were filled with gurus stating that investors should avoid those "lousy" small-cap and value stocks, as they were obviously poor investments. Small-cap and value funds experienced outflows of funds, and large-cap growth funds experienced inflows.

Think of the period from 1996 to 1998 as bag A, from which you were only able to draw a small sample, one with few observations. Think of the 73 years of data for which information on equity markets was available as bag B. While large-cap and growth stocks outperformed during that 3-year period (which can seem like a long time while you're in it), over the longer term we know that small-cap stocks outperformed large-cap stocks and value stocks outperformed growth stocks. From 1927 to 2010, while the S&P 500 rose 9.9 percent per year, the asset classes of small cap, small-cap value, and large-cap value rose 12.0, 15.0, and 11.7 percent, respectively.

Investors ignoring the much larger data set are making the same mistake as those who chose bag A on the basis of a small sample: They trust their intuition that the small sample is representative of the entire data set. The only difference between the two is that choosing bag A didn't cause you to lose any money. Basing investment decisions on small samples can lead to costly outcomes, particularly if a small and probably recent data series causes you to abandon a well-designed investment strategy.

A powerful illustration of incorrectly basing investment decisions on small data sets is the following tale. Every investor knows that stocks provide higher expected returns than bank certificates of deposit. However, for the 25-year period from 1966 to 1990, riskless one-month bank CDs outperformed large-cap growth stocks. If after 25 long years you abandoned your strategy of investing in the asset class of equities with higher respected returns and switched to bank CDs, you would have missed one of the greatest bull markets in history. Despite that lesson, some investors are all too willing to abandon their investment strategies based on much shorter-term results—often on just a few months of data, let alone just a few years.

It appears that making irrational decisions based on short-term results is an all-too-human pattern of behavior that affects a large number of investors. You can avoid the mistake of relying on small samples of data by making sure your decisions are based on long-term historical evidence, not on short-term data.

MISTAKE 5

Do You Let Your Ego Dominate the Decision-Making Process?

Behavioral finance is a fascinating field, taking what psychologists have learned about human behavior and applying it to investing. The insights provided by behavioralists help explain why investors act the way they do, sometimes in what appears to be irrational ways. The financial journalist Jonathan Clements put it this way: "When it comes to investing, we're a bunch of irrational, inconsistent, neurotic wimps."[1] One insight from the field of psychology is that individuals allow their egos to influence their investment decisions, leading to costly errors. Let's briefly explore some of the ways in which egos can get in the way of rational decision making.

There is a tremendous body of evidence showing that the vast majority of actively managed funds underperform their benchmarks, and the longer the time frame, the greater the likelihood of underperformance. While a few active funds do manage to beat their benchmarks, even an organization like Morningstar, with its extensive resources, has admitted that its star ratings have no predictive value for future performance. (They are very good, of course, at "predicting" past performance.) Therefore, what logic is there for you to believe you can forecast which of the few actively managed funds that outperformed in the past will continue to do so? Consider that the only ways you can be successful where Morningstar, and all other such rating services and newsletters, has failed is either to use a different system or to interpret the data differently and more correctly.

If you are going to use past performance to predict the future winners, the evidence is strong that your approach is likely to fail. What other way is there to identify future winners? Faced with the facts, some individuals are even willing to admit that it is very hard to identify such future winners. Their egos, however, lead them to conclude that somehow they will succeed where others fail. They thus end up playing a loser's game, where the odds of winning are so low that they are better off not playing.

Listen to Edward C. Johnson III, chairman of Fidelity Advisors: "I can't believe that the great mass of investors are going to be satisfied with just receiving average returns. The name of the game is to be the best."[2] This is what a typical investment advisor's pitch might be when confronted with an investor who asks about investing in index funds: "If you index [passively invest], you will get average rates of return. You don't want to be average, do you? Don't you think you can do better than that?" Both stockbrokers and Edward Johnson are appealing to the need to be "better than average." Listen carefully once again to Jonathan Clements: "It's the big lie that, repeated often enough, is eventually accepted as truth. You can beat the market. Trounce the averages. Outpace the index. Beat the street. An entire industry strokes this fantasy."[3]

The mistake Wall Street wants you to make is to fail to understand that by simply earning *market* returns, you will earn *greater* after-tax returns than the *average* investor. The reason is that the average actively managed fund underperforms its benchmark by well over 1 percent per year on a pretax basis and by far more on an after-tax basis. In addition, as you have seen from the studies on *investment* returns (TWRs) versus *investor* returns (DWRs), the active management of portfolios by individuals produces another substantial negative impact. In other words, by being a passive investor and earning *market* returns, you will likely outperform the average investor, including professional investors. The best way to be above average is not to play Wall Street's game of active investing.

The need to protect their ego also helps explain why individuals choose to invest in actively managed funds instead of passive investment vehicles. If the active manager they chose beats the benchmark, the investors take credit for being smart enough to choose the manager. If the manager underperforms, the manager gets the blame and is fired. From the ego's perspective, it is an "I win–I don't lose" game. If investors choose a passively managed investment vehicle, they have no one to blame except themselves. This becomes an "I win–I lose" game. The ego prefers not to play a game it might lose.

The same I win–I don't lose game applies to stock picking. If the stocks that individuals choose outperform, they take the credit. If the stocks underperform, the investors blame the broker, publication, or guru that recommended the stock. The ego is protected in either case.

Summary

You can avoid costly investment mistakes by not letting your ego enter into the investment decision-making process. As John Bogle, the founder of Vanguard, put it, "The realistic epitome of investment success is to realize the highest possible portion of the market returns earned in the financial asset class in which you invest—the stock market, the bond market, or the money market—recognizing and accepting that that portion will be less than 100 percent."[4] The best way to accomplish that objective is to invest in passively managed and tax-managed funds. Bogle notes they will be "a vast improvement over the 85 percent or so that the typical mutual fund has provided."[5]

MISTAKE 6

Do You Allow Yourself to Be Influenced by a Herd Mentality?

Sober nations have all at once become desperate gamblers, and risked almost their existence upon the turn of a piece of paper. . . . Men, it has been well said, think in herds; it will be seen that they go mad in herds, while they only recover their senses slowly, and one by one.

—Charles MacKay
*Extraordinary Popular Delusions
and the Madness of Crowds,* 1841

Psychologists have long known that individuals allow themselves to be influenced by the herd mentality, or the "madness of crowds," as Charles MacKay described it back in the 1840s. The herd mentality may be defined as a desire to be like others, to be part of the "action" or "scene."

Unfortunately, when it comes to investing, perfectly rational people can be influenced by a herd mentality. The potential for large financial rewards plays on the human emotions of greed and envy. However, allowing your investment decisions to be influenced by the madness of crowds can have a devastating impact on your financial statement.

Investing, especially in speculative assets, has become much more of a social activity. Today, investors often spend many of their nonworking hours online, reading, discussing, or simply gossiping about their investments. Of course, they discuss their successes with far greater frequency than they do their losses—contrary to the cliché that misery loves company. How can this be destructive to your financial health? Let's see.

Influenced by the herds, investors start betting huge sums on investments they know little or nothing about (perhaps can't even spell) or would not have even previously considered. If a particular madness lasts long enough, even very conservative investors may abandon long-held beliefs—feeling they have missed out on what the crowd deems "easy money" or a sure thing. They forget basic principles such as risk and reward and the value of diversification.

Thankfully, it's not a frequent occurrence, but bubbles do seem to appear with regularity. Certainly, the recent housing bubble comes to mind for many, but we're also only a few years removed from the technology (or dot-com) bubble. Going back a little further, we had a "tronics" bubble in the 1960s, when any stock with *-tronics* as a suffix soared to heights never even imagined. There have been enough manias that several wonderful books have been written on the subject. To avoid repeating mistakes of the past, you may consider reading Robert Shiller's *Irrational Exuberance*, Edward Chancellor's *Devil Take the Hindmost*, and Charles MacKay's *Extraordinary Popular Delusions and the Madness of Crowds*. MacKay's book is particularly noteworthy as it was written in 1841.

In his book, Shiller makes the strong case that mass psychology may at times be the dominant cause of stock price movements. While the market is very rational over the long term, for short periods it can become quite irrational. The "madness of crowds" takes over, and a new "conventional wisdom" is quickly formed. MacKay put it this way: "Every age has its peculiar folly: some scheme, project, or fantasy into which it plunges, spurred on by the love of gain, the necessity of excitement, or the force of imitation."[1] Sir Isaac Newton was reported to have said about the investment mania of his day, the South Seas Company, "I can calculate the motions of heavenly bodies, but not the madness of people."[2]

Shiller argues that "anyone taken as an individual is tolerably sensible and reasonable—as a member of a crowd, he at once becomes a blockhead."[3] In mass, blockheads can play a major role in the stock market. What are known as positive feedback loops lead to self-fulfilling prophecies—in the short term. Buying attracts more buying, and prices go up simply because they are going up. Buoyed by rising prices, investors become more confident, enticing more money into the market. Like a Ponzi scheme, the strategy works until it no longer works. Herding can create bubbles and, unfortunately, the devastating impact that results from the bursting of those bubbles. Let's see just how devastating the impact can be.

The twentieth century witnessed four periods when price-to-earnings (P/E) ratios reached historically lofty levels. The first occurred at the turn of the century. Prices had exploded as real earnings growth boomed. Corporate profits had doubled over the previous five years. The future was certainly optimistic, fueled by the dawning of a new era—a high-tech future. Sound familiar? The coincidence is almost eerie. What actually occurred? By June 1920, the stock market lost 67 percent of its real June 1901 value.

The second occurrence of lofty valuations occurred in 1929 after a spectacular bull market had sent P/E ratios far above previous peaks. By June 1932, the market had fallen more than 80 percent in real terms.

The third instance occurred in 1966. P/E ratios soared to levels reached only in the two previous "bubbles." By December 1974, real stock prices fell 56 percent and would not return to their January 1966 level until May 1992.

The fourth bubble reached its peak in March 2000 when the NASDAQ crossed the 5,000 level. Caught up in the mania of a high-tech revolution, investors had driven price-to-earnings ratios to heights never seen before. By March 2001, the NASDAQ had fallen 70 percent, its greatest drop ever.

How do we explain what Federal Reserve Chairman Alan Greenspan called the "irrational exuberance" of investors? Investors influenced by the herd can console themselves that if they are proved to be wrong, at least they are wrong along with everyone else. The consequences, both professionally and for one's own self-esteem, are far less than if you are wrong and alone in your choice of action. There is safety in numbers. This may help explain why even so-called professionals get caught in the herd.

Unfortunately, for rational investors who are able to resist the madness of crowds, there does not seem to be a systematic way to profit from manias. The reason is that there is no way to predict just how irrational prices might get. Burton Malkiel, professor of economics at Princeton University, put it this way: "We know in retrospect that stock prices tend to overreact and valuations revert to the mean. But it's never possible to know in advance when the reversion will occur. Even bubbles are only clear in retrospect."[4]

Understanding human behavior in combination with having the discipline to avoid the temptation of following the crowd and the noise of the moment is an important part of the winning investment strategy. Perhaps it is hard for human beings to stand still when all those around us are taking action, even when we know it is in our best interests to do nothing. The keys to staying disciplined, and avoiding becoming "irrationally exuberant," are

> Having a thorough understanding of how markets work. Bubbles inevitably burst since valuations cannot be justified by any likely economic assumptions. Always remember that while stock valuation is not a science, stocks are nothing more than financial instruments whose values are based on future earnings. Knowledge is power.

> Having a well-designed road map to achieving your financial goals. The road map, in the form of an investment policy statement, including a rebalancing table, will help to keep you from taking "scenic tours" of interesting investments best avoided.

> Having an understanding of how human behavior can impact investment decisions. Remember Anatole France's warning: "If fifty million people say a foolish a thing, it is still a foolish thing."

MISTAKE 7

Do You Confuse
Skill and Luck?

Investors attribute successes to their own brilliance, and
they attribute failures to bad luck. If you keep doing
that, at the end of the day you think you're a genius.
—Nicholas Barberis
Wall Street Journal, February 4, 2001

Imagine the following scenario: 10,000 individuals are gathered
together to participate in a contest. A coin will be tossed, and
they must guess whether it will come up heads or tails. Anyone
who correctly guesses the outcome of 10 consecutive tosses will be
declared a winner and will receive the coveted title of "coin-tossing
guru." Statistically, we can expect that after the first toss, 5,000 participants will have guessed right and 5,000 guessed wrong. After
the second round, the remaining participants will be expected to
be 2,500, and so on. After 10 repetitions we would expect to have
10 remaining participants who would have guessed correctly all
10 times and earned their guru status. What probability would
you attach to the likelihood that those 10 gurus would win the
next coin-toss competition? Would you bet they would win? The
answers are obvious. What does this have to do with investing?

Today, there are about as many mutual funds as there are
stocks. With so many active managers trying to win, statistics
alone dictate that some will succeed. However, beating the market is a zero-sum game—that is, since all stocks must be owned
by someone, for every active manager who outperforms the market, there must be one who underperforms. Therefore, the odds
of any specific manager being successful are at best 50-50 (before
considering the higher expenses of active managers). Using our
coin-toss analogy, we would expect that randomly half the active

managers would outperform in any one year, about one in four to outperform two years in a row, about one in eight to do so three years in a row, and so on. Yet far fewer actively managed funds outperform than would be randomly expected.

While no one would use the results of our coin-tossing contest to predict the next winner, a manager who beats the index for even one year is instantly accorded guru status, complete with write-ups in financial publications and appearances on CNBC. There is an old saying that even a blind squirrel will on occasion find a nut. Since there is no evidence of any persistence in fund performance beyond the randomly expected and there is no way to predict the future winners, investors appear to be interpreting the *accidental success* (picking a stock or mutual fund manager that outperforms) to be the result of skill. Investors make the similar mistake of interpreting *accidental failure* to be the result of bad luck.

The October 8, 2001, issue of *BusinessWeek* included a perfect example of the phenomenon of being fooled by randomness. The article, titled "Chicks' Picks Come Home to Roost," was a mea culpa by reporter Toddi Gutner. A year earlier she had written a column about the "Chicks laying nest eggs"—10 female friends and relatives using the Internet to run an investment club. Their portfolio had beaten the S&P 500 Index by 30 percent for the period October 1998 through September 2000. Instead of attributing this to randomness, the author gave them guru status—"have proved to be no financial birdbrains." The author never questioned that it might have been randomness. Instead, it had to be skill. The reason it had to be skill is that if it were a random event, there would be no story. The Chicks went on to publish a book imparting their wisdom, *Chicks Laying Nest Eggs: How 10 Skirts Beat the Pants Off Wall Street . . . and How You Can Too.*

To Gutner's credit, she admitted in her column that she might have been the birdbrain. She reported that the Chicks' portfolio had lost 35 percent from its inception nearly three years earlier through September 17, 2001. Compare this with a loss of just 16 percent for the S&P 500.[1]

You can avoid the mistake of confusing skill with luck by checking to see if an outcome is statistically significant or if it is more likely to have been a random, and therefore unpredictable, occurrence. In addition, you should make sure there is logic supporting the conclusion.

Do You Avoid Passive Investing Because You Sense a Loss of Control?

As they begin their investment journey, investors using mutual funds can choose one of two paths. They can choose either actively managed funds or passively managed vehicles such as index funds and exchange-traded funds (ETFs). The evidence is clear that the vast majority of individual investors would improve their outcomes if they adopted the passive strategy, and yet most investors choose the active path.

An important factor in this choice is that investors feel they are somehow in control with actively managed funds. Wall Street firms' understanding of this psychology is reflected in their advertisements for online trading espousing the "you're in control" theme. On the other hand, these same investors feel that passive investing involves a sense of loss of control over the risks and returns of their portfolios. Passive investors simply build diversified portfolios of passively managed funds, index funds, or ETFs that reflect their unique ability, willingness, and need to take risk, and then they rebalance when the market's moves have caused their portfolios to drift out of balance. The sense is the market, not the investor, is "in control."

It's a very human trait to want to take control and do something. Although using actively managed funds and actively managing their portfolios are strategies that give investors a sense of control, the reality is completely different. You simply need the right pair of looking glasses to have the correct perspective.

Financial economists have found that almost all investment returns are determined by a portfolio's exposure to three risk factors: equities, size (small versus large), and value (growth versus value). When fixed-income instruments are in the portfolio, then the determinants include the maturity (or more correctly the duration) and credit quality of the fixed-income assets. The problem is that when investors choose actively managed funds to build their portfolios, they cede control over the determinants of return to fund managers. Active managers try to time the market and select which stocks will outperform. If an active manager believes that a bear market will arrive, the fund will sell stocks and buy Treasury bills or possibly even sell stocks short. A small-cap fund might decide to buy large-cap stocks, a value fund might decide to buy growth stocks, and a domestic fund might decide to buy international stocks. These types of changes are called *style drift*, and it is style drift that causes investors to lose control over their asset allocation and thus the risk and reward of their portfolio.

Because investors in passively managed funds never have to worry about style drift, they retain complete control over the risks and rewards of their portfolio. By understanding that the efforts of active managers to select stocks and time the market have little impact on a portfolio's returns, you can avoid the mistake of using actively managed funds to provide yourself with a false sense of control.

We need to cover one other "take-control" strategy: the purchase by investors of individual stocks instead of actively managed funds. This strategy would seem to be the ultimate in controlling your own portfolio. However, in pursuing this course, you create two problems. First, you likely cannot achieve the extensive diversification that the use of mutual funds accomplishes. Second, the evidence tells us that investors who select their own stocks underperform appropriate benchmarks by significant margins. If you are considering taking control by buying individual stocks, you would do yourself a great service if you first consider whether your objective is to take control or to earn the greatest possible return for the risks you are willing to accept.

MISTAKE 9

Do You Avoid Admitting Your Investment Mistakes?

The average individual is highly risk averse. For example, studies have found that to entice the average person to accept an even-money bet (such as a coin toss), you must offer the person at least 2-to-1 odds. Studies have also found that the pain of a loss is at least twice as great as the joy we feel from an equivalent-sized gain. These behavioral traits lead to an investment mistake called *regret avoidance*, which could be simply described as refusing to admit mistakes.

Indeed, we seem to be hardwired to avoid admitting mistakes. Consider the following example from Karen Schulz, author of *Being Wrong*. Her friend Elizabeth got into an argument about whether Orion was a summer or winter constellation. She was absolutely convinced that Orion was a summer constellation, even though it was December and the two were standing outside looking at Orion. "I was so damned determined that I figured it was some sort of crazy astronomical phenomenon. My logic was something like, 'Well, everyone knows that every 52 years, Orion appears for 18 months straight.'" (For the record, it doesn't, and Elizabeth eventually paid up on her bet.)

Admitting investment mistakes is no easier. Most people have a natural tendency to avoid admitting when an investing decision didn't turn out as planned. This causes them to hold on to securities that have losses, because they can maintain the illusion that it is only a theoretical loss until it is realized. The act of selling would be viewed as an admission they had made an error. This perception, plus the amount of mental pain involved when losses are realized, causes investors to be reluctant to sell. How many times have you said to yourself or heard others say, "I will sell it when it gets back to what I paid for it"?

Avoiding the facts, however, doesn't change them. Regret avoidance leads to two investment mistakes. The first mistake is holding on to an asset until it recovers. What you paid for the security should have no bearing (except for the tax consideration) on whether you should continue to hold it. The right question to ask is: If I did not own any amount of a particular stock, would I buy any at the current price to fit my portfolio? If the answer is no, then you should sell it, because every day that you continue to own the security at current prices, you are effectively making a decision to buy it.

As Carol Tavris and Elliot Aronson, authors of *Mistakes Were Made (but Not by Me)*, note: "A richer understanding of how and why our minds work as they do is the first step toward breaking the self-justification habit. And that, in turn, requires us to be more mindful of our behavior and the reasons for our choices. It takes time, self-reflection, and willingness." But it's worth it because as Tavris and Aronson note, "If you can admit a mistake when it is the size of an acorn, it is easier to repair than when it has become the size of a tree, with deep, wide-ranging roots."

The second mistake caused by regret avoidance is missing the opportunity to harvest losses for tax purposes. If the loss is short term, the tax deduction obtained with the loss will be at the higher ordinary income tax rate, rather than the lower long-term capital gains rate. Harvesting the loss allows you to offset other gains in the portfolio, thereby reducing your tax bill.

If the asset with an unrealized loss still fits within the overall strategic asset allocation of the portfolio, one of two options should be considered when selling the stock or mutual fund. The first option is to simply sell the security and repurchase it after 31 days. This allows you to avoid the wash sale rule, which states that repurchasing the same or a substantially similar security within 30 days causes the two trades to be considered a wash, rendering the loss nondeductible. The other strategy is to swap the asset for a similar (but not substantially identical) security, such as buying an S&P 500 Index fund after selling a Russell 1000 fund. The two funds should perform very similarly.

You can prevent the paralysis induced by regret avoidance by remembering that tax-managing a portfolio is a very important part of the investment process. While we all would like to only have winners in our portfolio, realizing losses to obtain the tax benefit is part of the winning strategy. Once the loss is realized, you are less likely to make the mistake of buying the same security again if it no longer fits into your overall portfolio plan. If the losing asset is not in a taxable account, then the sell decision should be made as part of a regular portfolio review. Remember to ask yourself whether the asset still fits within the overall plan and if you would buy it today if you didn't currently own it.

MISTAKE 10

Do You Pay Attention to the "Experts"?

We rely on the advice of experts in many areas of everyday life. Nutritionists tell us to eat more fruits and vegetables and avoid heavily processed food. Fitness trainers tell us to get at least 30 minutes of exercise three times a week. You name the area of life—parenting, work, school, and so on—and there's no shortage of people offering advice on what you should (and if they're really pushy, must) do.

Investing is no different. CNBC keeps its airwaves filled with talking heads telling you what you should invest in or avoid. Financial publications have so-called experts predicting the directions of everything from the stock market to interest rates to the economy. As with most experts, you have to know when the advice is good and when it is harmful. And the evidence shows that listening to and acting on predictions from market gurus will most likely hurt your portfolio.

Many investors have seen their portfolios devastated despite having followed the advice of experts. They are left to wonder, "What went wrong?" (As Jim Cramer famously said to John Stewart of the *Daily Show*, "I got a lot wrong.") The answer is that the strategy of following the advice of "future tellers" disguised as experts is the wrong strategy. As investment legend Warren Buffett put it, "A prediction about the direction of the stock market tells you nothing about where stocks are headed, but a whole lot about the person doing the predicting."

David Freedman, in his outstanding book *Wrong*, explains how biases and corruption play a role in expert recommendations:

Most of us think of scientists as being devoted to uncovering truths, not pumping their career prospects. Less formal experts don't enjoy that sort of halo. To win promotion or even simply keep their jobs, law-enforcement officials have to wrestle with the sometimes vicious politics racking the administrations they serve, and stockbrokers desperately struggle to corral new customers lest they not survive the next round of pink slips. For such experts, actually being right isn't always the best path to career success. There have been endless accounts of doctors ginning up unnecessary or overpriced tests for patients carried out at labs in which the doctors are investors, of government officials who receive favors and kickbacks, or brokers churning accounts to raise commissions and so forth.

Freedman notes that a wide range of economists and even mathematicians, as well as many nonscientist financial experts, have been demonstrating quite clearly for about a century that no matter what technique you use to pick stocks, you're not likely to beat the market. The fact that "many of us still put our faith in, not to mention bet our life savings based on, the advice of, say a screaming, bouncing, bell-ringing television personality who claims to have special insight into the movements of stocks, is, I think, a sharp illustration of how some experts can ride straight-out irrationality to great personal success."

Freedman provides a great example of how people react to advice. He presents the case of an individual with back pain. He visits two doctors. Each reviews the MRI. The first states that he's seen many similar cases and that it's hard to say exactly what is wrong, and so he suggests trying Treatment A first and going from there. The second doctor states that he knows exactly what is wrong and what to do. Which doctor do you choose? Almost always people will choose the latter. Yet that might very well be the wrong choice. While we want certainty, it rarely exists. And it certainly doesn't exist in the investment world where returns so frequently are explained by unforecastable events such as Mideast revolutions, Japanese earthquakes and tsunamis, or the attack on the World Trade Center buildings.

This leads to investors' seeking the advice of the experts who most seem like they know what they're talking about. Yet political scientist Philip Tetlock demonstrated in his outstanding book *Expert Political Judgment*, that even professional economic forecasters don't make accurate forecasts with any persistence.

Tetlock found that the so-called experts who make prediction their business—who appear as experts on television and talk radio, are quoted in the press, and advise governments and businesses—are no better than the proverbial chimps throwing darts. He divided forecasters into two general categories: (1) foxes, who draw on a wide variety of experiences and for whom the world cannot be boiled down to a single idea, and (2) hedgehogs, who view the world through the lens of a single defining idea. The following are some of his most interesting findings:

> What distinguishes the worst forecasters from the not-so-bad is that while hedgehogs are more confident, they are wrong more often than foxes.
> What differentiates foxes from hedgehogs is that the foxes rarely see things as bad as they appear at the trough or as good as they look at the peak.
> Optimists tend to be more accurate than pessimists. Keep this in mind the next time you read a doomsday forecast.
> *What* experts think matters far less than *how* they think. We are better off turning to the foxes, who know many little things and accept ambiguity and contradiction as inevitable features of life, rather than turning to the hedgehogs, who reach for formulaic solutions to ill-defined problems.
> It made virtually no difference whether forecasters were Ph.D.s, economists, political scientists, journalists, or historians, whether they had policy experience or access to classified information, or whether they had logged many or few years of experience in their chosen line of work. The only predictor of accuracy was fame, which was negatively correlated with accuracy; the most famous— those more likely feted by the media—made the worst forecasts.
> Beyond a stark minimum, subject-matter expertise translates less into forecasting accuracy than it does into overconfidence—and the ability to spin elaborate tapestries of reasons for expecting "favorite" outcomes.
> Like ordinary mortals, experts fell prey to the hindsight effect— they claimed they knew more about what was going to happen than they actually knew before the fact. This systematic misre-membering of past positions may look strategic, but the evidence indicates that people sometimes truly convince themselves that they "knew it all along." Hindsight bias causes overconfidence.

One of our favorite sayings is that there are three types of investment forecasters: those who don't know where the market is going, those who know they don't know, and those who know they don't know but get paid a lot of money to pretend they do. In other words, they are playing an entirely different game. As Tetlock noted, they're "fighting to preserve their reputation in a cutthroat adversarial culture. They woo dumb-ass reporters who want glib sound bits. In their world, only the overconfident survive and only the truly arrogant thrive." He also noted that the same self-assured hedgehog style of reasoning that suppresses forecasting accuracy and slow belief updating translates into attention-grabbing bold predictions that are rarely checked for accuracy.

Freedman reaches this conclusion: "While it's clearly true that you should never trust experts blindly, there are many situations in which you should and even must trust them, and in which to do otherwise is nothing other than reckless." He advises that "more of us ought to be following consensus expert advice that seems well supported, is not terribly burdensome to implement and appears to have little downside, such as eating fish, getting exercise, putting money into tax-deferred savings plans, and so on." He goes on to note, "Yet many of us manage to avoid following advice that not only is espoused by a wide range of experts but seems so basic and well proven that to mistrust it would appear to defy logic." Passive investing falls into that category.

Yet despite the overwhelming body of evidence that there are no good forecasters, investors pay lots of attention to economic and market forecasts, often acting on them, altering even well-thought-out plans. Whenever we are asked to comment on some such forecast, our answer is always the same: regardless of how intelligent sounding the argument, you should almost certainly ignore it because the forecaster is no more likely to be right than if he or she were guessing the outcome of a coin flip. Our experience tells us that almost no one—that probably means you—is off the hook on this one.

MISTAKE 11

Do You Let the Price Paid Affect Your Decision to Continue to Hold an Asset?

Put yourself in the following situation: You are a wine connoisseur. You decide to purchase a few cases of a new release at $10 per bottle, and you store the wine in your cellar to age. Ten years later the dealer from whom you purchased the wine informs you that the wine is now selling for $200 per bottle. You have a decision to make. Do you buy more or sell your stock?

Faced with this type of decision, very few people would sell the wine—but very few would buy more. Given the appreciation in the wine's value, many might choose to save it to drink on special occasions. But the decision not to sell, while not buying more, is not completely rational. The wine owner is being influenced by what is known as the *endowment effect*. The fact that the wine is something you already own (an endowment) should not have any impact on your decision. If you would not buy more at a given price, you should be willing to sell at that price. Since you wouldn't buy any of the wine if you didn't already own any, the wine represents a poor value to you and thus should be sold.

The endowment effect causes individuals to make poor investment decisions. It causes investors to hold on to assets they would not purchase if they didn't already own any, because either the assets don't fit into the asset allocation plan, or they are viewed as so highly priced that they are poor investments from a risk-reward perspective. The most common example of the endowment effect is that people are reluctant to sell stocks or mutual funds that were inherited or were purchased by a deceased spouse. Typically, they say something like "I can't sell that stock; it was my grandfather's favorite, and he'd owned it since 1952." Or "That stock has been in my family for generations." Or "My husband worked for that company for 40 years;

I couldn't possibly sell it." Another example of the endowment effect involves stock that has been accumulated through stock options or some type of profit-sharing or retirement plan.

Financial assets are like the bottles of wine. If you wouldn't buy them at the market price, you should sell them. Stocks and mutual funds are not people. They have no memory, they don't know who bought them, and they won't hate you if you sell them. An investment should be owned only if it fits into your current overall asset allocation plan. Its ownership should be viewed in that context.

You can avoid the endowment effect by asking this question: "If I didn't already own the asset, how much would I buy today as part of my overall investment plan?" If the answer is "I wouldn't buy any" or "I would buy less than I currently hold," then you should develop a disposition plan. There is one further consideration to be given to disposing of an "endowment asset": there may be substantial capital gains taxes involved. If this is so, you might consider donating the stock to your favorite charity. By donating the financial asset in place of cash you would have donated anyway, you can avoid paying the capital gains tax.

MISTAKE 12

Are You Subject to the Fallacy of the "Hot Streak"?

In investment performance, the past is not prologue.
—Charles Ellis
Winning the Loser's Game

There is an amusing and insightful story from the world of statistics that has relevance to the field of investing. Each year a statistics professor begins her class by asking each student to write down the sequential outcome of a series of 100 imaginary coin tosses. One student, however, is chosen to flip a *real* coin and chart the outcome. The professor then leaves the room and returns in 15 minutes with the outcomes waiting for her on her desk and correctly picks the real outcome. How does she perform this magical act? She knows the report with the longest consecutive streak of H (heads) or T (tails) is highly likely to be the result of the real flip. Even though HHHHHHHHHH and HHTTHTTHHT are equally likely to occur, more people would be likely to write the latter, more random sequence.

Streaks randomly occur with greater frequency than people believe. For example, the odds of flipping a coin 20 times and getting either four heads or four tails in a row are 50 percent. Because people underestimate the frequency of streaks, they tend to assign far too much meaning to events that are highly likely to be random occurrences. One study even demonstrated that a "hot hand" in basketball was likely to be nothing more than a random event.[1] A statistician following a basketball team around for an entire season found the odds of a career 50 percent shooter's hitting the next shot were 50 percent, even if this player had just hit five shots in a row.

34

A common investment error is to jump on the bandwagon of an actively managed fund that has been successful in beating its benchmark a few years in a row. Investors perceive there is a causal relationship (such as the fund manager's being an investment guru) when, instead, the performance is more likely to be the result of a random event. If the odds of beating the benchmark in one year are 50 percent, then beating a benchmark three years in a row is just as likely as tossing three heads in a row. It is expected to occur about 12 percent of the time. With thousands of managers trying, it is likely that many will succeed. Unfortunately, if success is a random event, it has no predictive value.

In his book *A Random Walk Down Wall Street*, Burton Malkiel reported that he did extensive testing on whether an investor, by choosing the "hot" funds, could outperform the market. The results showed the ineffectiveness of a strategy that first chose the top 10, 20, 30, or more funds based on the performance of the previous 12 months and then one year later switched to the new top performers. This strategy produced results that were below both those of the S&P 500 Index and those of the average mutual fund. Similar results were found when Malkiel tried ranking funds by their past 2-, 5-, and 10-year track records.[2] And we think most investors would be surprised at the results of another study of the performance of mutual funds all the way back to 1962. Its author, Mark Carhart, came to the amazing conclusion that the top 10 percent performers in any one year are more likely to fall to the bottom 10 percent than repeat in the top 10 percent.[3]

The most dramatic example of the failure of the hot-hand strategy is the 44 Wall Street Fund. Thanks to its now long-forgotten manager David Baker, it generated even greater returns than Peter Lynch's Magellan Fund in the 1970s and ranked as the top-performing diversified U.S. stock fund of the decade. Unfortunately, 44 Wall Street ranked as the single worst-performing fund in the 1980s, losing 73 percent.[4] During the same period, the S&P 500 grew at 17.5 percent per year. The fund did so poorly that it was merged into the Cumberland Growth Fund in April 1993, which was then merged into the Matterhorn Growth Fund in April 1996.

Belief in the hot hand, even with 10 years of evidence, can be quite expensive. Each dollar invested in Baker's fund fell in value to just 27 cents. On the other hand, each dollar invested in the S&P 500 Index would have grown to just over $5. As you can see, believing that the past performance of active managers is a good predictor of their future performance can be expensive.

You can avoid the mistake of overreacting to events and following the hot hand by carefully considering whether the outcome might have been a random one. As investment manager Marty Whitman points out, "The gutters of Wall Street are strewn with the bodies of people who looked good for five years."[5] Examining long-term data can help reduce the risk of making this type of mistake. Using the coin-toss analogy, while three coin tosses that come up all heads would be considered random, if 100 coin tosses resulted in 95 percent heads, we would be wise to consider that we are not dealing with a fair coin.

Do You Confuse the Familiar with the Safe?

> People overconfidently confuse familiarity with knowledge.
> For every example of a person who made money on an
> investment because she used a company's product or
> understood its strategy, we can give you five instances where
> such knowledge was insufficient to justify the investment.
>
> —Gary Belsky and Thomas Gilovich
> *Why Smart People Make Big Money Mistakes*

When AT&T was broken up, shareholders were given shares in each of what were called the Baby Bells. A study done a short while later found that the residents of each region held a disproportionate number of shares of their local regional Bell. Each group of regional investors was confident its regional Baby Bell would outperform the others.[1] How else can you explain those investors having most of their eggs in one baby basket?

Other examples of "familiarity breeding investment" are Atlanta residents having owned a disproportionate share of Coca-Cola and St. Louis residents having owned a disproportionate share of Anheuser-Busch. Obviously, it isn't any safer to invest in Coca-Cola if you live in Atlanta than if you live in St. Louis. And it wasn't safer to invest in A-B if you lived in St. Louis than if you lived in Atlanta. The same bias leads investors all over the world to overweight their own domestic equities, typically allocating only about 10 percent to international equities. That figure should be closer to 50 percent for U.S. investors.

Investors tend to view domestic stocks as safer and better investments than international counterparts. One study found the expected *real* return to U.S. equities was 5.5 percent in the eyes of U.S. investors, but only 3.1 percent and 4.4 percent in the eyes of Japanese and British investors, respectively. Similarly, the expected return on Japanese equities was 6.6 percent in the eyes of Japanese investors, but only 3.2 percent and 3.8 percent in the eyes of U.S. and British investors, respectively.[2] Familiarity breeds overconfidence (or an illusion of safety), and lack of familiarity breeds a perception of high risk.

Many investors avoid adding international investments to their portfolios because they believe international investing is too risky. Is this perception accurate? A study by Debra Glassman and Leigh Riddick found that portfolio allocations by U.S. investors to foreign and domestic securities are consistent with the belief by investors that the standard deviations of foreign securities are higher by a factor of 1.5 to 3.5 than their historical value.[3] Why do investors make this mistake? In their paper, Hersh Shefrin and Meir Statman note:

> *The distinction between foreign stocks and domestic ones is an illustration of the distinction between risk, where probabilities are known, and uncertainty, where probabilities are not known. Familiarity with a security brings the situation closer to risk than to uncertainty. Uncertainty-averse investors prefer familiar gambles over unfamiliar ones, even when the gambles have identical risk.[4]*

Academics recommend that investors add international assets to their portfolios because they actually *reduce* risk. International equities do not move in perfect tandem with domestic equities. Therefore, the addition of international stocks to a portfolio should reduce the volatility (risk) of the *overall* portfolio. A study published in the Fall 1998 issue of the *Journal of Investing* sought to determine whether international equity diversification actually provided that theoretical risk reduction benefit.

The study covered the period 1970 to 1996. David Laster, of the Federal Reserve Bank of New York, examined the performance of portfolios with varying allocations to the S&P 500 Index and the MSCI EAFE Index. The study looked at portfolios with allocations of 10 percent S&P 500 and 90 percent MSCI EAFE, 20 percent S&P 500 and 80 percent EAFE, and so on. At the end of each year, each portfolio was rebalanced, correcting for market movements, to its original allocations.

Before reviewing the results of the study, it is important to note that during this period the S&P 500 outperformed the MSCI EAFE (12.3 percent versus 12.0 percent per year). In addition, the correlation of returns between the two indexes was 0.48, a fairly low figure. The study concluded that

> › Any combination of the S&P 500 and the MSCI EAFE outper-formed either index individually—a result of the low correlation.
> › Increasing the international allocation to as much as 40 percent *increased* the returns and *reduced* risk as measured by standard deviation (volatility).
> › Increasing the international allocation from zero to just 20 percent reduced the likelihood of negative returns by one-third.[5]

What is likely to surprise most investors is that adding international assets to a portfolio during a period when they underperformed actually resulted in higher returns and lower risk.

Risk and Expected Return

Let's assume that you do believe the United States is safer because the economic and political prospects are better (keeping in mind that investors in other countries also appear to believe their domestic market is safer). You should then conclude the United States has lower expected returns. Although this would not mean the United States was a poor place to invest, it is illogical to believe the United States is a safer place to invest while also believing the United States will provide higher returns. Risk and expected reward should be related.

There are other arguments for including international asset classes in a portfolio. U.S. investors have all their intellectual capital in the domestic market. Their ability to generate income from employment is tied to U.S. economic conditions. They also might own a home, which may constitute a large percentage of their assets. If the dollar falls in value on the currency markets, not only will the cost of imports rise, but the competitive pressures from cheap imports will also decrease, allowing domestic manufacturers to raise prices. This combination of events could lower living standards. Owning foreign assets acts as a hedge against such risk.

Investing in international equities surely involves risk, but so does investing in domestic equities. And the evidence suggests that including international equities within a portfolio reduces the overall risks of the entire portfolio. Think about it this way: Diversification is a form of insurance. And we only insure against bad things. International diversification provides us with insurance in case the U.S. capital markets and the dollar perform poorly.

MISTAKE 14

Do You Believe You Are Playing with the House's Money?

In their wonderful book *Why Smart People Make Big Money Mistakes*, Gary Belsky and Thomas Gilovich relate the following legendary tale. By the third day of their honeymoon in Las Vegas, the newlyweds had lost their $1,000 gambling allowance. That night in bed, the groom noticed a glowing object on the dresser. It was a $5 chip he had saved as a souvenir. The number 17 was on the chip's face. Taking this as an omen, he donned his green bathrobe, rushed down to the roulette tables, and placed the chip on the square marked 17. Sure enough, the ball hit 17. The 35:1 bet paid $175. He let his winnings ride, and once again the little ball landed on 17, paying $6,125. And so it went, until the lucky groom was about to wager $7.5 million. Unfortunately, the floor manager intervened, claiming the casino didn't have the money to pay should 17 hit again. Still clad in his bathrobe, the young man taxied to a better-financed casino. Once again he bet it all on 17, only to lose it all when the ball fell on 18. Broke and dejected, the groom walked back to his hotel room. "Where were you?" asked his bride. "Playing roulette." "How did you do?" "Not bad. I lost $5."[1]

The "Legend of the Man in the Green Bathrobe" illustrates "mental accounting." In the case of the man in the green bathrobe, mental accounting allowed him to think of the $7.5 million he lost as the "house's money," not his. As the following example illustrates, investors make this same mistake.

A good friend of Larry's had been either lucky or smart enough to buy Cisco at 5 per share. The stock represented a relatively small portion of his net worth. When the stock reached 80, his position in Cisco had become a substantial portion of his portfolio. When asked if he would buy any at the current price, he said no. Larry then stated that if he wouldn't buy any, he must believe either that it was too highly valued or that he was currently holding too much of the stock and it was too risky to have that many of his eggs in one basket. Despite the logic of the argument, Larry's friend steadfastly refused to sell some shares for the following reason: his cost was only 5, and the stock would have to drop about 95 percent before he would have a loss. Larry then asked him if he owned a green bathrobe.

A few months later Cisco had hit 13, and he was still holding it. Now, this man is one of the smartest people Larry knew. Yet mental accounting had caused him to make the same mistake as the man in the green bathrobe. He had considered his unrealized gain as the "house's money," instead of his own. Just as the man in the green bathrobe could have taken his chips and cashed them in, Larry's friend could have sold the stock at 80 and converted his unrealized gain into nice green cash.

Making the mental accounting mistake of believing you are playing with the house's money can be avoided by developing and having the discipline to adhere to an investment policy statement and a rebalancing table. This will force you to get up and walk away with the house's money if a position in a single asset grows beyond the maximum tolerance range established by your plan.

Do You Let Friendships Influence Your Choice of Investment Advisors?

Many people have a difficult time separating friendship from business. The inability to control this emotion can be costly, as the following story demonstrates.

Rick and Phil had been friends for more than 30 years. They celebrated every New Year by having lunch together, and so they got together in early January 2002. Inevitably, the conversation turned to investing. Rick and Phil shared the same stockbroker, Marvin, who was also a mutual longtime friend. The following is the conversation that took place:

RICK: How did you do last year?

PHIL: I did okay, I guess.

RICK: No, specifically, I mean what rate of return did you earn?

PHIL: You know, I have no idea.

RICK: And what has been your rate of return over the last 10 years?

PHIL: I have no idea.

RICK: And I never knew either until I finally decided to calculate the return on my investments. And I can tell you that I was unhappy with what I found. I think the bull market of the late nineties made us complacent. We enjoyed nominal returns that were pretty good, certainly from a historical perspective. I learned, however, that the stocks and mutual funds I owned provided well-below-market returns. So while I did okay, I should have been doing much better. "Luckily," the losses of the last few years caused me to take a serious look at the results. I have decided to seek another advisor. I asked coworkers and friends that had experienced better results and were happy with their financial advisor for recommendations. I already have several interviews set up.

PHIL: You mean you are actually going to fire Marvin?

RICK: Yes.

PHIL: How can you do that? You have been friends for a long time. Boy, that will be tough.

RICK: Yes, I know it will be tough. But the way I look at it is this: If Marvin is truly my friend, he should want what is best for me. And if his friendship is based solely on the fact that he is my stockbroker, then he really isn't my friend anyway. If the price of friendship—all the commissions and fees I have paid to his firm—is putting my ability to retire and live the lifestyle I desire at risk, then the price is simply too high.

PHIL: I hear you, but I just don't think I could do it.

The following year Rick and Phil got together again. Once again the conversation turned to investing. Rick told Phil that he had hired a financial advisory firm with which he was pleased. And this was despite the fact that the equity portion of his portfolio had lost about 11 percent. He pointed out that there were three reasons that he was pleased with his decision to change advisors. The first was that while his equity portfolio had lost 11 percent, the market had actually fallen twice as much. It was the first time in years that his portfolio had outperformed the market.

The second reason Rick was pleased with his decision was that for the first time in his life he actually had a financial plan in place. It was one that was tailored to his unique situation, and it was integrated into a well-designed estate and tax plan as well.

The third reason that Rick was pleased with his decision was that he had now adopted a passive investment strategy, and so he was no longer paying attention to the stock market. This allowed him to pay more attention to both his golf game and his wife—and as a result he had being doing much better with both!

Phil then asked Rick how it had gone when he told Marvin he was no longer going to be his investment advisor. As expected, Marvin was upset. Rick discovered their friendship was based entirely on their business relationship. He brought Phil a copy of *The Only Guide to a Winning Investment Strategy You'll Ever Need* with his advisor's card.

Phil read the book, and while it made lots of sense to him, he still did nothing. It was just too hard to fire a friend, and 2003 was turning out to be a much better year.

January 2004 rolled around, and it was time for their annual lunch. This time the wives joined. And when the conversation turned to investing, Rick asked Phil if he had made any decision about his advisor. Phil said that he had not but that he had a much better year in 2003. His equity portfolio was up over 25 percent. Rick pointed out that while that was a great number, his globally diversified portfolio was up almost twice that at over 49 percent! Phil's wife, Phyllis, then asked Rick to explain more about his approach—which he proceeded to do, emphasizing the part about having a well-designed plan. Rick's wife added that she was much happier too, as Rick no longer spent time watching CNBC or reading financial publications.

When Phil got home, Phyllis asked him about their investments and the difference between the performance of Rick's and their portfolio. It was the first time she had ever asked Phil to go over the performance of their portfolio. Despite the important role investments played in her ability to retire to a desired lifestyle, she had never paid attention to their investments before. Phil went over the entire history. When he had finished, she told Phil that she was calling Rick's advisor to set up a meeting.

The next week the meeting was held, and Phil and Phyllis were both impressed with the logic of the investment strategy and the competence of the advisor. They shook hands with the advisor and told him they would get back to him shortly. When they got home, Phyllis told Phil that she was impressed and thought they should change advisors immediately. Phil agreed that he was impressed but that he just could not get himself to face Marvin and tell him that he was no longer going to be his advisor. Phyllis made the decision simple: "Either you do it, or I will."

All too often investors continue to work with advisors despite poor results because it is difficult to fire an advisor who is also a friend, and even more difficult to fire one who is a relative. The moral of this story is that you are best served by evaluating the true cost of those relationships, keeping in mind that true friends want what is best for you and do not put their self-interest above your own.

PART 2

Ignorance Is Not Bliss

Do You Fail to See the Poison Inside the Shiny Apple?

In the classic fairy tale *Snow White and the Seven Dwarfs*, the evil Queen arrives at Snow White's cottage disguised as an old peddler woman. Despite being warned by the seven dwarfs not to open the door for anyone or to accept any gifts, Snow White answers the door. The Queen uses the girl's naiveté against her and lures Snow White into taking a bite from a poisoned apple. Falling into a sleeping death, Snow White can only be awakened by love's first kiss.

The moral of the story is that children should be wary of old ladies who come knocking at their door tempting them with treats. It is more than likely that the old lady has a hidden agenda. The broker-dealer community knows that individual investors lack sufficient knowledge about the bond market, which makes exploiting them as easy as tempting Snow White. Unfortunately for those investors, Prince Charming will not be riding in on a white horse to save them or their portfolios.

The Games Brokers Play—at Your Expense

Brokers exploit the naiveté of investors in several ways. The first is through markups (when an investor buys a bond) and markdowns (when an investor sells a bond). It is unfortunate that the SEC does not require a broker-dealer to disclose the amount of markup or markdown charged. The result is that transaction costs in bond trades can be like icebergs, where the largest part is hidden beneath the surface.

When buying bonds, the danger is that because the only required disclosure is the transaction fee (which is an administrative fee, not a commission), most investors assume it is the only cost they will incur—typically a nominal amount such as

$25 or even less. However, this is typically just the tip of the iceberg. Markups and markdowns can be quite large since there is little in the way of regulations to prevent abuses. The following will likely shock most investors.

In a May 2002 ruling, SEC administrative law judge Lillian A. McEwen dismissed fraud charges brought by the SEC and the Municipal Securities Rulemaking Board against a Los Angeles broker. McEwen concluded, "Markups and markdowns on municipal securities ranging from 1.87 to 5.64 percent were not excessive and did not violate the securities fraud laws."[1]

There are other ways for brokers to transfer wealth from their clients to their own pockets. The first example relates to the maturity of the bonds that brokers prefer to sell. Investors need to be aware that the size of the impact of a markup or markdown on the yield of a bond is negatively related to its remaining term to maturity. For example, a bond with a remaining maturity of just one year will see a return impact of about 1 percent for each 1 point of markup or markdown. However, the impact on yield is reduced as the term to maturity lengthens because the markup will be "amortized" over a longer time. Consider the following example.

A bond with a remaining term of just 1 year is yielding 3 percent and trading at par (100). A markup of even 1 percent would be hard to hide, as the yield to maturity would drop by more than 1 percent to 1.98 percent. On the other hand, if the bond had a remaining term of 10 years, the yield to maturity would fall to about 2.85 percent. And if the bond had a remaining term of 25 years, the yield to maturity would fall to about 2.93 percent. The longer the maturity, the less the impact on yield to maturity, and the easier it is to hide the markup.

Now imagine a broker wanting to take a markup of 4 points on the same bond. That would be hard to do with a bond with just 1 year remaining to maturity, because the yield to maturity would then be negative—the investor would pay 104 for a bond that in 1 year would return his $100 in principal and just $3 of interest. On the other hand, the impact on the yield to maturity of a bond with 25 years to maturity would be only about 0.31 percent per year.

It isn't hard to guess which maturities brokers push when selling bonds to individual investors. Unfortunately, not only do investors end up paying large transaction fees, but they also end up taking more price risk than would be typically prudent. As an example, we were asked to review the bond holdings of an 86-year-old investor. We found that there were many bonds with maturities of more than 20 years. Now there is probably no good reason for an 86-year-old to own bonds with maturities well beyond his life expectancy. In addition, the greatest risk to this investor was inflation, and longer-term bonds have the most inflation risk.

And as is typically the case, the investor had a long relationship with the broker, who worked with a prestigious firm. Unfortunately, the trust he had in both the long relationship and the firm was misplaced.

Double Dipping

One of Larry's favorite *Seinfeld* episodes is the one where George was caught double dipping his chip. One of the guests pointed out that George's action was a hazard to the health of the other guests. Brokers also engage in double dipping—a practice that is hazardous to the wealth of investors. Let's examine how the double dip works in the bond world.

Brokers exploit individual investors by selling premium bonds that have call dates that are much closer than the maturity date. The bonds sell at a premium as a result of their high coupons (the attraction) relative to current market rates. The higher-than-market coupon means that the issuer will likely call the bond at the first opportunity. Consider the following example.

A bond with a remaining term to maturity of 25 years is carrying a coupon of 6 percent. The current market rate for similar bonds is now 4 percent, and the bond can be called at 101 in 1 year. Despite the relatively high coupon (2 percent above the current market rate) and the long remaining term to maturity, the bond should not be trading much above the call price of 101 because of the nearness of the call date and the high likelihood that the bond will be called by the issuer. Let's assume the bond is trading at 103. Now the broker decides to add a markup of 5 points and sells the bond to the investor at 108. While the yield to maturity is about 5.6 percent, well above current market rates, the bond will almost certainly be called in 1 year. Assuming it is called at 101, the investor will have earned the coupon of 6 percent and lost 7 points in price, producing a net loss of 1 percent. As you can see, the investor was actually sold a bond with a negative expected return! This is not as rare as you might think. But it gets worse. When the bond is called, the broker will advise the investor of the call. The investor now has to reinvest the cash, and the broker gets to "double-dip."

For a variety of reasons, the prudent approach to buying bonds is to be sure that if the bond is callable, you have at least 80 percent call protection. (For example, if there are 10 years remaining until maturity, the earliest it could be called is at least 8 years).

If you are concerned that you have been taken advantage of, there's a solution. We recommend that you take a list of your current holdings along with the original transactions slips (showing what is called the CUSIP number and the date of the trade) to an independent financial advisor. The advisor can analyze your holdings to see if the types of abuses we have discussed have taken place (including uncovering the size of the markups or markdowns that were charged).

While it is likely too late to do anything about prior abuses, there is no reason to allow them to continue once you are aware of the games brokers play at your expense. Preventing them will allow you to take that trip to Hawaii, instead of paying for the broker's trip.

Do You Confuse Information with Knowledge?

> Prominent media journalism is a thoughtless process of providing the noise that can capture people's attention.
> —Nassim Nicholas Taleb
> *Fooled by Randomness*

> Something that everyone knows isn't worth knowing.
> —Bernard Baruch

In the world of investing, there is a major difference between information and knowledge. Information is facts, data, or someone's opinions. Knowledge, on the other hand, is information that is of value. Confusing the two is a major mistake. Let's take a look at what we call the "information paradox."

At the core of the efficient market hypothesis is that *new* information is disseminated to the public so rapidly and completely that prices instantly adjust to new data. If this is the case, investors can consistently beat the market only with either the best of luck or inside information (on which it is illegal to trade). The logical conclusion seems *illogical* to most investors: if information is valuable, it has no value. Thus, we have the information paradox.

There is a very simple and logical explanation of the paradox: the reason that valuable information has no value is that unless you are the only one to know it, the market has already incorporated it into prices. The only other way you can exploit information is to interpret that information differently from the way in which the market collectively interprets it. The example below should illustrate the logic of the information paradox. Any investor who has ever purchased a stock based on a recommendation from a broker (or from a financial publication, a CNBC guest, and so on) will be able to relate to this situation:

BROKER: We just have to buy IBM.

INVESTOR: Why should I buy IBM?

BROKER: Our analyst that covers IBM is a genius. She graduated first in her MBA class at Harvard. She then graduated first in her class at MIT, receiving a Ph.D. in electrical engineering. She worked for 10 years at IBM in product development and 10 more in marketing and sales. She then joined our firm and has been our technology analyst. She has personally visited all IBM plants and research facilities; she has also visited with all competitors. She even visited with all of IBM's major customers to check on how they perceive IBM products and service and on the status of new orders. And she met with IBM's suppliers to check on the quality of their work. The stock is currently selling at 100. Given the great new pipeline of 100 great new products and the growth in sales that will result, the stock is worth 200 if it's worth a penny.

INVESTOR: That sounds great. Let's buy 1,000 shares.

Let's assume everything the broker said was absolutely true. There is a logical reason for you to ignore all such prognostications—there is something wrong with the picture. An alternative version of our hypothetical phone call will illustrate why. This version, however, will be one totally unfamiliar to all investors *and* also will be one they will never hear:

BROKER: Though we do have a very smart analyst covering IBM, there are 65 other very smart analysts covering IBM. They all have MBAs from top schools and lots of experience. They are all highly paid and motivated. They all work diligently to gather the facts. They all have the same information our analyst does. If the other analysts thought IBM was worth 200, the stock would already be trading there. Do you think all those smart people would let a stock that is worth 200 sit there at 100 without rushing to buy it? The reason IBM is trading at 100 is that the market as a whole thinks it is only worth 100, not

200. However, our analyst thinks the rest of the world has got it wrong. Only our analyst really knows this stuff, and the rest of the smart analysts are simply misinterpreting the information. We really need to buy IBM.

INVESTOR: …[dial tone]

We think it is safe to say that if you had heard the second conversation instead of the first, rather than agreeing to buy IBM, you would have laughed and hung up. You will note, however, that although the second conversation is far more likely to reflect the truth, this conversation never occurs. Why? It is not in the broker's interest for you to know the truth. He wouldn't make any money.

There is an alternative way to regard the advice of a stockbroker. Let's assume the broker actually has the investor's interest at heart and truly believes that his firm's analyst is a great analyst, can ferret out information others cannot, and can do a better job of interpreting the information. Though it is possible that all brokers may have their clients' interests at heart and also believe their firm's analyst is the best, all the analysts cannot be above average, let alone the best. Is it logical to believe the analyst at Morgan Stanley is superior and knows more than the analyst at Goldman Sachs or Janus? Actually, it doesn't even matter. What really matters is the clear evidence that it is highly unlikely that any one individual over time will be able to identify securities the rest of the market has somehow mispriced.

There is another problem with following the broker's advice. Suppose that you do buy IBM and it proceeds to rise in value. Now what? Since IBM had about a 50-50 chance of outperforming the market, how do you know the analyst's correct prediction was based on skill and not a matter of luck? Many analysts become famous on just a single recommendation. There are numerous examples, but perhaps the most compelling is that of Elaine Garzarelli. While working at Shearson Lehman, Ms. Garzarelli correctly forecast the 1987 crash. Shearson Lehman began to widely tout her ability to call market moves and rewarded her for her successful prognostications with a mutual fund of her own to manage. Let's look at her record.

By June 30, 1994, the fund she was managing, the Smith Barney/Shearson Sector Analysis Fund, had risen in value by just

38 percent over the 5 years she was in charge, underperforming the Dow Jones Industrial Average (DJIA) by about 50 percent. In May 1996, the DJIA surpassed 5,700, and this well-known market guru, who had left Shearson Lehman to form her own firm, advised her clients to invest aggressively. Almost immediately, the market underwent a sharp correction, falling over 400 points. She then reversed direction, advising her clients to sell. Once again the market reversed course. By November, the DJIA had crossed 6,500. In January 1997, with the market approaching 7,000, Ms. Garzarelli reversed position once again and advised her clients to buy. By April, the market had dropped to under 6,400.

The next time you watch CNBC and listen to an analyst or fund manager tout even a hundred good reasons why to buy a specific stock or equities in general, keep the information paradox in mind as well as these three thoughts:

1. *Capturing incremental insight is very difficult, if not impossible, to achieve.* The reason is that security analysts are competing with many other smart and highly motivated people researching the same stocks. Competition among all the professional active managers ensures the market price is highly likely to be the correct price.
2. *Think about where you just heard the new insightful information— on national television.* In the unlikely scenario this information *was* a secret, it no longer is. The same analogy could be made for recommendations from any of the high-profile publications such as *Barron's*, *BusinessWeek*, *Fortune*, *Forbes*, *Money*, or *SmartMoney*.
3. *As Rex Sinquefield, former cochairman of Dimensional Fund Advisors, points out,* "Just because there are some investors smarter than others, that advantage will not show up. The market is too vast and too informationally efficient."[1]

Let's see how expensive confusing "noise" with valuable information can be. Brad Barber and Terrance Odean's study "All That Glitters: The Effect of Attention and News on the Buying Behavior of Individual and Institutional Investors" hypothesized that individual investors are likely to be net buyers of what they called "attention-grabbing" stocks.

Their main finding was that individual investors tend to be net purchasers of stocks on high-attention days:

> › Days that those stocks experience high abnormal trading volume
> › Days following extreme price moves
> › Days on which stocks are in the news

In looking at stocks experiencing unusually high trading volume, Barber and Odean found that individuals made nearly twice as many purchases than sales of those stocks.

Barber and Odean also found that individual investors tend to be net buyers of both the previous day's big winners and big losers. Following the same pattern, individual investors also tend to be net buyers of companies on days that those companies are in the news—whether the news is good or bad.[2]

Unfortunately for these individual investors, they fail to recognize how efficient markets work. They fail to understand that the information grabbing their attention is already incorporated into the price of the stock—and the speed of the stock market's response to new information is startling. A study on the after-trading-hours quarterly earnings announcements of 100 NYSE and 100 NASDAQ firms found that the majority of the price response is realized during the *opening* trade. For earnings announcements that occurred during trading hours, the results were not much different. For NYSE stocks the price adjustment occurred during the first several postannouncement trades. For NASDAQ stocks the price adjustment was concentrated in the very first postannouncement trade.[3]

The result is that investors make the mistake of confusing information (the attention-getting news) with knowledge they can use to buy an undervalued (mispriced) stock. This leads, unfortunately, to the poor trading results that Barber and Odean have consistently found in their studies.

The bottom line is that individual investors generate negative results by paying attention to the noise of the market, even before the costs of the trades. If investors ignored the noise, not only would they earn better returns, but they would also lead more productive lives (getting to spend their time on more important issues than trying to beat the market).

MISTAKE 18

Do You Believe Your Fortune Is in the Stars?

The brand that has emerged as dominant in the
1990s is not Fidelity, Putnam, or even Merrill
Lynch—but instead is Morningstar.
—R. Pozen
The Mutual Fund Business, 1998, p. 75

I own last year's top-performing funds.
Unfortunately, I bought them this year.
—Anonymous

Perhaps the most common approach to selecting mutual
funds is to rely on the popular rating service provided by
Morningstar that rates funds using a star system similar to the
one used by film critics. Ads touting four- and five-star ratings
are found everywhere. Investors must believe the stars have predictive value. One study covering the period January through
August 1995 found that an amazing 97 percent of fund inflows
went into four- and five-star funds, while three-star funds experienced outflows.[1]

The question is, Should you place your fortune in the stars?
Morningstar itself provides us with evidence on how successful a
strategy that is.

Each June, Morningstar examines how its ratings are doing.
It looks to see how each rating group has done over the ensuing
years, comparing the performance of the funds given five stars
with the performance of those that received just one star.

Let's take a look at some of the results. What is most interesting is that Morningstar touted the results of its class of 2004—its five-star domestic funds outperformed its one-star funds by 2.8 percent per year. What Morningstar failed to emphasize is that by 2009 the funds given five stars in 2004 now had a five-year rating of just 3.2. And those same funds now had a ranking of 41, outperforming just 59 percent of all actively managed funds. In other words, the five-star rating was a poor predictor of future ratings. We can make that claim because studies show the average actively managed fund underperforms its appropriate benchmark by over 1.5 percent per year. Thus, outperforming 59 percent of a lousy group is damning with faint praise.

And the 2004 group was the one Morningstar was boasting about. The 2007 group of five-star funds had so far managed to underperform the one-star group! The 2005 group of five-star funds now had a three-year rating of just 3.1. Even worse, the 2006 group had a three-year rating of just 2.9.[2]

The evidence is overwhelming that while active management gives you the hope of outperformance, the far greater likelihood is underperformance. And for taxable investors the hurdles are even greater. In the 1996 annual report of Berkshire Hathaway, Warren Buffett provided this advice: "Most investors, both institutional and individual, will find that the best way to own common stocks is through an index fund that charges minimal fees. Those following this path are sure to beat the net results (after fees and expenses) delivered by the great majority of investment professionals. Seriously, costs matter."[3]

A perfect illustration of this is the 2010 study Morningstar did comparing the predictive value of its star ratings with the predictive value of expense ratios. Morningstar found that expense ratios were a better predictor than star ratings.[4]

The bottom line is that using Morningstar's ratings system is like driving forward while looking in the rearview mirror.

MISTAKE 19

Do You Rely on Misleading Information?

"*Warning: Returns shown contain biases we are not required to report.*" The SEC should require this disclosure for the advertisements of many mutual funds. Without this type of disclaimer, the majority of investors are unaware they are making investment decisions based on reported returns that either are outright misrepresentations of the returns earned by investors or at the very least are misleading representations. The reported returns of many funds are distorted because of biases in the data. Let's look at the two biases for which mandatory disclosures should be required.

The first is known as *survivorship bias*. Funds that have poor performance disappear, most often by merging a poorly performing fund into a better-performing one. Unfortunately, only the performance reporting disappears, not the poor returns. Let's see why survivorship bias is so important.

In 1986, Lipper Analytical Services reported that the then-existing 568 stock funds returned 13.4 percent. By 1996, the 1986 performance had magically improved to 14.7 percent. The 1.3 percent improvement was a result of the disappearance of 24 percent of the original funds—and the fact that only the 1986 performance of the funds still in existence 10 years later was used in the new computation.[1]

The second bias in data comes from the use of what are known as *incubator funds*. Incubator funds are newly created funds seeded by mutual fund families with their own capital and not available to the public.

Here is an example of how this works. A fund family creates several small-cap funds, possibly even under the same manager. Each fund might own a different group of small-cap stocks. The fund family incubates the funds, safe from public scrutiny. After a few years, the fund family brings public only the fund with the best performance. Magically, the performance of the other funds disappears. Unfortunately, the SEC has ruled that fund families are allowed to report the prepublic performance of incubator funds. Thus, we have the potential for a huge distortion of reality.

To make matters worse, a large fund family might provide a tiny incubator fund with a relatively large allocation of a hot initial public offering (IPO). Given the small amount of assets in an incubator fund, the fund's returns could be supercharged, clearly a distortion of what might be expected once a fund went public. Fortunately, the SEC has taken some action against this type of distortion. In 1999 it fined the Van Kampen Growth Fund, a unit of Morgan Stanley Dean Witter, $125,000 for not adequately disclosing the role IPOs had in the strong first-year gain of the fund. The fund was started as an incubator fund in 1996 and rose 62 percent that year.[2] Another example of the abuse of the system came in May 2000 when Dreyfus agreed to pay nearly $3 million to resolve charges from both the New York state attorney general and the SEC that the firm had made inadequate or false disclosures about the role of IPOs in returns.[3] It would seem the logical solution to this distorted reporting is to prohibit the advertising of returns before a fund is made available to the public.

As you can see, even with fund families playing within current SEC rules, there exists the possibility for a distortion of both the actual returns received by investors and the potential for repeat performances. Fuller disclosure might help, but since many investors don't read the fine print, the public would be better served if the practices were simply prohibited. At least being aware of the potential for bias in the data might help prevent poor investment decisions.

When you hear a claim about the performance of a mutual fund or a group of funds, make sure the data presented contain none of the biases discussed above. In addition, you should take very seriously the SEC's warning on using past performance as a predictor. As we have seen, this warning is required for a good reason.

Do You Only Consider the Operating Expense Ratio When Selecting a Mutual Fund?

> We all know that active management fees
> are high. Poor performance does not come
> cheap. You have to pay dearly for it.
> —Rex Sinquefield

> The shortest route to top quartile performance is
> to be in the bottom quartile of expenses.
> —John Bogle

Many investors know that when it comes to investing, costs matter. To outperform their benchmarks, active managers must not only be able to select the right stocks and time the market successfully; they must do so while more than recovering the costs of their efforts.

When deciding on their choice of mutual funds, many investors consider only the operating expense ratio. The main reason for this error is probably the fact that the operating expense ratio is the only expense currently published. Unfortunately, not only is the operating expense ratio but one of many costs, but in many cases it is the least of the costs involved, especially for taxable accounts. The cost of the other expenses—trading costs, taxes, and the cost of cash—goes unreported. These costs are nonetheless real and are manifested in lower returns.

Let's examine the other expenses that mutual fund investors incur and their impact on returns.

The Cost of Cash

The least understood hidden cost is the *cost of cash*. The cost of cash occurs when a mutual fund holds a cash position instead of being fully invested in the market. A study by Russ Wermers found that nonequity holdings reduced returns for the average actively managed equity fund by 0.7 percent per year.[1] The greater the cash position held, the greater the impact. Unfortunately, the past average cash holding of an actively managed fund may not be a good predictor of the future. Therefore, you might use Wermers's estimate when considering an active fund. With index funds or other passive investment vehicles being virtually fully invested, the cost of cash will be negligible.

Trading Expenses

The average actively managed fund now has turnover of about 100 percent, and the cost of all that turnover—commissions, bid-offer spreads, and market impact costs—can easily exceed 1 percent. Depending on the index it is attempting to replicate, the typical passively managed fund will have turnover of between 3 and 25 percent (lower for passive large-cap and growth funds and greater for passive small-cap and value funds).

Morningstar studied the negative impact of the turnover of active managers. It divided mutual funds into two categories: those with an average holding period greater than 5 years (less than 20 percent turnover) and those with an average holding period of less than 1 year (turnover greater than 100 percent). Over a 10-year period, Morningstar found that low-turnover funds rose an average of 12.87 percent per year, while high-turnover funds gained only 11.29 percent per year on average.[2]

Trading costs are generally much higher for funds that invest internationally. Not only are commissions and bid-offer spreads generally higher than they are in the United States, but some countries also impose what is called a *stamp duty*. In addition, fees can be very high. For example, in the United Kingdom commissions average 35 basis points, the stamp duty is 50 basis points, and custodial fees are 6 basis points, for a total of 91 basis points, even before considering the cost of the bid-offer spread.[3]

Market Impact Costs

Active managers incur larger "market impact" costs than do index funds. Market impact is what occurs when a mutual fund wants to buy or sell a large block of stock. The fund's purchases or sales will cause the stock to move beyond its current bid (lower) or offer (higher) price, increasing the cost of trading. The cost of market impact will vary, depending on many factors (fund size, asset class, turnover, etc.), and it can be quite substantial.

Research organization Barra noted that a fairly typical case of a small- or mid-cap stock fund with $500 million in assets and an annual turnover rate of between 80 and 100 percent could lose 3 to 5 percent per year to market impact costs—far more than the annual expenses of most funds.[4]

Without access to the specific data, it is very hard to estimate a fund's market impact costs. However, you can at least consider high turnover as an indicator of the size of the impact. Also, the smaller the market capitalization of the stocks the fund owns, the greater the impact.

Taxes

Unfortunately, we have not come to the end of the road of fund expenses. In fact, we have not yet covered what is often the greatest expense for taxable accounts: the burden of taxes. Take one example: For the 15-year period ending June 30, 1998, the Vanguard S&P 500 Index Fund provided pretax returns of 16.9 percent per year. The fund lost 1.9 percent per year to taxes. Its after-tax return of 15 percent meant the fund's tax efficiency was 89 percent. The average actively managed fund provided pretax returns of 13.6 percent and after-tax returns of just 10.8 percent. Losing 2.8 percent per year to taxes resulted in a tax efficiency of just 79 percent.[5] Fortunately, after-tax returns data is now available from services such as Morningstar. Recently, they have become an SEC reporting requirement.

It may be said that the long-term goal of investing is to multiply the eggs in our baskets. Yet too many investors focus on producing more eggs (getting high returns) while paying little attention to the fox (costs) that perpetually robs the henhouse.

If you ignore the fox, soon there will be nothing left to produce more eggs.[6] You can avoid this mistake by analyzing a fund's turnover and tax efficiency; then using information in this chapter, you can estimate the total costs of investing in a fund.

Do You Fail to Consider the Costs of an Investment Strategy?

> Overwhelmingly, mutual funds extract enormous sums from investors in exchange for providing a shocking disservice. That is, mutual funds charge their investors big fees and usually fail to deliver returns that beat the market.
>
> —David Swensen
> Chief Investment Officer, Yale Endowment Fund

Investment strategies that produce market-beating results are obviously attractive to investors. Attributing great skill to the creators of the strategy, investors frequently adopt that strategy—all too often with disappointing results. One reason, as we have already seen, is that the past is not a good predictor of future performance. Also, investors are prone to attribute skill to what might be a function of luck, since many strategies rely on patterns that might be the result of random events. And there is another reason: although strategies do not entail costs, implementing them does. Let's look at some examples that demonstrate that it is a long way from a market-beating strategy to market-beating results. The first involves *BusinessWeek*.

The July 24, 2000, issue of *BusinessWeek* contained an analysis of Gene Marcial's 1999 stock picks. The article concluded that Marcial's stock-picking results were "sensational," noting that Marcial's picks trounced both the DJIA and the S&P 500 indexes.

Larry Putnam, a contributing writer for the Web site Indexfunds.com, took a closer look at *BusinessWeek*'s claim.[1] When analyzing mutual funds or stock picks, it is important to make sure you are making apples-to-apples comparisons, something *BusinessWeek* failed to do and thus provided misleading information. Putnam compared the price performance of Marcial's 155 stock picks with their appropriate benchmarks. Here is a summary of what he found:

> Of Marcial's 155 picks, 85 of them (55 percent) traded on the NASDAQ and AMEX. These are typically smaller-cap and technology-related stocks.
> The other 70 picks (45 percent) traded on the NYSE. These are more typically large-cap growth stocks.
> When you compare Marcial's picks with a portfolio that is weighted 55 percent NASDAQ and 45 percent S&P 500, his 155 picks should have increased in price an average of 25.5 percent for the 6-month period.

Marcial's picks were up 26 percent. Compared with the predicted 25.5 percent increase, the 26 percent reported increase for Marcial's stock selections no longer look "sensational." It is important to note that Marcial's picks were up an average of 8.8 percent the day after they appeared in print. It is highly unlikely that investors were able to take advantage of the first-day price rise.

The picks also ignore trading costs (bid-offer spreads) and commissions. This is particularly important when you consider that nearly half of Marcial's picks were priced under $15, and about one-third were priced below $10. Stocks with such low prices are typically very small-cap stocks that carry much greater trading costs than do large caps. For example, at the time, the bid-offer spread (an estimate of trading costs) for the largest 10 percent of stocks was just 0.65 percent. However, for the smallest 10 percent of stocks, it was almost 7 times as great at 4.3 percent. Then consider that you have to add in commissions (buy and sell) as well.

Once you subtract all estimated trading costs, Marcial's supposedly impressive returns no longer look so hot. In fact, using any reasonable estimate of the costs, implementing a "Marcial" strategy would have produced returns that were below an appropriate benchmark. Another consideration is that this analysis ignored the potentially large tax implications of such an active stock-picking strategy. Putnam's work points out how easily investors can be misled by ambiguous information.

An example of failing to consider the costs of following an investment strategy is the aforementioned study by Russ Wermers, whose results confirmed the findings of other studies on the stock-picking skills of security analysts:

> › In 13 of the 20 years encompassed by the study, the stocks selected by active managers outperformed the S&P 500 Index. The average for the 20-year period was 0.7 percent per year.
> › The 0.7 percent advantage provided by stock selection skills (exploiting the mistakes of individual investors) was more than offset by expenses incurred in the effort.

Wermers's study found the returns of active managers were reduced by approximately

> › 0.8 percent due to fund operating expenses.
> › 0.8 percent due to transaction costs.
> › 0.7 percent per year due to holding nonequity assets. Active managers generally hold some amount of cash (or cash equivalents) in attempts to time the market while waiting to find what they perceive to be an undervalued security, or they hold the cash as reserves to meet shareholder redemptions. Some managers even hold longer-term fixed-income investments in an attempt to outperform equities.

The total negative impact of expenses was 2.3 percent per year. And the study did not include the impact of taxes, which would have had an additional negative impact on returns.[2]

Perhaps the most amusing example of "it's a long way from strategy to outcome" was Wade Cook Financial's Internet site, which solicited investors to pay up to $7,995 for two-day stock-trading seminars. The company's advertising claimed that some of its students obtained investment returns of 15 percent a month. However, its 10-K report filed with the Securities and Exchange Commission disclosed that Wade Cook Financial lost $2 million, or 89 percent of its own money, in the market in 2000. "Either Wade is unable to follow his own system, which he claims is simple to follow, or the system doesn't work," said Deb Bortner, director of the Washington State Securities Division and president of the North American Securities Administrators Association.[3]

The bottom line is this: it is often a long way from the theoretical results of a strategy to the actual results that can be obtained. Keep this in mind the next time you read about a market-beating strategy.

Do You Confuse Great Companies with High-Return Investments?

One of the most persistent and incorrect beliefs among investors is that "growth" stocks have provided (and are expected to provide) higher returns than "value" stocks. Growth stocks are stocks of the glamorous high price-to-earnings (P/E) or low book-to-market (BtM) companies, while value stocks are the stocks of distressed companies, trading at low P/E ratios and high BtMs. The problem arises from the confusion between *earnings* generated by growth companies and *returns* earned by their shareholders. Let us explain.

It is true that growth companies *outearn* value companies. For example, for the period ending in 2010, the return on assets for growth stocks was 9.2 percent per year, compared with the 3.7 percent return on assets for value stocks. During the same period, however, the average annual return to investors in value stocks was 14.9 percent per year—40 percent higher than the 10.7 average annual return to growth stock investors.

The explanation for this seeming anomaly is that investors discount the future expected earnings of value stocks at a higher rate than they discount the future earnings of growth stocks. This more than offsets the faster earnings growth rates of growth companies. The high discount rate results in low current valuations for value stocks and higher expected future returns relative to growth stocks. Why do investors use a higher discount rate for value stocks when calculating the current value? The following example should provide a clear answer.

Let's consider the case of two similar companies, Wal-Mart and Kmart. Most investors would say that Wal-Mart is a far better run company and a safer investment. If an investor could buy either company at the same market capitalization (say $20 billion), the obvious choice would be Wal-Mart. It not only has far higher current earnings but also is expected to produce much faster growth of future earnings. Investors recognizing this opportunity would buy shares of Wal-Mart (driving its price up) and sell shares of Kmart (driving its price down).

Now let us say that Wal-Mart's market value rises relative to Kmart until the two have the same *expected* future rate of return—say $40 billion for Wal-Mart and $10 billion for Kmart. Given that Wal-Mart is perceived to be the better company, and therefore a less risky investment, investors would still choose Wal-Mart. The reason is that although we now have equal expected returns, there is less perceived risk in owning Wal-Mart. So our process of investors buying Wal-Mart and selling Kmart continues until the expected return of owning Kmart is sufficiently greater than the expected return of owning Wal-Mart to entice investors to accept the higher risk. The size of the price differential (and thus the difference in future expected returns) is directly related to the difference in perceived risk. Given that Wal-Mart is perceived to be a much safer investment than Kmart, the price differential may have to be very large to entice investors to accept the risk of owning Kmart.

Would these price changes make Wal-Mart "overvalued" or "highly valued" relative to Kmart? The answer is "highly valued." If investors thought Wal-Mart was overvalued relative to Kmart, they would sell Wal-Mart and buy Kmart until equilibrium was reached. Instead, the high relative valuation of Wal-Mart reflects low perceived risk. Wal-Mart's future earnings are being discounted at a low rate, reflecting the lower perceived risk. This low discount rate translates into low future expected returns. Risk and expected reward are inversely related. Kmart's future earnings are discounted at a high rate. It therefore has a relatively low valuation, reflecting the greater perceived risk. However, it also has a high expected future return.

There are three very common characteristics of value stocks that are associated with firms in distress: high volatility of dividends, high ratio of debt to equity, and high volatility of earnings. The high perceived risk translates into high-risk premiums demanded by investors and thus low current prices and high future expected returns.

Our hope is that you now understand why growth stocks have provided, and are likely to continue to provide, lower returns than value stocks, despite having much higher growth rates of earnings. It is a simple risk story.

There is a related problem that investors have regarding growth stocks. They wonder, how can growth stocks, with their high prices, be considered safe investments? The explanation is that investors are confusing *business* (operating) risk with *price* risk. Kmart has more *business* risk than Wal-Mart. Therefore, the price of Kmart's stock falls until investors are compensated for the *business* risk.

On the other hand, *stock* risk, or *price* risk, increases with increases in the P/E ratio. This concept can be clarified by an analogy related to the fixed-income markets. Long-term bonds have greater price risk than short-term bonds—the longer the maturity, the greater the risk. For example, if interest rates rise 1 percent, a 1-year note will fall in value by about 1 percent, a 10-year note by about 7 percent, and a 30-year bond by about 13 percent. Here is the analogy to growth and value stocks.

Growth stocks are like long-term fixed-income instruments. Because of their high P/E and low BtM ratios, much of their value is derived from expected earnings far into the future. For value stocks, on the other hand, because of their low P/E and high BtM ratios, most of their current value is derived from liquidation value and expected earnings in the near future. As we saw, when interest rates go up, long-term (long-duration) fixed-income assets fall in value more than short-term fixed-income assets. The same is true of equities. Thus, when the rate at which you discount future earnings increases (because either the risk-free rate or the risk premium rose), growth stocks will fall in price more than value stocks. So growth stocks have more price risk than value stocks in a similar manner to long-term Treasury bonds having more price risk than short-term Treasury notes.

There is another reason that growth stocks might be considered to have more price risk. The less the perceived likelihood of a company failing to reach its projected earnings, the lower the risk premium and the higher the stock price. Taken to an extreme, a stock with very little perceived risk might be said to be "priced for perfection." Simply put, there is little room for any upside surprise. If everything goes as expected, you get low returns (because of the low-risk premium). On the other hand, if anything goes wrong, the risk premium might rise sharply, and the stock could fall dramatically. This is the type of price risk that existed in the NASDAQ 100 stocks that were trading at astronomical P/E ratios prior to our entering the new millennium. Conversely, with value stocks being so distressed, there is far less likelihood of disappointment (when the risk premium would rise further) and lots of opportunity for upside surprise (the risk premium would fall, and the price would rise dramatically).

Some value stocks are so distressed due to such high perception of risk, they have a high upside potential if the risk premium falls.

Let's look at another example of why growth stocks with their high P/E ratios have a high degree of *price* risk. Keep in mind that a high P/E ratio reflects both the market's expectation for rapid growth in earnings and investor perception of low *business* risk. Anyone who follows the market closely has observed that frequently when a growth stock misses its forecasted earnings by even just a few cents, its stock falls dramatically—seemingly far out of proportion to the small shortfall in earnings.

The explanation is simple. Let's assume we have a high-flying technology stock with projected earnings of $1 per share and selling at $100 per share. Let's also assume that earnings come in at only $0.90. The shortfall in earnings might cause the price to drop to 90, given the 100 P/E ratio. However, the shortfall in earnings will also likely affect the risk premium, causing it to rise. Let's further assume the rise in the perception of *business* risk causes the risk premium to rise so that the P/E ratio now falls to a still sky-high 80. Instead of falling just 20 percent as the P/E ratio fell, the price falls further due to the combination of the fall in the P/E ratio and the shortfall in earnings. The stock will actually fall to 72, for a drop of 28 percent. It is the rise in the risk premium (perception of *business* risk) that causes the sharp fall, not the 10 percent shortfall in earnings.

We hope we have now resolved the seeming conundrum of the riskiness of value and growth stocks, as well as their expected returns. To summarize, it is the perception of a high degree of *business* risk, and thus a high-risk premium applied to valuations, that causes the price of value companies to be distressed. The same high-risk premium creates high expected future returns. It is the perception of low *business* risk, and thus a low-risk premium applied to valuations, that causes the price of growth stocks to be elevated. It is high prices that create the perception that there's much greater *price* risk in growth stocks than in value stocks. However, what you need to understand is that investors believe there's much less likelihood of that business risk of growth stocks appearing. Otherwise, if they perceive the risk to be greater, the price would be lower.

There is a simple principle to remember that can help you avoid making poor investment decisions. Risk and *expected* return should be related. If prices are high, they reflect low perceived risk. Thus, you should expect low future returns, and vice versa. This does not make a highly priced stock a poor investment. It simply makes it a stock that is perceived to have low risk and thus low future returns. Thinking otherwise would be like assuming government bonds are poor investments when the alternative is junk bonds.

Do You Understand How the Price Paid Affects Returns?

> Probably the question heard most frequently is: "How high can stocks go?" To the unsophisticated observer there appears to be no maximum price.
> —*New York Times*, August 21, 1929

When forecasting investment returns, many individuals make the mistake of simply extrapolating recent returns into the future. Bull markets lead investors to expect higher future returns, and bear markets lead them to expect lower future returns. However, you need to understand that the price you pay for an asset has an impact on future returns.

A two-step process determines equity prices. First, future earnings are forecast. Then the present value of those earnings is calculated by discounting them at the *risk-free rate* (the rate on riskless short-term instruments such as a one-month Treasury bill) plus a *risk premium* (the size of which is commensurate with the amount of perceived risk). The lower the riskless rate or the risk premium, the higher the present value, and vice versa. Let's explore how this works.

If the risk premium of an asset class falls (as investors perceive less risk), two things occur. First, investors in that asset class benefit from a one-time increase in the price of the asset, as future earnings are now discounted at a lower rate. This is similar to the impact of falling interest rates on bond prices.

The second impact is on future expected returns. Since risk premiums are a reflection of future expected returns, the falling risk premium reflects lower future returns. This process is exactly the opposite of what investors perceive when they extrapolate the recent outperformance of an asset class into the future.

Let's examine some of the historical data to see if we can make any useful observations about the size of risk premiums and future expected returns, or at least the changes in them. We will examine the valuation metrics of price-to-earnings ratios and book-to-market values.

The average historical P/E ratio for the market has been around 15. A study covering the period 1926 through the second quarter of 1999 found that an investor who bought stocks when the market traded at P/E ratios of between 14 and 16 earned a median return of 11.8 percent over the next 10 years. This was remarkably close to the long-term return of the market. The S&P 500 returned 11.0 percent per year for the 74-year period 1926 to 2000.

Let's now look at the returns investors received when they bought stocks when the perception of risk was low (such as during a bull market) and when the perception of risk was high (such as during a bear market). Investors who purchased stocks when the P/E ratios were greater than 22 (when investors were highly optimistic and buying stocks enthusiastically) earned a median return of just 5 percent per year over the next 10 years.

Conversely, investors who purchased stocks when the P/E ratios were below 10 earned a median return of 16.9 percent per year over the next 10 years. Investors who bought stocks when the P/E ratios were below 10 (when seemingly no one wanted to own stocks) outperformed investors who bought stocks when the P/E ratios were above 22 (when seemingly everyone was jumping on the equity bandwagon) by almost 12 percent per year.[1]

You can avoid the mistake of simply extrapolating recent returns into the future by understanding and remembering how market prices are determined and how risk premiums impact future returns. It also helps to avoid the extremes in overconfidence and despair that bull and bear markets respectively bring.

And finally, it helps to remember the old cliché to buy low and sell high. Buying in bear markets is how you buy low. The simplest way to implement the buy-low/sell-high strategy is to build a portfolio that is highly diversified by asset class and then regularly rebalance. Through the process of periodically rebalancing your portfolio, you will automatically be selling the asset classes where risk premiums have fallen and prices have thus risen (on a relative basis), and you will be buying those where risk premiums have risen and prices have thus fallen (on a relative basis).

Do You Believe More Heads Are Better Than One?

Heavy advertising, the ease of making trades, and the growth of 401(k) and other retirement plans have all combined to fuel the interest in investing. Along with the social aspect of sharing investing success stories, these factors have also probably fueled the interest in investment clubs. The question is: Are more heads better than one when it comes to investing? Professors Brad Barber and Terrance Odean sought the answer to that question in their study, "Too Many Cooks Spoil the Profit: The Performance of Investment Clubs." The study covered 166 investment clubs, using data from a large brokerage house, from February 1991 to January 1997.[1] Here is a summary of their findings, which include all trading costs:

> The average club lagged a broad market index by 3.8 percent per year, returning 14.1 percent versus 17.9 percent.
> Sixty percent of the clubs underperformed the market.
> When performance was adjusted for exposure to the risk factors of size and value, the alphas (performance above or below benchmark) were negative even before transaction costs. After trading costs, the alphas were on average −4.4 percent per year.

Though these findings are not surprising given all the evidence on the failure of active managers to beat their benchmarks, they do conflict with data from the National Association of Investment Clubs (NAIC). The study noted that several articles in the *Wall Street Journal* and *New York Times* claimed that NAIC surveys show that 60 percent of investment clubs outperform, rather than showing that 60 percent of the clubs underperform. There are three good possible explanations.

First, as with actively managed funds, there is likely to be survivorship bias in the data—clubs that perform poorly might break up. Second, there is likely to be reporting bias in the data—clubs that perform poorly are less likely to report results than clubs that do well. In fact, only about 5 to 10 percent of all investment clubs return the NAIC's survey.[2] Third, there may be clubs that simply miscalculate returns.

There were some other interesting findings from Barber and Odean's study:

> Despite trading less than individuals (65 percent annual turnover compared with 75 percent for individual investors), and therefore incurring lower trading expenses, clubs produced lower returns than individual investors—showing that at least when it comes to investing, fewer heads may be better.
> The clubs would have been far better off if they never had traded during the year—beginning-of-the-year portfolios outperformed their actual holdings by 3.5 percent per year. The reason was that the stocks they sold outperformed the stocks they bought by over 4 percent per year.

The conclusion is that investment clubs have something in common with individual investors—trading is hazardous to their financial health. Barber and Odean concluded: "Investment clubs serve many useful functions. They encourage savings. They educate their members about financial markets. They foster friendships and social ties. They entertain. Unfortunately, their investments do not beat the market."

Do You Believe Active Managers Will Protect You from Bear Markets?

We are the first to admit that during bear markets actively managed funds begin with an advantage over passively managed ones and that the value of index funds falls during bear markets. The advantages that active managers have in bear markets are a result of maintaining reserves both to meet redemption requests and to hold investment funds available as they seek the next great stock to buy. This cash reserve, because cash is a poorly performing asset class in bull markets, is one of the reasons active managers underperform in bull markets. In bear markets, however, cash becomes king. Theoretically anticipating bear markets, active managers can reduce their exposure to equities and protect their investors from the type of losses that index funds experience (since index funds are always virtually 100 percent invested). Unfortunately, the videotape reveals that active managers offer no such protection. Let's look at some of the evidence.

Just prior to one of the worst bear markets in the post–World War II era (1973–1974), mutual fund cash reserves stood at only 4 percent. They reached about 12 percent at the ensuing low. In mid-1998, when the Asian Contagion bear market arrived, cash reserves were just 5 percent. Compare this with the 13 percent level reached at the market low in 1990, just prior to beginning the longest bull market in history.[1] It seems fund managers are very good at executing a buy-high/sell-low strategy.

A Lipper Analytical Services study provided further evidence on the failure of active managers to outperform in bear markets, despite their advantages. Lipper studied the six market corrections (defined as a drop of at least 10 percent) from August 31, 1978, to October 11, 1990, and found that while the average loss for the S&P 500 Index was 15.1 percent, the average loss for large-cap growth funds was 17.0 percent.[2]

And consider this bit of amazing evidence. Goldman Sachs studied mutual fund cash holdings from 1970 to 1989. The study found that mutual fund managers miscalled *all* nine major turning points.[3] You could not get all nine turning points wrong if you tried!

The 2009 Spring/Summer issue of the *Vanguard Investment Perspectives* provides us with further and more recent evidence. Vanguard's study, covering the period 1970 to 2008, examined the returns of active funds during the seven periods when the Dow Jones Wilshire 5000 Index fell at least 10 percent and the six periods when the MSCI EAFE Index fell by at least that amount. Despite acknowledging survivorship bias in the data, Vanguard found:

> *It didn't matter whether an active manager was operating in a bear market, a bull market that precedes or follows it, or across longer-term cycles.* The combination of cost, security selection, and market timing proved a difficult hurdle to overcome.
> *Success can be explained at least in part by style exposures.* For example, during the bear market of September 2000 to March 2003, while the U.S. total market lost more than 42 percent, the Russell 1000 Value Index fell just 21 percent. Once active funds were compared with their style benchmarks, there was no consistent pattern of outperformance. This was confirmed by Standard & Poor's finding that the majority of funds in eight of the nine domestic equity style boxes were outperformed by indexes in the negative markets of 2008. Results were similar during the bear market of 2000 to 2002.
> *Past success in overcoming this hurdle didn't ensure future success.* The degree of attrition among winners from one period to the next indicated that successfully navigating one or even two bear markets might be more strongly linked to simple luck than to skill.

Vanguard concluded, "We find little evidence to support the purported benefits of active management during periods of market stress."[4]

In the face of so much evidence, only people who are unwilling to give up on long-held opinions will continue to believe that active managers can protect investors from bear markets.

MISTAKE 26

Do You Fail to Compare Your Funds with Proper Benchmarks?

The recent bear market gave active managers and their faithful another chance to declare that it was once again a stock pickers' market and that active management would prove to be the winning strategy. Unfortunately, this is an old canard that is trotted out every so often in an attempt to keep alive the myth that active management is the winning strategy and to keep investors paying high fees for poor, inconsistent, and tax-inefficient performance. However, when proper light is shed on the subject, the canard is exposed as having no basis in fact.

Active managers point to their successes in periods like 1977 to 1979, when 85 percent, 69 percent, and 80 percent, respectively, of the actively managed funds outperformed the S&P 500 Index; and 1991 to 1993, when 55 percent, 54 percent, and 60 percent, respectively, did so. The claim is that those were stock pickers' kind of years—as opposed to the years 1994 to 1998, when no more than 22 percent of the active funds accomplished that feat. The problem with the claim of being a stock pickers' market is that it doesn't hold up to scrutiny. The reason is that the claimants are using an apples-to-oranges comparison to make their case. The conclusions are drawn because of confusing indexing with the exclusive use of the S&P 500.

For the time period 1963 to 1998, there were just 14 years (39 percent) when more than 50 percent of active managers beat the S&P 500.[1] Of those 14 years, 13 were years when small caps (as represented by the CRSP 6-10 index through May 1986 and the passively managed DFA Small Cap Fund thereafter) beat large caps. The one exception was 1974, when 53 percent of active managers beat the S&P 500 and small caps underperformed that index by about 2 percent.

The explanation for the seeming outperformance of active managers in those 14 years is that the average actively managed fund holds stocks with a smaller average market cap than the weighted market cap of the S&P 500. And it is asset allocation, not stock selection or market timing, that determines almost all differences in returns. This can be seen when we compare the performance of actively managed funds with the performance of a small-cap benchmark in the 14 years when more than 50 percent of the actively managed funds outperformed the S&P 500. Here is what we find:

> A small-cap index (or fund) outperformed the average actively managed fund in 12 of the 14 years.
> The only two years when the average actively managed fund beat both the S&P 500 and a small-cap benchmark were 1966 and 1974—both years of bear markets in both small- and large-cap stocks.
> There were seven other years when small-cap stocks outperformed large-cap stocks. In not a single one of those periods did more than 50 percent of active managers beat the S&P 500.[2]

The data should come as no surprise. When small-cap stocks outperform large-cap stocks, managers holding stocks with an average market cap less than that of the S&P 500 should (and do) perform relatively better. Unfortunately, the S&P 500 is the wrong benchmark. Actively managed funds should always be benchmarked in a way that ensures an apples-to-apples comparison. Small-cap funds should be compared with a small-cap index, and large-cap funds should be compared with a large-cap index. The same is true for value and growth funds.

Mark Carhart's classic study of the mutual fund industry determined that once you accounted for style factors (small cap versus large cap and value versus growth), the average actively managed fund underperformed its benchmark on a pretax basis by 1.8 percent per year.[3]

To gain further perspective on active management, let's take a longer-term look at the performance against two benchmarks, the Wilshire 5000 and the Russell 3000, which are broader indexes than the S&P 500 Index. For the 5-, 10-, and 15-year periods ending in 2000, only 16 percent, 16 percent, and 17 percent, respectively, of actively managed funds outperformed the Wilshire 5000. Only 14 percent, 14 percent, and 15 percent, respectively, of actively managed funds outperformed the Russell 3000.[4] These data should be enough to convince almost anyone that active management is a loser's game.

It's not that you can't win; it's just that the odds of doing so are so low that it doesn't pay to play. But for those who need further evidence, these data do not even contain all the bad news. First, the evidence is based on pretax returns. Since actively managed funds are inherently more tax inefficient than index funds, it is a virtual certainty that on an after-tax basis the percentage of out-performers would have been much lower. Second, the data contain survivorship bias, which negatively impacts returns further.

To avoid making this type of mistake, make sure that you compare the performance of an actively managed fund against its appropriate passive benchmark. If it is a small-cap fund, make sure you compare it with a small-cap index such as the S&P 600. If it is a small-cap value fund, it should be compared with a bench-mark such as the S&P SmallCap 600 Value Index, and so on.

MISTAKE 27

Do You Focus on Pretax Returns?

If index funds look great before taxes, their performance
is almost unbeatable after taxes, thanks to their low
turnover and thus slow realization of capital gains.

—Jonathan Clements
Wall Street Journal, December 22, 1998

While I was at Morgan Stanley Dean Witter, I never once
came across a broker talking to a client about the problems
turnover creates with mutual fund investing. Nor capital
gains tax. Nor the effect the tax has on lowering the
investor's true rate of return. Simply put, the idea or notion
of after-tax returns was shoved aside and under the rug.

—Ted Lux
Ex-stockbroker, *Exposing the Wheel Spin on Wall Street*

Our experience is that most investors focus on the pretax
returns of their investments, despite the fact that investors in taxable accounts don't get to spend pretax returns, only
after-tax returns. Most investors are simply not aware of how
devastating an impact taxes can have on returns. Let's see the
role taxes play in determining after-tax returns.

Although the effect of paying taxes may be minimal in any
one year, it becomes substantial over long periods. A study
commissioned by Charles Schwab demonstrated how great an
impact this stealth attack has on returns. Schwab measured the
performance of 62 equity funds for the period 1963 to 1992.
It found that while each dollar invested would have grown to

$21.89 in a tax-deferred account, it would only have produced $9.87 in a taxable account for a high-bracket investor.[1] For high-tax-bracket investors, the study also found that for the 10-year period ending December 1992, Vanguard's S&P 500 Index fund would have outperformed 92 percent of actively managed funds after taxes.[2]

A simulated study covering the 25-year period ending in 1995 examined the effects of expenses and taxes on returns. This study assumed that a hypothetical fund

> Matched the performance of the S&P 500
> Had turnover of 80 percent
> Incurred expenses of 1 percent

The study found that the typical investor received only 41 percent of the preexpense, pretax returns of the index. The government took 47 percent of the returns, and this finding doesn't even consider how state and local taxes affected the returns or if the investor were subject to the highest tax brackets.[3]

Let's look at several studies that cover shorter investment horizons. Robert Jeffrey and Robert Arnott showed the impact of taxes on returns in their study of 71 actively managed funds for the 10-year period 1982 to 1991. They found that while 15 of the 71 funds beat a passively managed fund on a pretax basis, only 5 did so on an after-tax basis.[4]

Morningstar studied the five-year period 1992 to 1996 and found that diversified U.S. stock funds gained an average of 91.9 percent. Morningstar then assumed that income and short-term gains were taxed at 39.6 percent and long-term capital gains at 28 percent; the result was that after-tax returns dwindled to 71.5 percent, a loss of 22 percent of the returns.[5] As you can see, even over short investment horizons, taxes can destroy returns.

Individual investors are beginning to awaken to the important role that fund distributions play in after-tax performance. This has been one of the driving forces behind the rapid growth of ETFs and index and other passively managed funds. Many fund families have taken this issue to the next level by creating passively managed funds that are also tax-managed. These tax-managed funds strive both to minimize fund distributions and to maximize the percentage of distributions that will be in the form of long-term capital gains. They accomplish this by implementing the following strategies:

> Maintaining low turnover
> Attempting to avoid realization of short-term gains
> Harvesting losses by selling stocks that are below cost, in order to offset realized gains in other securities
> Selling the appreciated shares with the highest cost basis
> Trading around dividend dates
> Ensuring that revenue from securities lending does not exceed the operating expenses of the fund

Taxes are probably the largest expense that investors incur, even greater than management fees or commissions. Therefore, ignoring the impact of taxes on the returns from taxable accounts is one of the biggest mistakes you can make. You can avoid this mistake if you keep the following points in mind. The burden of taxes provides an almost insurmountable hurdle for active managers to overcome. Because of the important impact of taxes on returns, passively managed funds that are also tax-managed should be the investment vehicles of choice for taxable accounts. If you do choose to use actively managed funds, they are best held in a tax-deferred account, where the high turnover won't impact after-tax returns.

Do You Rely on a Fund's Descriptive Name When Making Purchase Decisions?

How many legs would a sheep have if you called its tail a leg?
Four. Because calling its tail a leg doesn't make it one.
—Abraham Lincoln

Several academic studies have come to the conclusion that asset allocation (how investments are allocated among various asset classes in a portfolio) determines the vast majority of not only the returns but also the risks of a portfolio:

> A study by Gary P. Brinson, L. Randolph Hood, and Gilbert L. Beebower, "Determinants of Portfolio Returns," demonstrated that 94 percent of the differences in returns resulted not from market timing or stock selection, but from "asset allocation" decisions.[1]
> In another study of 31 pension plans, representing $70 billion of total assets under management, Eugene Fama, Jr., found that asset allocation determined over 97 percent of returns.[2]
> And finally, a study by Roger G. Ibbotson and Paul D. Kaplan, analyzing the 10-year performance of 94 balanced mutual funds and the 5-year performance of 58 pension plans, concluded that approximately 100 percent of a portfolio's absolute return is explained by asset allocation.[3]

Whether the number is 94 or 100 percent doesn't really matter. The evidence is very clear that asset allocation determines the vast majority of the risk and reward of a portfolio.

Given that conclusion, the most important decision that investors can make is the asset allocation decision. This is the one that will determine the long-term performance of the portfolio. Once investors decide on their investment policy (asset allocation), they must choose which funds to use as the building blocks of their portfolio. One choice involves implementing the strategy with active or passive managers. If investors choose passive managers, they can be highly confident that the specific investment style will be adhered to, as the fund will simply be replicating the asset class or index it represents. There is no such assurance with active managers. With active managers, you cannot even rely on the fund's name when making a choice. Let's look at two examples.

It is April 2001, and an investor would like exposure to U.S. large-cap value stocks. Believing that the fund's name describes its investment style, the investor chooses the PBHG Large-Cap Value Fund. As of March 31, 2001, the fund's weighted average book-to-market value was 0.14. At the time, the most "growthy" 10 percent of stocks had a BtM of 0.14 or lower. This was certainly not a value-oriented fund. Using the academic definition of value—the top three deciles as ranked by BtM by the Center for Research in Security Prices (CRSP)—a fund would have to have a weighted average BtM of 0.92 or higher to be considered a value fund. Even using a more liberal definition of value as the top 50 percent of stocks as ranked by BtM, value would be defined as stocks with a BtM of about 0.6 or greater. By contrast, the DFA Large Cap Value Fund, a passive asset class fund, had a BtM of well over 1.

As another example, in March 2001 investors seeking exposure to the asset class of U.S. small-cap stocks might have chosen the Aquinas Small-Cap Fund, which had a median market cap of almost $2.4 billion. There is no definition of small-cap stocks that would include a fund in which over 50 percent of the stocks had a market capitalization that large. In fact, that level would place the median market capitalization in the top 30 percent of all stocks as ranked by the CRSP. In contrast, the passively managed DFA Small Cap Fund had a median market cap of less than $100 million, and its passively managed Micro Cap Fund had a median market cap of about $50 million.

A fitting analogy would be to take a black horse, paint it with white stripes, and call it a zebra. Of course, no matter what the color, the horse would still be a horse. The lesson is that you should not choose a fund, even an index fund, by its name. Instead, you should carefully check its weighted average book-to-market and market capitalization levels. That is the simplest way to tell the true nature of a fund.

Do You Believe Active Management Is a Winner's Game in Inefficient Markets?

Even many devotees of active portfolio strategies have conceded that the efficiency of the market for U.S. large-cap stocks is so great that attempting to add value through active management is unlikely to produce positive results. They do cling, however, to the idea that active management is likely to add value in less efficient markets. The asset class for which the active management argument is made most strongly is the emerging markets—an "inefficient" asset class if there ever was one. As the following tale will demonstrate, believers in active management have a major problem—there isn't any evidence to support their claim.

Aaron and David were good friends. One day after work in early 2009, they got together for a drink. Aaron told David that because of the poor performance of the actively managed mutual funds in his portfolio, he decided to fire his financial advisor. He told David that he had recently met with his CPA, who had several years ago expanded his practice to include investment advice. Aaron was persuaded by his CPA's explanation about how the securities markets were efficient and why active management was likely to result in below-benchmark performance. He went on to explain that the CPA had provided him with a comparison of the returns of the funds he had owned with those of comparable index and other passively managed funds. That comparison, especially on an after-tax basis, convinced him it was time to stop trying to beat the market. He was going to become a passive, buy-and-hold investor.

David, who considered himself a knowledgeable investor, agreed that indexing was a good strategy in large-cap stocks of developed countries. However, in emerging markets where the competition for information is far less, surely active management is likely to be the winning strategy. Aaron respected David's knowledge and thought what he had said made sense. He went back to his CPA to ask him if passive management was the right strategy for every asset class or just for large-cap stocks.

The CPA told Aaron that the question "Does active management work in less efficient markets?" was one of the most asked questions he gets, and so they set up a meeting for the following day. The conversation went as follows:

> **CPA:** Aaron, if a market is inefficient, we should see evidence of actively managed funds outperforming passively managed funds in inefficient markets. In preparation for our meeting, I used the Morningstar database to provide us with a list of the 54 actively managed emerging market stock funds with a full 10-year track record for the period 1999 to 2008. During this period the average actively managed fund returned 9.1 percent. Now contrast that return with the returns of the three passively managed funds run by Dimensional Fund Advisors. Its Emerging Markets Value Fund returned 13.4 percent, outperforming 94 percent of the actively managed funds. Its Emerging Markets Small Cap Fund returned 11.5 percent, outperforming 76 percent of the actively managed funds. And its Emerging Markets Fund returned 9.5 percent, outperforming 62 percent of the actively managed funds.
>
> **AARON:** Okay, you have me convinced. But can you help me understand why the performance of these funds is so poor when it seems likely the competition for information is less than it is in the market for U.S. large-cap stocks?
>
> **CPA:** Aaron, that is a great question. The answer is that while there may be informational inefficiencies in the emerging markets, the evidence is clear that active managers have not been able to exploit them on a persistent basis. I think there are three intuitively simple explanations. First, transaction costs in the emerging markets are generally much higher than they are in the United States and other developed markets. Thus, the hurdles that must be overcome are greater. Second, there are generally not that many stocks in any one emerging market that have sufficient liquidity for an actively managed fund to consider purchasing. This limits the ability for active managers

to add value through security selection. The third explanation is that active funds typically have much higher operating expenses.

Summary

We can draw three conclusions from the data:

1. The emerging markets are not as inefficient as the active managers claim.
2. The costs of operating an emerging market fund, plus the costs of trading in the less liquid markets of these countries, are so great that once other expenses (including taxes) are considered, active managers are unlikely to add value.
3. Because turnover is much greater in actively managed funds, trading costs hit them harder than passively managed funds.

There are many myths perpetuated by the Wall Street establishment and the financial media. That active management is the winning strategy in less efficient markets is just one of them. As the historical evidence demonstrates, active management is highly unlikely to outperform in even the allegedly inefficient emerging markets. In fact, the evidence suggests that active managers perform just as poorly in the "inefficient" markets as they do in the more efficient markets of the developed nations.

Do You Fail to Understand the Tyranny of the Efficiency of the Market?

Behavioral finance is the study of human behavior and how that behavior leads to investment errors, including the mispricing of assets. Pricing anomalies present a problem for those who believe in the efficient market hypothesis. However, the real question for investors is not whether the market persistently makes pricing errors. Instead, the real question is whether the anomalies are exploitable after taking into account real-world costs. In other words, if behavioral finance is to have merit as an investment strategy alternative to passive investing, one should be able to observe investors who have successfully used its theories and produced abnormal returns.

The authors of the study "Behavioral Finance: Are the Disciples Profiting from the Doctrine?" identified 16 self-proclaimed or media-identified behavioral mutual funds—funds that attempt to take advantage of discoveries from the field of behavioral finance.[1]

The authors analyzed the behavioral funds to determine whether they successfully attract investment dollars and also if their strategies earn abnormal returns for their investors. The following summarizes their findings:

> Behavioral funds successfully attracted investment dollars at a significantly greater rate than index and corresponding actively managed nonbehavioral funds. Investors apparently believe that the pricing errors are persistently exploitable.
> While the funds do outperform S&P 500 Index funds, the explanation for the outperformance is that they load very heavily on the high-minus-low factor (meaning they have significant exposure to

value stocks). After adjusting for risk, they do not earn abnormal returns.

> Behavioral mutual funds are tantamount to value investing and not much more.

There Is Smoke, but No Fire

While behavioral finance has gained substantial attention in academia and seems to be gaining greater acceptance among practitioners, there doesn't seem to be any evidence to support the raison d'être for the funds—that anomalies can be identified and exploited on a persistent basis. Even if there are anomalies, there are two simple and plausible explanations for the findings of the study. The first is that strategies have no costs, but implementing them does. A strategy may appear to work on paper, but the costs of implementation can exceed the size of the pricing errors. The second is that once an anomaly is discovered and attempts are made to exploit it, the very act of doing it will serve to reduce or eliminate the size of the pricing error. Those who seek to exploit market anomalies almost inevitably find that the markets are tyrannical in their efficiency. The following examples demonstrate that point.

The Tyranny of the Efficient Markets

Richard Thaler is one of the leaders in the field of behavioral finance. As we discussed, the basic hypothesis of behavioral finance is that, due to behavioral biases, markets make persistent mistakes in pricing securities. An example of a persistent mistake is that the market underreacts to news—both good and bad news are only slowly incorporated into prices. Fuller and Thaler Asset Management was formed to exploit such errors.

Fuller and Thaler Asset Management offers two funds based on behavioral theories: Undiscovered Managers Behavioral Growth Fund and Undiscovered Managers Behavioral Value Fund. (Note that JPMorgan acquired these funds in January 2004. However, Fuller continued as a subadvisor.) To test the behavioral theories, we will compare the performance of these funds with the performance of the DFA Small Cap Fund and its Small Cap Value Fund, respectively. The DFA funds are managed based on the belief that markets are efficient, and so stock selection and market-timing efforts are eschewed. Thus, we have a real live test of the behavioral theory and the efficiency of the market.

For the 10-year period 2001 to 2010, the Behavioral Growth Fund returned 3.4 percent per year. This compares with the 8.3 percent per year return of the DFA Small Cap Fund. The Behavioral Value Fund returned 9.4 percent per year. The DFA Small Value Fund returned 11.1 percent. There certainly doesn't seem to be any evidence of the ability to exploit inefficiencies in the market.

Further Evidence

LSV Asset Management was formed in 1994 by professors Josef Lakonishok, Andrei Shleifer, and Robert Vishny. Together, they have published more than 200 academic papers on investing and the field of behavioral finance. Their research is the foundation for LSV's investment strategy. The basic premise of their investment strategy is that superior long-term results can be achieved by systematically exploiting the judgmental biases and behavioral weaknesses that influence the decisions of many investors. These include the tendency to

> Extrapolate the past too far into the future
> Wrongly equate a good company with a good investment irrespective of price
> Ignore statistical evidence
> Develop a "mindset" about a company

They believe that the market persistently misprices securities and that pricing mistakes can be exploited.

While LSV is basically an institutional money manager, it runs three mutual funds: the LSV Value Equity Fund, the LSV Conservative Value Equity Fund, and the LSV Conservative Core Equity Fund. Lakonishok, the chief executive officer of LSV, also manages the HighMark Small Cap Value Fund.

To test whether the hypothesized inefficiencies can be exploited, we can compare the performance of these funds against the passively managed funds of DFA. Since the LSV Conservative Value Equity Fund and the LSV Conservative Core Equity Fund both have inception dates of 2007, and we want to look at longer-term data, we will confine our comparison to just the other two funds.

Again, we look at the 10-year period 2001 to 2010. The LSV Value Equity Fund returned 5.2 percent per year. The similar DFA Large Cap Value Fund returned 5.3 percent per year. Now let's look at the performance of the HighMark Small Cap Value Fund. It returned 8.0 percent per year. The similar DFA Small Cap Value Fund returned 11.1 percent per year—the behavioral fund underperformed a passive benchmark by 3.1 percent per year.

Based on the evidence, it seems that exploiting inefficiencies is a lot harder than identifying them.

The Failed Quest

We have seen how some of the leading academics have applied their theories on market inefficiency and failed in their quest for the Holy Grail of alpha. There does not seem to be evidence in favor of the behavioral theory being an implementable strategy. The case can be made that if there ever was a time when the theory would have worked, it no longer appears to be true. The tyranny of the efficiency of markets and the wisdom of crowds make for a very powerful opponent indeed.

Do You Believe Hedge Fund Managers Deliver Superior Performance?

Hedge funds, a small and specialized niche within the investment fund arena, attract lots of attention. Hedge funds differ from mutual funds in several ways:

> They are not generally available to individuals unless they have high net worths.
> Unlike the typical broadly diversified mutual fund, they generally have highly concentrated large positions in just a few securities.
> They have broad latitude to make large bets (either long or short) on almost any type of asset, be it a commodity, real estate, currency, country debt, stocks, or something else.
> Management generally has a significant stake in the fund, limited regulatory oversight, and strong financial incentives, from fees that typically range from 1 to 2 percent per year plus 20 percent of profits.

Hedge fund managers seek to outperform market indexes such as the S&P 500 Index by exploiting what they perceive to be market mispricings. Studying their performance would seem to be one way of testing the efficient market hypothesis and the ability of active managers to outperform their respective benchmarks.

A study by AQR Capital Management covered the five-year period ending January 31, 2001. The data for the study came from CSFB/Tremont's database. The study found that the average hedge fund had returned 14.7 percent per year, lagging the S&P 500 Index by almost 4 percent per year. In addition, the study concluded that many hedge funds were taking on significantly greater risk by investing in highly illiquid securities. Seems that while index funds may be boring, they make better investment vehicles.[1]

The 2006 study "The A, B, Cs of Hedge Funds: Alphas, Betas, and Costs" covered the period from January 1995 through March 2006 and found the average hedge fund had returned 8.98 percent per year, lagging the S&P 500 Index by 2.6 percent per year. Equally important, this study included the bear market of 2000 to 2002 (the type of market when hedge funds are supposed to perform the best).[2]

And finally, we have data for the period from 2003 through 2010. As the following table demonstrates, the HRFX Global Hedge Fund Index of hedge funds underperformed every major equity asset class.

2003–2010	ANNUALIZED RETURN (%)
HFRX Global Hedge Fund Index	2.8
Domestic Indexes	
S&P 500 Index	6.7
MSCI US Small Cap 1750 Index	12.0
MSCI US Prime Market Value Index	7.1
MSCI US Small Cap Value Index	11.2
Dow Jones Select REIT Index	11.1
International Indexes	
MSCI EAFE Index	10.0
MSCI EAFE Small Cap Index	15.0
MSCI EAFE Value Index	10.4
MSCI Emerging Markets Index	21.6

The large fees (usually around 2 percent of assets) and the incentive-based compensation (usually around 20 percent of any profits obtained) attract many successful mutual fund managers to the hedge fund arena. Compensation that was in the hundreds of thousands as a mutual fund manager becomes millions as a hedge fund manager. Unfortunately, the persistence of performance, just as in the mutual fund arena, doesn't justify the faith of investors. According to Stephen T. Brown, professor at NYU's Stern Business School, "Half of them [ex-mutual fund managers] that survive the first six months are dead two years later."[3] Buried along with them are investor assets.

Summary

Hedge fund investing appeals to investors because of the exclusive nature of the club. It also offers the potential of great rewards. Unfortunately, the evidence is that hedge fund managers demonstrate no greater ability to deliver above-market returns than do active mutual fund managers. At the same time that investors in hedge funds were earning below-market returns, they were (in many cases) assuming far more risk—although they were probably unaware they were doing so. The following is a list of some of those risks:

> › Hedge funds lack the daily liquidity of mutual funds.
> › Hedge funds lack transparency—a requirement for prudent decision making. Hedge funds cause investors to lose control over their asset allocation (since investors don't know what their hedge funds are invested in).
> › Hedge funds tend to invest in highly risky assets and often compound that risk by taking on large amounts of leverage.
> › Hedge funds don't combine well with equities. The correlation of hedge funds to equities has a nasty tendency to turn high at the wrong time.

In addition to these risks, hedge funds also tend to be highly tax inefficient and show no persistent performance beyond the randomly expected, meaning there is no way to identify the few winners ahead of time.

Yes, a few hedge managers will succeed. However, the real tests are these two questions: Do more succeed than is randomly expected? Is there persistence in performance? As the historical record suggests, the answer to these questions is no, and so investors should logically avoid investing in hedge funds.

MISTAKE 32

Are You Subject to the Money Illusion?

The most costly of all follies is to believe
in the palpably not true.
—H. L. Mencken

Magic, or conjuring, is the art of entertaining an audience by performing illusions that baffle and amaze, often by giving the impression that something impossible has been achieved. Specifically, optical illusions are tricks that fool your eyes. Most magic tricks that fall into the category of optical illusions work, however, by fooling both the brain and the eyes together at the same time.

Fortunately, most magical illusions don't cost the participants anything, except perhaps some embarrassment at being fooled. However, basing investment strategies on illusions can be very damaging, leading investors to make all kinds of mistakes. There are many illusions in the world of investing. The process known as *data mining* creates many of them. Unfortunately, identifying patterns that worked in the past does not necessarily provide you with any useful information about stock price movements in the future. As Andrew Lo, a finance professor at MIT, points out, "Given enough time, enough attempts, and enough imagination, almost any pattern can be teased out of any data set."[1]

The stock and bond markets are filled with wrongheaded data mining. David Leinweber, of First Quadrant Corp., illustrates this point with what he calls "stupid data-miner tricks." Leinweber discovered that the single best predictor of the S&P 500 Index has historically been butter production in Bangladesh.[2] His example is a perfect illustration of the fact that the mere existence of a correlation does not necessarily give it predictive value. Some logical reason for the correlation to exist is required for it to have credibility. For example, there is a strong and logical correlation between the level of economic activity and the level of interest rates. As economic activity increases, the demand for money, and therefore its price (interest rates), also increases.

One of the illusions with great potential for creating investment mistakes is known as the *money illusion*. The reason it has such great potential for creating mistakes is that it relates to one of the most popular indicators used by investors to determine if the market is undervalued or overvalued, known as the *Fed model*.

In 1997, in his monetary policy report to Congress, Fed chairman Alan Greenspan indicated that changes in the ratio of prices in the S&P 500 to consensus estimates of earnings over the coming 12 months have often been inversely related to changes in long-term Treasury yields.[3] Following this report, Edward Yardeni, at the time a market strategist for Morgan Grenfell, speculated that the Federal Reserve was using a model to determine if the market was fairly valued—that is, how attractive were stocks priced *relative* to bonds. The model became known as the "Fed model," despite no acknowledgment of its use by the Fed.

Using the "logic" that bonds and stocks are competing instruments, the model uses the yield on the 10-year Treasury bond to calculate "fair value," comparing that rate with the E/P ratio (the inverse of the popular P/E ratio). For example, if the yield on the 10-year Treasury were 4 percent, then fair value would be an E/P of 4 percent, or a P/E of 25. If the P/E is greater (lower) than 25, then the market is considered overvalued (undervalued). If the same bond were yielding 5 percent, then fair value would be at a P/E of only 20. The logic is that higher interest rates create more competition for stocks, and this should be reflected in valuations. Thus lower interest rates justify higher valuations, and vice versa.

Since Yardeni coined the phrase, the Fed model as a valuation tool has become conventional wisdom, and unfortunately for investors, conventional wisdom is often wrong. (The earth is flat was once conventional wisdom.) There are two major problems with the Fed model.

The first relates to how the model is used by many investors. Yardeni speculated that the Federal Reserve used the model to compare the valuation of stocks *relative* to bonds as competing instruments. The model says nothing about absolute expected returns. Thus stocks, using the Fed model, might be priced under fair value relative to bonds, and they can have either high or low expected returns. However, the expected return of stocks is not determined by their relative value to bonds. Instead, the expected return is determined by the current dividend yield plus the expected growth in dividends. This is an important point that seems to be lost on many investors. The result is that investors who believe that low interest rates justify a high valuation for stocks, without the high valuation impacting expected returns, are likely to be highly disappointed (and perhaps not have enough funds with which to live comfortably in retirement). The reality is that when P/Es are high, expected returns are low, and vice versa.

The second problem with the Fed model, leading to a false conclusion, is that it fails to consider that inflation has a different impact on corporate earnings than it does on the return on fixed-income instruments. Over the long term, the nominal growth rate of corporate earnings has been in line with the nominal growth rate of the economy, and the real growth rate of corporate earnings has been in line with the real growth of the economy.[4] Thus, the *real* growth rate of earnings is not impacted by inflation in the long term. On the other hand, the yield to maturity on a 10-year bond is a nominal return, and, therefore, the *real* return on the bond will be negatively impacted by inflation. The error of comparing a number that is not impacted by inflation with one that is leads to the *money illusion*. Let's explain why we have a money illusion.

We begin by assuming that the real yield on a 10-year Treasury inflation-protected security (TIPS), a riskless instrument, is 2 percent. If the expected long-term rate of inflation is 3 percent, then a 10-year Treasury bond would be expected to yield about 5 percent (the 2 percent real yield on TIPS plus the 3 percent expected rate of inflation). According to the Fed model, that would mean a fair value for stocks at a P/E of 20 (E/P of 5 percent). Let's now change our assumption to a long-term expected rate of inflation of 2 percent. This would cause the yield on the 10-year bond to fall from 5 to 4 percent, causing the fair-value P/E to rise to 25. But this makes no sense. Inflation does not impact the real rate of return demanded by equity investors. Therefore, over the long term, it should not impact valuations.

In addition, as stated above, there is a very strong relationship between nominal earnings growth and inflation over the long term. In this case, a long-term expected inflation rate of 2 percent, instead of 3 percent, would be expected to lower the growth of nominal earnings by 1 percent. However, it would have no impact on real earnings growth over the long term (the only kind that matter). Because the real return on bonds is impacted by inflation while real earnings growth is not, the Fed model compares a number that is impacted by inflation with a number that is not (resulting in the money illusion).

Let's also consider what would happen if the real interest component of bond prices fell. The real rate is reflective of the economic demand for funds. Thus, it is reflective of the rate of growth of the economy. If the real rate falls due to a slower rate of economic growth, interest rates would fall, reflecting the reduced demand for funds. Using the same example from above, if the real rate on TIPS fell from 2 to 1 percent, that would have the same impact on nominal rates as a 1 percent fall in expected inflation and, therefore, the same impact on the fair-value P/E ratio—causing fair value to rise. However, this too does not make sense. A slower rate of real economic growth means a slower rate of growth in corporate earnings. Thus, while the competition from lower interest rates is reduced, so will be future earnings. Since corporate earnings have grown in line with nominal GDP growth over the long term, a 1 percent lower long-term rate of growth in GDP would lead to a 1 percent lower expected growth in corporate earnings. Thus, the benefit of falling interest rates would be offset by the equivalent fall in future expected earnings. Of course, the reverse would be true if a stronger economy caused a rise in real interest rates. The negative effect of a higher rate of interest would be offset by a faster expected growth in earnings. The bottom line is that there is no reason to believe stock valuations should change if the *real* return demanded by investors has not changed.

Clifford S. Asness studied the period 1881 to 2001. He concluded that the Fed model did not have any predictive power in terms of absolute stock returns—the conventional wisdom is wrong. (As we discussed, however, this is not the purpose for which Yardeni thought the Fed model was used. In keeping with the purpose for which the model was designed, it would have been more appropriate for Asness to study the relative performance of stocks versus bonds given the "signal"—undervalued or overvalued—the model was giving.)

Asness also concluded that the P/E ratio does have strong forecasting powers over 10-year horizons. Thus, the lower the P/E ratio, the higher the expected returns to stocks, regardless of the level of interest rates, and vice versa.[5]

There is one other point to consider. A stronger economy, leading to higher real interest rates, should also be expected to lead to a rise in corporate earnings. The stronger economy reduces the risks of equity investing, which could cause investors to demand a lower risk premium. Thus, it is possible that higher interest rates, if caused by a stronger economy and not higher inflation, could actually justify higher (not lower) valuations for stocks. The Fed model, however, would suggest that higher interest rates mean that stocks are less attractive. And, of course, the reverse would be true if a weaker economy led to lower real interest rates.

Summary

While gaining knowledge of how a magical illusion works has the negative effect of ruining the illusion, understanding the "magic" of financial illusions is beneficial to investors, as it should help them avoid mistakes. In the case of the money illusion, understanding how the money illusion is created will prevent investors from believing that an environment of low (high) interest rates allows for either high (low) valuations or high (low) future stock returns. Instead, if the current level of prices is high (a high P/E ratio), that should lead one to conclude that future returns to equities are likely to be lower than has historically been the case, and vice versa. It is also important to note that this does not mean that investors should either avoid equities because they are "overvalued" or increase their allocations because they are "undervalued." It simply means that if the P/E is higher than the historic average, investors should not expect future returns to be as great as their historical average.

Many factors impact the future returns to stocks. We hope, however, that you are now convinced that the Fed model should not be used to determine if the market is at fair value or not.

MISTAKE 33

Do You Believe Demographics Are Destiny?

I n October 1999, the book *The Roaring 2000s: Building the Wealth and Lifestyle You Desire in the Greatest Boom in History* was published. The author was Harry Dent, a demographer. The book was a bestseller. Its main investment theme was both simple and compelling:

> First, the population of the United States is rapidly aging.
> Second, the aging population will boost the demand for certain products and services, benefiting those sectors—specifically the stocks of companies related to the health-care sector of the economy. The earnings of these companies would rise rapidly as a result of the greatly increased demand.
> Third, individuals can benefit from these trends by investing in stocks of companies in those sectors of the economy.

This type of advice follows what can be called the conventional wisdom on investing—identify companies that will benefit from economic and other trends and will thus have rapidly rising earnings. Unfortunately, as newspaper columnist Don Marquis noted, "An idea is not responsible for the people who believe in it."

Let's imagine that an investor received a copy of Harry Dent's book as a present in 2000. He read the book and was impressed with the compelling case made by Dent. Particularly compelling to our investor is that, unlike economic forecasting, demographic forecasting can be considered a science. He decides that in order to best take advantage of the valuable knowledge imparted to him, he should invest his entire nest egg in Vanguard's Health Care Fund. This would concentrate his assets in the sector that would benefit the most from the trends Harry Dent identified. In addition, Vanguard is a highly respected firm, and its funds are known for their low costs.

Just as a precaution, our investor checks the track record of the fund. For the five-year period 1995 to 1999, the fund had provided an annualized rate of return of 24 percent. Then in 2000, it returned 59.3 percent. That was the cherry on the ice cream sundae. Thus, our intrepid investor boldly invests his entire nest egg in the fund on January 1, 2001. Let's check the record to see what kind of returns our investor earned and also to see if he was rewarded for taking the risk of concentrating his assets in just one sector of the economy.

For the 10-year period 2001 through 2010, the Vanguard Health Care Fund provided an annualized returned of 4.9 percent. Particularly impressive was that it outperformed the S&P 500 Index by 3.5 percent per year. However, that performance is not quite so impressive when compared with the performance of other domestic asset classes. The following table presents the returns of five domestic passively managed asset class funds run by Dimensional Fund Advisors and five similar index funds run by Vanguard as well as an equally weighted and annually rebalanced portfolio from both fund families.

2001 to 2010

FUND	ANNUALIZED RETURN (%)	FUND	ANNUALIZED RETURN (%)
DFA Real Estate	10.5	Vanguard Real Estate	10.7
DFA Small Value	11.1	Vanguard Small Cap Value	7.9
DFA Micro Cap	9.6	Vanguard Small Cap	7.2
DFA Large Value	5.3	Vanguard Value	2.1
DFA Large Company Fund (S&P 500 Index)	1.4	Vanguard S&P 500	1.4
Equally weighted and annually rebalanced portfolio	7.8	Equally weighted and annually rebalanced portfolio	6.0

How would the diversified investor, who did not have all his eggs in one health-care basket and thus clearly took less risk, have performed? The DFA portfolio outperformed by 2.9 percent, while the Vanguard portfolio outperformed by 1.1 percent. From the data it would be impossible to conclude that one was rewarded for taking such concentrated risk. In addition, the period spans two of the worst bear markets, and health-care stocks are supposed to be "defensive," protecting you during such periods. There was no need to concentrate risk in one sector of the economy.

This should also serve as a reminder to not make the mistake of confusing *information* with *knowledge*. If you read Harry Dent's books, you would say he makes sense. However, before leaping to invest in individual stocks or mutual funds based on Dent's (or any guru's) insightful analysis, investors need to consider the following: Is Harry Dent the only person who knows the demand for health care will rise as the population ages? Aren't all investors aware of this? Doesn't the market already incorporate this knowledge into current prices? If the market is aware of this information, it has already been incorporated into prices. Therefore, the knowledge cannot be exploited.

Summary

We hope that you have learned that you should never confuse information with knowledge. Possession of an insight is not sufficient. You can only benefit if other traders do not have the insight yet. And if you have such information, it is highly likely to be inside information, upon which it is illegal to trade. We also hope that you have learned that broad diversification is the prudent investment strategy.

Do You Follow a Prudent Process When Choosing a Financial Advisory Firm?

When it comes to home repairs, individuals can be catego-rized into two broad groups: those who hire professionals and the do-it-yourselfers. Of course, there are those who belong to the do-it-yourself group who shouldn't and would be much better off hiring professionals.

When it comes to investing, there are also those same two groups. And like the do-it-yourselfers, there are those who are in the group and shouldn't be. They feel they shouldn't pay pro-fessionals for something they believe they can do just as well. Unfortunately, the evidence from academic studies demonstrates that there are few individuals with the knowledge and discipline to be successful investors.

There are also individuals who recognize they have neither the knowledge nor the discipline required to be successful on their own. They also recognize that a good financial advisory firm can add value in many ways, such as allowing them to focus their attention on the more important things in their lives. They know that even if they had the skills to do it themselves, the time spent on financial matters is time not spent with family and friends. And they place a greater value on that time than the cost of paying a firm. For those who recognize the value of a good financial advisory firm, the following advice is offered.

Finding a Trusted Advisory Firm

Surveys show that along with financial expertise, investors look for people they can trust. Trust, however, is an intangible qual-ity. It cannot be quantified in the same way one can look at a baseball player's batting average. Therefore, our recommendation is that you require potential financial advisory firms to make the following 11 commitments to you. Doing so will give you the greatest chance of avoiding conflicts of interest and achieving your financial goals.

1. Our guiding principle is that our advice will always be in your best interest.
2. We provide you with care following a fiduciary standard—the highest legal duty that one party can have to another.
3. We are a fee-only investment advisor—avoiding the conflicts that commissioned-based compensation can create.
4. We fully disclose potential conflicts.
5. Our advice is based on the latest academic research, not on our opinions.
6. We are client centric—we don't sell any products, only advice.
7. We provide a high level of personal attention—each client works with a team of professionals and will develop strong personal relationships with team members.
8. We invest our personal assets, including our profit-sharing plan, based on the same set of investment principles, and in the same or comparable securities, that we recommend to our clients.
9. We will develop an investment plan that is integrated into estate, tax, and risk management (insurance) plans. The overall plan will be tailored to your unique situation.
10. Our advice is always goal oriented—evaluating each decision not in isolation, but in terms of its impact on the likelihood of success of the *overall* plan.
11. Our comprehensive wealth management services are provided by individuals that have CFP, PFS, or other comparable designations.

Summary

There are certainly some individuals who have the knowledge, time, interest, and discipline to develop an investment plan, integrate it into a well-designed estate, tax, and risk management plan, and then manage the plan (rebalance and tax-loss harvest) on an ongoing basis in a cost- and tax-efficient manner, as well as adapt the plan to meet changing circumstances and the passage of time. Unfortunately, the evidence is that far fewer people have those skills than believe they have them.

Fortunately, if you would be best served by hiring a professional advisory firm, good advice doesn't have to be expensive. However, bad or untrustworthy advice almost always will cost you dearly, no matter how little you pay for it. Therefore, you should perform a thorough due diligence before choosing a firm. That due diligence not only should include a request that the advisor make the aforementioned 11 commitments to you but also should include a careful review of the form ADV—a disclosure document setting forth information about the firm, including the investment strategy, fee schedules, conflicts of interest, regulatory incidents, and so on. A careful due diligence will minimize the risk of having to make expensive repairs.

PART 3

Mistakes Made
When Planning an
Investment Strategy

Do You Understand the Arithmetic of Active Management?

We are not afraid to follow the truth wherever it may lead, nor to tolerate any error so long as reason is left free to combat it.
—Thomas Jefferson

In 1991, William Sharpe wrote a paper, "The Arithmetic of Active Management." Using simple arithmetic, he proved that active management, in aggregate, must be a loser's game. Sharpe's "proof" demonstrated that this holds true not only for the broad market, but for subsectors of the market (e.g., small stocks or emerging market stocks). It also showed that the conclusion holds true in both bull and bear markets. The reason is simple: all stocks must be owned by someone.[1]

The Mathematics of Investing

A simple example will demonstrate conclusively that active investing must, in aggregate, be a loser's game. The market is made up of two types of investors, active and passive. For the purpose of this example, let's assume that 70 percent of investors are active and that 30 percent of investors are passive. (It does not matter what percentages are used. The outcome will be the same.) Let's further assume that the market returns 15 percent per year for the period in question. We know that a passive strategy (like owning Vanguard's total stock market fund) must earn 15 percent on a pre-expense basis. What rate of return, before expenses, must the active managers have earned? The answer must also be 15 percent. The following equations show the math:

Total stock market = active investors + passive investors
X = Rate of return earned by active investors
15% (100%) = X% (70%) + 15% (30%)
X must equal 15%

If one active investor outperforms because he overweighted the top-performing stocks, another active investor must have underperformed by underweighting those very same stocks. The investor that outperformed originally bought those winning securities from someone. Since passive investors simply buy and hold, the stock must have been sold by another active investor. In aggregate, on a preexpense basis, active investors earn the same market rate of return as do passive investors. Note that if we substituted the S&P 500 Index (or small-value stocks or emerging market stocks) for the total stock market, we would reach the same conclusion. It does not matter which asset class we are discussing—the math is the same. And the math doesn't change if the bull is rampaging or the bear comes out of hibernation: active management must earn the same pre-expense gross return as passive management, regardless of asset class or market condition.

The Evidence

The findings of numerous studies have provided evidence that Sharpe was correct (as he must be). And, importantly, studies have consistently found that past performance is a poor predictor of future performance, especially when it comes to good performance. (Bad performance is likely to continue if it is the result of high expenses.)

One such study by the Zero Alpha Group, "Survivorship Bias and Improper Measurement," provides further evidence on "the loser's game." The study examined the 10-year period 1995–2004. The authors used Morningstar's well-known style boxes to place actively managed funds into their appropriate category and then compared the returns with the appropriate S&P/Barra

index. They used the CRSP database because it is free of survivorship bias. The following table presents the return of the S&P/Barra index minus the return of the actively managed funds within the appropriate style box.

	Value	Blend	Growth
U.S. large	1.5%	3.2%	2.2%
U.S. mid	4.0%	4.3%	4.7%
U.S. small	1.6%	0.3%	0.2%

In all nine categories, the average actively managed fund underperformed its appropriate benchmark.

The next table shows the degree to which survivorship bias overstates historic returns if it is not accounted for.

	Value	Blend	Growth
U.S. large	−1.0%	−1.9%	−0.6%
U.S. mid	−2.0%	−2.4%	−1.4%
U.S. small	−1.1%	0.4%	−1.5%

In eight of the nine categories, survivorship bias inflated returns. The one exception is likely an anomaly that results from a measurement error. It is unlikely that funds that had actually performed well would ever be sent to the "mutual fund graveyard." It is also important to note that if survivorship bias was not accounted for, then it would appear that in some categories actively managed funds beat their benchmarks (small blend and small growth).[2]

There are two important conclusions that investors should draw from the above data. First, investors should be wary of claims of market inefficiency and management skill. The results supporting such a claim are likely to be due to improper measurement, such as using the wrong benchmark, or, in the case of individual funds, randomness. Second, as Sharpe demonstrated, active management is a loser's game whatever the asset class, whether markets are efficient or inefficient. The reason is simple: costs matter.

MISTAKE 36

Do You Understand That Bear Markets Are a Necessary Evil?

A necessary evil can be defined as something that is unpleasant or undesirable but is needed to achieve a result. Investors should view bear markets as a necessary evil. Let's explore why.

Perhaps the most basic principle of modern financial theory is that risk and *expected* return are related. Stocks are riskier than one-month Treasury bills. Since they are riskier, the only logical explanation for investing in stocks is that they must provide a higher *expected* return. However, if stocks always provided higher returns than one-month Treasury bills, investing in stocks would not entail any risk, and there would be no risk premium. In fact, in 24 of the 85 years from 1926 through 2010 (or close to 30 percent of the time), the S&P 500 Index produced negative returns. In addition, there have been periods when the S&P 500 produced severe losses:

> January 1929–December 1932, it lost 64 percent.
> January 1973–September 1974, it lost 43 percent.
> April 2000–September 2002, it lost 44 percent.
> November 2007–February 2009, it lost 51 percent.

The very fact that investors have experienced such large losses leads them to price stocks with a large risk premium. From 1926 through 2010, the S&P 500 has provided an annual risk premium over one-month Treasury bills of 7.7 percent. If the losses that investors experienced had been smaller, the risk premium would also have been smaller. And the smaller the losses experienced, the smaller the premium would have been. An indicator of how risky stocks were is that the annual standard deviation of the equity risk premium was 19.9 percent, or 2.6 times as great as the premium itself.

The bottom line is that bear markets are necessary to the creation of the large equity risk premium we have experienced. Thus, if investors want stocks to provide high expected returns, bear markets should be considered a necessary evil. We can extend this logic to the risks of investing in small-cap and value stocks.

Small-Cap and Value Stocks

Small companies are riskier than large companies. Therefore, the market prices small-cap stocks to provide higher returns than large-cap stocks. From 1926 through 2010, small-cap stocks provided an annual premium of 3.1 percent. However, small-cap stocks have not always outperformed large-cap stocks. For example:

> January 1969–December 1974, small-cap stocks underperformed large-cap stocks by a total of 47 percent.
> January 1986–December 1990, small-cap stocks underperformed large-cap stocks by a total of 33 percent.
> January 1994–December 1998, small-cap stocks underperformed large-cap stocks by a total of 30 percent.

If small-cap stocks always outperformed, there would be no risk of investing in them relative to investing in large-cap stocks, and there would be no risk premium.

Further evidence of the risk of investing in small-cap stocks is that while the small-cap risk premium has been 3.1 percent, the annual standard deviation of the premium has been 11.8 percent, almost four times the premium.

We also know that value companies are riskier than growth companies. Therefore, the market prices value stocks to provide higher returns than growth stocks. From 1926 through 2010, value stocks have provided an annual premium of 4.6 percent. However, value stocks have not always outperformed. For example:

> March 1934–March 1935, value stocks underperformed growth stocks by a total of 43 percent.
> June 1998–February 2000, value stocks underperformed growth stocks by a total 44 percent.

As with small-cap stocks, if value stocks always outperformed, there would be no risk of investing in them relative to investing in growth stocks, and there would be no risk premium.

And as is the case with the small-cap premium, the value premium is volatile. The annual standard deviation of the value premium, at 11.1 percent, has been almost 2.5 times the premium.

Risk Premiums and Investment Discipline

The bottom line is that the outperformance of stocks relative to Treasury bills, small-cap stocks relative to large-cap stocks, and value stocks relative to growth stocks is not a free lunch. There are risks involved. And it is a virtual certainty the risks will show up from time to time. Unfortunately, we cannot know when or for how long the periods of underperformance will last, nor how severe they will be. Therefore, a necessary ingredient for investment success is to have the discipline to adhere to your investment plan, ignoring the noise of the market and the emotions (greed and envy in bull markets and fear and panic in bear markets) fueled by the noise.

Summary

Bear markets are a necessary evil, because their existence is the reason the stock market has provided the large risk premium and the high return that investors have had the opportunity to earn.

The bottom line for investors is this: If you don't have a plan, immediately sit down and develop one. Make sure the plan anticipates bear markets and outlines what actions you will take when they occur (doing so when you are not under the stress that bear markets create). Put the plan in writing in the form of an investment policy statement and an asset allocation table and sign it. That will increase the odds of adhering to it when you are tested by the emotions caused by both bull and bear markets. And then be sure to stay the course, altering your plan only if your assumptions about your ability, willingness, or need to take risk have changed.

MISTAKE 37

Do You Treat the Highly Likely as Certain and the Highly Unlikely as Impossible?

> People are commonly biased in several directions: They are
> optimistic; they overestimate the chances that they will
> succeed, and they overestimate their degree of knowledge, in
> the sense that their confidence far exceeds their "hit rate."
> —Amos Tversky

One of the biggest and most common mistakes investors make is to treat investment risk as if it isn't really risk. Individuals don't generally make this mistake in other areas of their lives. In fact, when it comes to most noninvestment decisions, they generally act in a risk-averse manner. The following example illustrates the point.

Imagine that you are a 30-year-old married male, you are the main income earner in your family, and you have two young children. You have recently finished paying off your college debts, have just used most of your savings for the down payment on your dream home, and have a very large monthly mortgage payment. You are a nonsmoker, eat a healthy diet, and exercise regularly. You also happen to have good genes—everyone in your family has lived a long life. Your life expectancy is probably something like 50 more years or longer. Given these facts, should you buy life insurance to provide for your family in the event of your early death?

Despite the odds of your early death being very low, virtually everyone would buy the insurance. The reason is that while there is a low likelihood of dying early, there is still uncertainty, or risk. In addition, the cost of being wrong (dying uninsured) is very high. In this case, individuals do not treat the highly unlikely—premature death—as impossible. They don't treat the highly likely—living a long time—as certain. Yet when it comes to investment decisions, this is exactly the type of mistake people often make.

One of the most important considerations involves identifying investors' risk tolerance (or ability to accept risk). One possibility is to use a guideline table, such as the one that follows.

MAXIMUM TOLERABLE LOSS (%)	MAXIMUM EQUITY EXPOSURE (%)
5	20
10	30
15	40
20	50
25	60
30	70
35	80
40	90
50	100

When examining acceptable levels of risk, individuals should remember the bear markets of 1973 to 1974, 2000 to 2002, and 2008. Then they should identify the maximum amount of loss they could tolerate without losing sleep, panicking and selling, or losing the discipline to rebalance. It's important to keep in mind that there's no guarantee that future bear markets won't be more severe than previous ones. The reason investors have experienced a risk premium for investing in equities is because there is risk involved. The majority of the investors in 2000 never experienced the pain of the 1973 to 1974 bear market. Or if they did, they probably had little invested at the time, as it was early in their investment careers. In addition, it was a long time ago. The only major bear market most baby boomers probably experienced prior to 2000 occurred in October 1987, and it was so short that the market closed the year higher than it had started. In addition, the following year the S&P 500 rose almost 17 percent. The new generation of investors was thus "taught" (or led to believe) that bear markets were an opportunity to buy on any dip in equity prices, as any dip would prove to be very short term (i.e., risk isn't risk). This is the equivalent of believing there is no risk in the stock market or of treating risk as if it isn't risk.

The problem with this kind of thinking is that people begin to treat the highly unlikely as impossible. This causes them to overstate their tolerance for risk and have too high an equity allocation. In turn, this creates the danger that if a bear market arrives, their heavy exposure to equities will cause them more pain than they can withstand. They may then either panic or be forced to sell because they simply cannot accept the possibility of further losses. This is what happened to many investors when the bear markets of 2000 to 2002 and 2008 occurred.

You can avoid the mistake of treating the highly likely as certain and the highly unlikely as impossible by remembering the basic economic principle that risk and *expected* (not guaranteed) reward are related. If the investments you are planning to make provide a higher return than riskless short-term government instruments, then there is both risk and uncertainty. The greater the expected difference in returns, the greater the uncertainty and the greater the risk. You should also keep in mind the following advice from Peter Bernstein: "Even the most brilliant of mathematical geniuses will never be able to tell us what the future holds."[1]

MISTAKE 38

Do You Take Risks Not Worth Taking?

In March 2003, Larry met with a husband and wife who were both 71 years old and had financial assets of $3 million. Unfortunately, their portfolio was worth $13 million three years earlier. Larry knew that the only way they could have experienced that kind of loss was if they held a portfolio that not only was all, or almost all, equities but also was heavily concentrated in U.S. large-cap growth stocks, and especially technology stocks. They confirmed that this was correct.

Larry asked the couple if they had been able to double their portfolio to $26 million instead, would that have led to any meaningful change in the quality of their lives? The response was a definitive no. Larry then told them that he assumed the experience of watching the $13 million shrink to $3 million was very painful. They agreed. He then asked them why they had taken the risks created by failing to diversify their portfolio. The wife turned to the husband and punched him in the arm while exclaiming, "I told you so." Some risks are not worth taking. Prudent investors do not take more risk than they have the ability, willingness, or need to.

In late March 2000, Larry met with an executive of Intel. His net worth at the time exceeded $10 million and, with the exception of his home, was almost totally in the stock of his employer. At the time, Intel was trading at around 70. Despite acknowledging the risks of this strategy, he was so confident of the outlook for his company that he would not consider selling the stock. Despite Larry's best efforts, there was no convincing him to sell.

Larry met the Intel executive two years later, with the stock now at about 30 and his financial assets now down more than 50 percent. Unfortunately, there was still no convincing him to diversify his holdings. He met him again a year later, with the stock now at about 16. And there was still no convincing him.

There are some risks not worth taking. Never have more than a very small percentage of your assets in the stock of any one company, especially your employer.

Investing is about taking risk. Prudent investors know, however, there are some risks that are worth taking and some that are not. And prudent investors know the difference. When the cost of a negative outcome is greater than one can bear, the risk should not be taken, no matter how great the odds of a favorable outcome appear to be.

Do You Confuse Before-the-Fact Strategy with After-the-Fact Outcome?

I'm a big believer in diversification, because I am totally convinced that forecasts will be wrong. Diversification is the guiding principle. That's the only way you can live through the hard times. It's going to cost you in the short run, because not everything will be going through the roof.

—Paul Samuelson

Imagine that you are Phil Jackson, coach of the Los Angeles Lakers. It is the fifth game of the championship series, and your team is ahead three games to one. LeBron James has just scored a basket with 10 seconds to go, giving the Miami Heat a 1-point lead. You call a timeout to set up the last play. Your star, Kobe Bryant, has had a relatively poor game, scoring just 15 points, and he has not shot well. On the other hand, Luke Walton has had a career game, scoring 25 points on almost perfect shooting. For whom do you call the last play, Bryant or Walton? Virtually everyone would set the play up for Bryant, one of the greatest players in history. It would not be rational to ignore career statistics and make a decision based on just one game. Unfortunately, Bryant misses the shot. In truth, while the decision was clearly the correct one, we should not be surprised. Given his career statistics, we would expect him to make the shot only about 50 percent of the time.

It is now the sixth game, and the same situation arises. Once again you call the play for Bryant. To your great disappointment, he misses again. Amazingly, the same situation arises in the final game. Once again you call on Bryant to hit the big shot. And again he misses. While the outcome was disappointing, surely everyone would agree the strategy of having your best player take the last shot was the right one.

This example is one of confusing strategy and outcome. Nassim Nicholas Taleb, the author of *Fooled by Randomness*, had the following to say on confusing strategy and outcome:

One cannot judge a performance in any given field by the results, but by the costs of the alternative (that is, if history played out in a different way). Such substitute courses of events are called alternative histories. Clearly the quality of a decision cannot be solely judged based on its outcome, but such a point seems to be voiced only by people who fail (those who succeed attribute their success to the quality of their decision).[1]

When it comes to investing, our ability to foresee which alternative history will play out is no clearer than it is for a basketball coach to see who should take the final shot.

The risks and rewards of diversification can be easily demonstrated by examining the period from 1975 through 2010. During this period the S&P 500 Index returned 11.8 percent, while the MSCI EAFE Index returned 11.4 percent. However, a diversified portfolio that was 50 percent S&P 500 and 50 percent MSCI EAFE and was rebalanced annually returned 11.9 percent.

Now let's imagine that you are an investor starting out on January 1, 1990. From 1975 through 1989, the diversified portfolio outperformed the S&P 500 by almost 3 percent per year (19.5 versus 16.6). Having seen the historical evidence and understanding the logic of diversification, you decide to invest in a globally diversified portfolio. Unfortunately, your timing is lousy. Over the next decade, the S&P 500 Index outperforms the diversified portfolio by about 11 percent (18.2 versus 7.3). After having the discipline to stick with your portfolio for 10 years, the disappointing outcome causes you to abandon your strategy. Of course, as soon as you bail out, the globally diversified portfolio once again begins to provide superior returns. From 2000 through 2008, it outperformed the S&P 500 by 2.2 percent per year (–1.4 versus –3.6). Then from 2009 through 2010 they provided similar returns, with the S&P returning 20.6 percent compared with the 20.2 percent return of the diversified portfolio.

The fact that you were unhappy with the outcome of the strategy of diversification doesn't mean the strategy was incorrect or the outcome was unexpected. Just as Kobe Bryant will occasionally miss 8 of 10 shots, a diversified strategy might underperform for 8 out of 10 years or even over much longer periods. Don't make the mistake of confusing strategy with outcome.

Unfortunately, too many investors have entered what John Bogle calls the "Age of Investment Relativism."[2] Investor satisfaction or unhappiness (and therefore the discipline required to stick with a strategy) seems to be determined to a great degree by the performance of the investor's portfolio relative to some index—an index that shouldn't even be relevant to an investor who accepts the wisdom of diversification. Relativism, sadly, can best be described as the triumph of emotion over wisdom and experience. The history of financial markets has demonstrated that today's trends are merely "noise" in the context of the long term. Bogle also cited an anonymous portfolio manager who warned, "Relativity worked well for Einstein, but it has no place in investing."[3]

Chasing the latest fad or hot asset class has proved to be a losing strategy and the result of confusing strategy and outcome. It is important for you to understand that the individual portions of your investment plan will perform differently over time. This is why it is important to build the plan with unique and low-correlating building blocks (asset classes). Unfortunately, as James Gipson, then manager of the Clipper Fund, wrote, "Diversification for investors, like celibacy for teenagers, is a concept both easy to understand and hard to practice."[4] Because of the risk of diversification, it is important for you to determine just how much *tracking error* to major benchmarks you are willing to live with as a trade-off for the benefits of diversification. Tracking error is the amount by which the performance of a portfolio (or fund) differs from the performance of a benchmark (such as the S&P 500).

Diversification means accepting the fact that parts of the portfolio will behave entirely differently from the portfolio itself. Choosing the appropriate level of tolerance for tracking error will help keep you disciplined. The less tracking error you are willing to accept, the more the equity portion of your portfolio should look like the S&P 500 Index. On the other hand, if you choose a marketlike portfolio, it will be one that is not very diversified by asset class and will have no international diversification. At least between these two choices (avoiding or accepting tracking error), there is no free lunch. It is almost as important to get this right as it is to determine the appropriate equity–fixed-income allocation. If you have the discipline to stick with a globally diversified passive asset class strategy, you are likely to be rewarded for your discipline.

Do You Believe Stocks Are Risky Only If Your Horizon Is Short?

> Buying stocks today is not the easy choice that it would be if we had a time machine and could go back into U.S. history.
>
> —Terry Burnham
> *Mean Markets and Lizard Brains*, p. 171

For the period 1926 to 2010, the S&P 500 Index returned 9.9 percent per year, outperforming long-term Treasury bonds by 4.4 percent per year. It was favorable returns such as these that led Jeremy Siegel, in his bestselling book *Stocks for the Long Run*, to declare that stocks were only risky if your investment horizon was short. Siegel presents the evidence on returns in the United States all the way back to the early 1800s to support his claim.

The claim that stocks are not risky if your horizon is long is based on just one set of data (the United States) for one period (albeit a long one). In other words, if stocks are only risky when your horizon is short, we should see evidence of this in other markets. Unfortunately, investors in many other markets did not receive the kind of returns U.S. investors earned. As you shall see, U.S. returns might just have been the result of what has been called "the triumph of the optimists."

It is January 1, 1949, and U.S. investors are looking back on the last 20 years of equity returns. They find the S&P 500 Index had returned 3.1 percent per year, underperforming long-term government bonds by 0.8 percent per year. (So much for the argument that stocks always beat bonds if your horizon is 20 years or more.) And how did the world look to U.S. investors at that time? Did it appear to be an encouraging environment for investing in stocks? In fact, the world looked like a pretty risky place to investors. They had endured two world wars and the Great Depression, an Iron Curtain had fallen across Europe, the Cold War was heating up, trouble was brewing in Korea (which would again throw much of the world into war on June 25, 1950), and there was now the threat of a nuclear war. The world looked so risky that stocks were trading at a P/E of about 6!

The world turned out to be a far less risky place than it appeared to investors in 1949, and investors were rewarded for the risks they took. The result was that U.S. investors enjoyed spectacular returns, partly as a result of the dramatic fall in the equity risk premium demanded by investors. For the period 1949 to 2010, the S&P 500 Index returned 11.2 percent per year, 5.2 percent above the return on long-term government bonds.

The lesson we learn from this tale is that while it is true that the longer your investment horizon the greater your *ability* to take the risk of investing in stocks (because you have greater ability to wait out a bear market without having to sell to raise capital), stocks are risky no matter the length of your investment horizon. In fact, that is exactly why U.S. stocks have *generally* (but not always) provided such great returns over the long term. Investors know that stocks are always risky. Thus, they price stocks in a manner that provides them with an expected risk premium. In other words, stocks have to be priced low enough that they will attract investors with a risk premium that is large enough to compensate them for taking the risk of equity ownership. In 1949, because the world looked like a very risky place in which to invest, the risk premium was very large (as P/E ratios were very low). Because the risks that investors were concerned about did not show up, investors were rewarded for taking the risks that they would.

If you are not yet convinced that stocks are risky no matter the investment horizon and that the United States may just have gotten the "lucky draw," consider the case of investors in Egyptian equities. In 1900, the Egyptian stock market was the fifth largest in the world. Those investors (along with equity investors in Cuba and Russia) are still waiting for the return *of* their capital, let alone the return *on* capital. Or consider that in the 1880s there were two promising countries in the Western Hemisphere that were receiving capital inflows from Europe for development purposes: the United States and Argentina. One group of long-term investors was rewarded, while the other was not. And finally, consider the case of Japanese investors. In 1989, the Nikkei Index hit a peak of almost 40,000. Twenty-two years later, it was still down about 75 percent. Do you think that long-term Japanese investors believe that stocks are not risky in the long run?

Summary

Stocks are risky no matter the length of your investment horizon. Therefore, the markets price stocks in a manner that provides investors with an expected risk premium. And because the majority of investors are risk averse, the equity risk premium has historically been large.

Investors should carefully evaluate their own unique ability, willingness, and need to take risk and should never take more risk than is appropriate to their personal situation. It is also important to remember these words of caution from Nassim Nicholas Taleb: "History teaches us that things that never happened before do happen."[1]

Do You Try to Succeed Even When Success Is Highly Unlikely?

> People think of trading as playing tennis against a
> wall. They can position themselves perfectly, and they
> can return the ball just right. But when they trade,
> it is real tennis that they are playing against very
> skilled players, including professional players.
>
> —Meir Statman
> *Wall Street Journal*, November 24, 1998

As we have seen, it is a common human trait to be overconfident of our skills. Even when individuals will admit that a task is difficult, there is still a tendency toward overconfidence. This is certainly true when it comes to identifying active managers who will outperform the market in the future. Presented with the evidence on the failure of active managers to outperform, a frequent response is, "The data only represent the average fund. By instituting simple screens you can easily eliminate many losers." Typical suggestions are to eliminate those funds with poor performance, high expenses, high turnover, or short manager tenure.

By *carefully* selecting funds, rather than looking at all funds, investors may feel they can identify funds that will outperform. This approach has a logical appeal, and it will likely improve the results compared with those of all actively managed funds. However, it is not likely that it will result in market-beating performance. In fact, after reading this section, our hope is that you will agree that it is not logical to think that you can identify the future winners, even with the most logical of approaches.

Consider the following. It seems logical to believe that if anyone could beat the market, it would be the pension plans of U.S. companies. Why might you think this is a good assumption? First, pension plans control large sums of money. They have access to the best and brightest portfolio managers, each clamoring to manage the billions of dollars in these plans (and earn large fees). Pension plans can also invest with managers that most individuals don't have access to because they don't have sufficient assets to meet the minimums of these superstar managers. And because of their size, pension plans almost certainly pay lower fees than individual investors would even if they had access to the same managers.

Second, it is not even remotely possible that these pension plans ever hired a manager who did not have a track record of outperforming their benchmarks, or at the very least matching them. Certainly they would never hire a manager with a record of underperformance.

Third, it is also safe to say that they never hired a manager who did not make a great presentation, explaining why the manager had succeeded and would continue to succeed. Surely the case presented was a convincing one.

Fourth, many, if not the majority, of these pension plans hire professional consultants—such as Frank Russell, SEI, and Goldman Sachs—to help them perform due diligence in interviewing, screening, and ultimately selecting the very best of the best. Frank Russell, for example, has boasted that it has more than 70 analysts performing more than 2,000 interviews a year. And you can be sure that these consultants have thought of every conceivable screen to find the best fund managers. Surely they have considered not only performance records, but also such factors as management tenure, depth of staff, consistency of performance (to make sure that a long-term record is not the result of one or two lucky years), performance in bear markets, consistency of implementation of strategy, turnover, and costs. It is unlikely that there is something that you or your financial advisor would think of that they had not already considered.

Fifth, unless they hire an advisory firm, individuals would rarely have the luxury to personally interview money managers and perform as thorough a due diligence as do these consultants.

So how does the performance of pension plans stack up against risk-adjusted benchmarks? The study "The Performance of U.S. Pension Plans" sought the answer to that question. The study covered 716 defined benefit plans (1992–2004) and 238 defined contribution plans (1997–2004). The authors found that their returns relative to benchmarks were close to zero. They also found that there was no persistence in pension plan performance. Thus, despite the conventional wisdom, past performance is not a reliable predictor of future performance. Importantly, they also found that neither fund size, degree of outsourcing, nor company stock holdings were factors driving performance. This finding refutes the claim that the large pension plans are handicapped by their size. Small plans did no better. Importantly, the authors concluded, "The striking similarities in performance patterns over time makes skill differences highly unlikely."[1]

Counterproductive Activity

A study by Amit Goyal and Sunil Wahal provides us with further evidence on the inability of plan sponsors to identify investment management firms that will outperform the market *after* they are hired. Goyal and Wahal examined the selection and termination of investment management firms by plan sponsors (public and corporate pension plans, unions, foundations, and endowments). They built a data set of the hiring and firing decisions by approximately 3,700 plan sponsors from 1994 to 2003. The data represented the allocation of more than $737 billion in mandates to hired investment managers and the withdrawal of $117 billion from fired investment managers. The following is a summary of their findings:

> Plan sponsors hire investment managers after large positive excess returns up to three years prior to hiring.
> The return-chasing behavior does not deliver positive excess returns thereafter.
> Post-hiring excess returns are indistinguishable from zero.
> Plan sponsors terminate investment managers after underperformance, but the excess returns of these managers after being fired are frequently positive.

> If plan sponsors had stayed with the fired investment managers, their returns would have been larger than those actually delivered by the newly hired managers.[2]

It is important to note that these results did not include any of the trading costs that would have accompanied transitioning a portfolio from one manager's holdings to the holdings preferred by the new manager. In other words, all the activity was counterproductive.

Summary

Those on Wall Street need and want you to play the game of active investing. They know that your odds of outperforming appropriate benchmarks are so low that it is not in your interest to play. However, they need you to play so that *they* (not you) make the most money. They make it by charging high fees for active management that persistently delivers poor performance. The financial media also want and need you to play so that you "tune in." That is how *they* (not you) make money.

However, you don't have to play the game of active management. Instead, you can earn market (not average) rates of return with low expenses and high tax efficiency. You can do so by investing in passively managed investment vehicles such as index funds and passive asset class funds. Then you are virtually guaranteed to outperform the majority of both professionals and individual investors. In other words, you win by not playing. This is why active investing is called the loser's game. It is not that the people playing are losers. And it is not that you cannot win. Instead, it is that the odds of success are so low that it is imprudent to try.

Returning to our starting point, is it logical for you to believe that you can predict which actively managed funds will outperform, or are you overconfident of your skills? If you are trying to find the great fund managers who will outperform in the future, ask yourself: What am I going to do differently, in terms of identifying the future winning fund managers, than did the pension plans and their consultants? Surely these organizations have thought of eliminating from consideration the poorly performing funds and the high-cost funds. And if you are not going to do something different, what logic is there in playing a game at which others with superior resources have consistently failed? Or is it that you believe that you can interpret the data more correctly than have others with far more resources?

Do You Understand the Importance of Saving Early in Life?

There are two reasons why the best time to invest is when you have funds available to do so. First, there is a substantial body of evidence which suggests that efforts to time investments are nonproductive. Second, but more significant, is the importance of compounding. The following examples of investors Sally, Sam, Jane, and John will illustrate the powerful effects of compounding.

Sally begins to save $5,000 a year at age 25. She continues to save this amount for 10 years, until age 34, at which point she stops saving. Sam, on the other hand, waits until age 35 to start saving. He then saves $5,000 a year for the next 30 years. At the end of 10 years, Sally will have invested $50,000. At the end of Sam's 30-year program, he will have invested $150,000, or three times as much as Sally did. But this is not the end of the story.

Assuming a 10 percent per year compound rate of return, Sally will have generated a portfolio of about $1.4 million by age 65. Despite Sam's having saved and invested three times as many dollars, his portfolio will have grown to only $820,000. When Sally and Sam are 75, their two portfolios will have grown to $3.6 million and $2.2 million, respectively.

If Jane waits until age 45 to begin investing, she must save $24,000 each year for the next 20 years to achieve the same portfolio as Sally. Remember, Sally only had to put aside $5,000 for 10 years. If John waits until age 55 to begin an investment program, he will have to save $87,000 a year for 10 years to reach the same goal. This illustrates the powerful roles that time and compounding play in investment outcomes. The moral is simple: if you can put off buying the high-dollar stuff you want, but don't need, in your early years and instead put a reasonable amount into a passively invested diversified asset class portfolio, you should be able to acquire a whole lot of those desired goods later in life.

MISTAKE 43

Do You Fail to Evaluate the Real Cost of an Expenditure?

Larry has a good friend we shall call Louis. While discussing financial plans, Larry asked about the expense of the private school education Louis was providing for his child.

Louis had the choice of either paying $10,000 for the private school education or sending his child to the local public school. Louis and his wife decided the $10,000 additional cost was a good *investment*. Larry offered Louis an alternative perspective on how to evaluate the cost of the expenditure, as he was underestimating the true costs.

Larry pointed out that had Louis chosen to send his child to the public school, he would have had $10,000 additional funds available to invest each year for the next 12 years. The dollars invested would then be available in his retirement. The next logical question was the amount of retirement income Louis was sacrificing to provide the private school education. Here are the assumptions used in presenting the answer:

> › Louis is 35 years old and wishes to retire and begin to withdraw funds from his retirement account at age 65.
> › Private school costs $10,000 a year, increasing at an assumed inflation rate of 3 percent per year.
> › Twelve years of private education will be required.
> › Return on investment will be 10 percent per year.
> › Upon retirement, Louis will withdraw a conservative 4 percent of the portfolio, adjusted for inflation, each year.

Using these assumptions, Louis would have an additional portfolio of $1,645,996 at age 65. This would allow him to withdraw an additional $65,840 the first year and then adjust upward for inflation thereafter. In today's dollars, that equated to $26,335 per year in additional buying power.

The point of the exercise was not to convince Louis to send his child to a public school, but to help him understand the true cost of that private education: Louis was likely to have $26,335 less per year in today's dollars to spend in retirement.

Certainly, the question of whether to send a child to a public or private school should not be decided on a purely economic basis. However, one should understand the true implications of any expenditure decision. This type of analysis should be done for any major expenditure in order to properly evaluate the full implications of the decision.

Do You Believe Diversification Is the Right Strategy Only If the Investment Horizon Is Long?

On one of Larry's favorite investing Web sites, there was a discussion about the benefits of diversification. One poster suggested that since his investment horizon was relatively short (10 years), he did not want to take the chance of investing in such risky asset classes as international equities, emerging markets, small-cap stocks, and value stocks. While agreeing that the poster's investment horizon should affect his asset allocation decision, Larry suggested that he came to the wrong conclusion. In fact, as we hope you will agree, the shorter your investment horizon, the greater the need for diversification across asset classes.

The length of the investment horizon should affect your equity–fixed-income asset allocation decision. The longer the horizon, the more likely it is that equities will outperform fixed-income instruments. Also, the longer the horizon, the greater your ability to wait out a bear market. With that in mind, you might use the following table to help you decide on an equity–fixed-income allocation:

INVESTMENT HORIZON	MAXIMUM EQUITY ALLOCATION (%)
0–3 years	0
4 years	10
5 years	20
6 years	30
7 years	40
8 years	50
9 years	60

10 years	70
11–14 years	80
15–19 years	90
20 years or longer	100

It is important to keep in mind that the ability to take risk (length of investment horizon) is only one consideration in developing a portfolio. Among the other considerations are the willingness and the need to take risk.

Once we have determined the equity–fixed-income allocation, we must decide on the specific allocation we desire among the various equity asset classes. Using the Fama-French indexes, we can compare the returns of various asset classes for the period 1927 to 2010:

Small value—15.0%
Large value—11.7%
Large growth—9.3%
Small growth—8.8%

As you can see, the difference between the highest-returning and lowest-returning asset class was 6.2 percent per year. Also consider that from 1970 through 2010, the S&P 500 Index returned 10.0 percent, while the MSCI EAFE Index returned 10.1 percent.

However, when the investment horizon is still long, though somewhat shorter than 30 years, there have been large differences in returns. Let's look at a few examples, beginning with the MSCI EAFE and S&P 500.

For the period 1971 to 1988, the S&P 500 underperformed the MSCI EAFE by 6.2 percent per year (17.2 percent to 11.0 percent). Now imagine yourself as a U.S. investor who in 1971 had *only* an 18-year horizon and therefore didn't want to take the risk of owning international stocks. From 1989 through 2000, the S&P 500 outperformed the MSCI EAFE by 11.4 percent per year (16.7 percent to 5.3 percent). Now imagine yourself as a foreign investor in 1989 with just an 11-year horizon and thus unwilling to take the risk of owning U.S. stocks.

Next let's look at a U.S. example. Although small value stocks outperformed large growth stocks by 5.7 percent per year over the entire 84-year period from 1927 to 2010, for the 23-year period 1966 to 1988 they outperformed by 9.3 percent per year (16.9 percent to 7.6 percent). Imagine yourself in 1966 with *just* a 23-year horizon and therefore not wanting to take the risk of owning small value stocks.

Although diversification across nonhighly correlating asset classes is the winning strategy no matter what the investment horizon, you should note that diversification across equity asset classes is actually more important as the investment horizon shortens. This is because any one asset class can underperform by very large amounts over even fairly long horizons, let alone relatively short ones. If your investment horizon is very short, then the way to control risk is to increase your allocation to short-term fixed-income assets, not to increase your allocation to any one equity asset class, no matter how safe you think it to be.

Do You Believe That This Time It's Different?

It has seemed to be taken for granted in speculative
circles that this is a market of "manifest destiny,"
and that destiny is to go continuously forward.
—*New York Times*, September 1929

Those who cannot remember the past
are condemned to repeat it.
—George Santayana

In the late 1990s, the financial media were filled with stories on the dramatic changes in our economy fostered by the Internet and biotechnology revolutions, along with the spectacular performance of the heavily technology-weighted NASDAQ. With those stories came the clarion call, "It's a different investment world." Investors were being told that all the old rules about valuations and risk and reward no longer applied. It no longer mattered what price you paid for a great company. You would ultimately be rewarded.

All rational arguments against this line of thinking were dismissed with the claim, "This time things are different." The following is a summary of that new era's investing strategy:

It's a new world order. It's the new new thing. Investors should own great companies at any price. Never discard the right company just because the price is too high. It's different this time. The Internet is changing the world. It's a great revolution, supercharging the economy. The United States clearly is the leader in technology, and productivity is growing at the fastest rate ever. We dominate the Internet, biotech, and financial services sectors. That is where the future is. Besides, the U.S. free enterprise system has proved it's the best model. Others have to now catch up. Just look at returns over the last few years. The opportunity is enormous. You can't afford to miss out. The future for New Age companies like AOL, Amazon, Cisco, Priceline, and the like is so bright and obvious. How can you possibly go wrong?

Mutual funds that jumped on the technology bandwagon provided spectacular returns for the early investors in this new era. New funds and new products such as QQQ (an exchange-traded fund designed to replicate the performance of the tech-heavy NASDAQ 100) were created at breakneck speed as investors stampeded into this New Age "gold rush."

However, for students of financial history, there was a great amount of similarity between the New Age investing and the go-go era of the early 1960s. Investors in that era heard the same clarion calls as we then entered the computer revolution. At that time, there was a group of stocks called the "Nifty Fifty." They were known as "one-decision" stocks: stocks that should be bought no matter the price and simply held forever (hence the term *one decision*). Let's go to the videotape to see the results of that "This time things are different" era.

From 1963 through 1968, five leading go-go funds (Enterprise Fund, Fidelity Capital, Fidelity Trend, T. Rowe Price New Horizons, and Ivest) provided cumulative returns of 344 percent, nearly 3½ times the return of the S&P 500 Index. The assets of the five funds increased an astounding 17 times, from $200 million to $3.4 billion.

Over the next six years, however, the story was quite different. Those same funds fell a cumulative 45 percent, about 2½ times as much as the 19 percent fall for the S&P 500.[1] When thinking about these figures, keep the following points in mind.

First, a drop of 45 percent has a much greater impact than an increase of the same percentage. For example, if you start with an investment of $100 and it rises 90 percent in the first year and falls 45 percent in the second, while your average annual return is +22.5 percent, your annualized return is only about 2 percent per year.

Second, many individuals invested in the funds after some or much of the gains were already achieved. Thus, many (if not most) investors earned nothing like those 344 percent cumulative returns. On the other hand, the funds did have $3.4 billion under management when the bubble burst. It is quite possible (perhaps even likely) that the average investor in the five funds not only would have underperformed the S&P 500 Index during the full 12-year period but might actually have lost money.

Returning to our go-go Nifty Fifty era, it is also worth noting that not a single stock from that Nifty Fifty group managed to outperform the S&P 500 over the next quarter century.[2]

If we had a videotape playing back for us the wisdom of the investment gurus of the new era 1960s, it would sound remarkably similar to the "wisdom" of the last decade of the twentieth century. In the 1960s, it was the same technology revolution story. A few companies eventually succeeded. However, many more failed. And most failed to justify the valuations placed on them. Here is a sampling of the hot technology stocks of 1968—and what happened to them when that bubble burst.

Hot Tech Stocks of 1968

COMPANY	1968 HIGH	1970 LOW	DROP (%)	P/E AT HIGH
Fairchild Camera	102	18	−82	443
Teledyne	72	13	−82	42
Control Data	163	28	−83	54
Mohawk Data	111	18	−84	285
Electronic Data	162	24	−85	352
Optical Scanning	146	16	−89	200
Itek	172	17	−90	71
University Computing	186	13	−93	118

Source: *Dun's* (1971); itulip.com.

Note the P/E ratios of those once high flyers and the size of their eventual collapse in price. Note, too, the similarity between what happened to 1968's hot stocks and what happened in 2000 to the new era tech stocks, especially the dot-coms.

There really was no reason to think that the Internet revolution would have any bigger impact than the previous society-changing inventions such as the automobile, air travel, TV, radio, or computers. (RCA hit 114 in 1929, and it took almost 60 years for it to recover to that level. How's that for a sure thing?)

Remember that technology benefits everyone. In fact, it often benefits the users more than the inventors and eventual industry winners—even if you can somehow identify them ahead of time. Besides, even if you are right about technology's great future, are you the only one who knows this? If not, the market has already incorporated this great future into current prices. (Remember, that is how prices reach lofty levels.) The only way to outperform the market is to exploit pricing mistakes by others. Bear in mind, the evidence is very clear that great earnings do not necessarily translate into great returns. Low-earning value companies have historically provided much higher investment returns (as compensation for their greater risk) than high-earning growth companies.

Summary

You can avoid the mistake of thinking this time is different by studying financial history. You will learn that there is nothing new or different, only the financial history you don't know. As Alan Greenspan noted in his address to Congress on February 26, 1997, "Regrettably, history is strewn with visions of such new eras that, in the end, have proven to be a mirage."[3]

MISTAKE 46

Do You Fail to Tax-Manage Your Portfolio Throughout the Year?

Even investors who are taxwise make the mistake of not tax-managing their portfolios throughout the year. Just as there are tax-management strategies that mutual funds can employ to improve their tax efficiency, there are similar strategies that you can use. Let's quickly review the strategies that a taxwise fund uses:

> Strategically harvests losses by selling stocks that are trading below their cost basis. The losses can be used to offset realized gains and to minimize taxes.
> Sells highest cost basis purchases to minimize gains and maximize losses. To know which shares have the highest cost basis, a fund must keep track of the cost basis of each share it purchases. When selling a portion of the shares owned, the fund sells the shares with the highest cost basis, minimizing taxes.
> Never willingly realizes short-term gains. Not selling any shares until the holding period is sufficient to qualify for the lower long-term capital gains rate.
> Trades around dividend dates—not buying shares of a company's stock just prior to the date of record for dividend payments to shareholders. Note the ex-dividend date is not the same as the date of record. The ex-dividend date is the date after the record date when the dividend is "separated" from the stock. The stock then trades at a lower price, net of dividends.
> For passive asset class funds: expands the buy range to a buy-and-hold range. For example, DFA's Small Cap Fund buys stocks whose market cap places them within the smallest 8 percent. However, to reduce trading costs, the portfolio will not sell a stock until its market cap exceeds the smallest 10 percent of companies

or becomes one of the 1,000 largest companies, whichever is higher. This is in contrast to an index fund, which generally will sell a stock as soon as it leaves the benchmark index (although some indexes have incorporated this concept to improve returns).

By mimicking those strategies, in conjunction with other techniques, you can improve your after-tax returns. Tax-aware investors know they should check their portfolios at the end of the year to see if there are losses that can be harvested to offset other gains. To maximize the benefit of harvesting losses, the specific lot identification method should be used. By doing so, an investor would be selling the lot with the highest cost basis, thus minimizing the current gains or maximizing the current loss and the current deduction.

However, it is a mistake to wait to harvest losses until the end of the year. Harvesting is a full-time job. One reason is that a fund might have a loss that can be harvested during the year, but by year-end it will have recovered. In that case, the opportunity to harvest the tax loss would be lost. In addition, it is typically important to take any short-term loss before it becomes long term. Short-term losses first offset short-term gains that are otherwise subject to higher ordinary income tax rates, while long-term losses first offset long-term gains that are otherwise subject to lower long-term rates. An investor who harvests a loss resets the cost basis to a new lower level. The tax rate differential then provides the opportunity to arbitrage the tax system. Let's see how that might work.

Assume an investor buys a fund at $100 on January 1. Two months later, it is trading at $50. The investor sells the fund. The loss is characterized as short term since the fund was held for less than one year. If we assume a 40 percent ordinary federal income tax rate, the investor will have a $20 tax savings. The net loss is $30. The investor also immediately purchases a very similar fund with the $50 proceeds of the sale. (Buying the same fund or a substantially identical fund within 30 days of the sale negates the deduction. Buying a similar fund, such as an S&P 600 ETF to replace a Russell 2000 fund, is acceptable.)

Let's jump forward one year and a day. Both the fund sold and the one purchased have risen to $100. Holding the first fund would mean no gain or loss and no tax deduction in the prior year. On the other hand, by harvesting the loss and replacing the original fund with the similar fund, this investor now has a gain of $50 on which he would have to pay taxes at the long-term capital gains rate. Let's assume that it is 20 percent. Thus, he owes taxes of $10 and has a net gain of $40. Not only did he pick up a $10 arbitrage of the tax system (received a $20 deduction and paid only $10, or had a net loss of $30 and net gain of $40), but he also gained the time value of the tax deduction for a full year. Note that he did not have to sell the fund in March 2010. If he continued to hold it, the tax on the unrealized gain would be deferred until the fund was sold.

When realizing a loss, an investor has the choice of reinvesting immediately in a similar fund (assuming one is available) or waiting out the required 31 days necessary to avoid the wash sale rule. Which is the winning strategy?

Stocks are always riskier than bonds (and therefore have higher expected returns); thus the winning strategy is always to reinvest. In addition, if you waited the 31 days, you would not be adhering to your plan, and also your equity allocation would be different for those 31 days if the proceeds weren't immediately reinvested.

And finally, the evidence is that if you are out of the market for a month, the odds of missing a large positive month are much greater than missing a large negative one.

For example, for the period 1926 to 2008, there were 170 months out of 996 (or 17.1 percent) where the stock market return was more than 5 percent. On the other hand, there were only 103 months with losses in excess of 5 percent. Thus, there was a 66 percent greater chance of missing a big gain than a big loss.

So at the time you sell, you should buy a similar fund. Keep in mind that if there is another loss 31 days later, you can swap back, get another deduction, and again reset your basis.

There are many funds and ETFs that make good substitutes for one another. However, you also need to keep in mind that to avoid the wash sale rule, you cannot sell and buy two instruments that are *substantially* identical in nature. It is likely the IRS would disallow the deduction. Therefore, you should be careful in your choice of alternatives.

There is another important tax strategy of which you should be aware. If you have held a fund for more than a year, you should always check to see what estimated distributions the fund plans to make during the year—specifically focusing on the amounts that will be ordinary income, short-term capital gains, and long-term capital gains. Most funds make distributions once a year, usually near the end of the year; but some make them more frequently, and sometimes funds make special distributions. You can usually obtain this information from your fund prior to the record date. It is important to check to see if there are going to be large distributions that will be treated as either ordinary income or short-term gains.

If this is true, then you might benefit from selling the fund before the record date. By doing so, the increase in the net asset value will be treated as long-term capital gains—and taxes will be at the lower long-term rate. If the fund making the large payout is selling for less than your tax basis, you certainly should consider selling the fund prior to the distribution. Otherwise you will have to pay taxes on the distribution, despite having an unrealized loss on the fund—a tax hell for an investor if ever there was one.

Just as a tax-managed fund trades around dividend dates (or avoids purchasing a stock about to pay a dividend), it is also important for you to avoid making purchases of mutual funds just prior to the ex-dividend date. You will be taxed on income you didn't really earn.

Finally, just as you would with tax-managed funds, you should generally avoid intentionally taking any short-term gains. (Simply wait until the long-term holding period is achieved.) For individuals, this last point refers to the rebalancing table that should be part of the investment policy statement. Rebalancing is important, as it allows you to control your portfolio's asset allocation. Without it, market movements will cause style drift.

However, because rebalancing in taxable accounts generally involves paying taxes (since you are selling winners to buy losers), it should be done only when significant style drift has occurred. This is why you should consider using a 5/25 rule to determine when to rebalance, rebalancing only when an asset (or asset class) has drifted either an absolute 5 percent from its target or a relative 25 percent. Either of these two measures can trigger the need to rebalance. For example, if an asset class has a target of 30 percent, rebalancing should occur any time the actual allocation falls below 25 percent or rises above 35 percent (the absolute 5 percent rule is the determining factor). If an asset class has a target of 10 percent, the rebalancing would be triggered at either 7.5 percent or 12.5 percent (the relative 25 percent rule is the determining factor). By allowing a bit of drift to occur, you can minimize the impact of taxes without losing control over the risks and rewards of your portfolio.

Tax-managing a portfolio is a very important part of the winning strategy. It is also a full-time job. By waiting until year-end to do tax planning, opportunities to tax-manage might be lost.

MISTAKE 47

Do You Let Taxes Dominate Your Decisions?

Minimizing the impact of taxes on returns is an important part of the winning strategy. However, many investors make the mistake of letting the avoidance of taxes drive investment decisions, often with disastrous results. The following example will illustrate the point.

It is August 2004, and an investor has bought 200 shares of Google and was lucky enough to buy those shares at a price of 100. The $20,000 investment was 5 percent of his $400,000 portfolio, half of which was in Treasury bonds. The stock skyrocketed. In December 2007, Google crossed 700. His shares were worth $140,000 and represented almost 25 percent of his portfolio, which had grown to $600,000. In addition, his equity allocation had grown from 50 percent to almost 70 percent.

The investor recognized that his portfolio was considerably more risky both by having as much as one-quarter of his portfolio in a single stock and by having a higher allocation to equities. However, selling would result in a large capital gains tax. Assuming a total federal and state tax rate of 20 percent, the tax on his $120,000 gain would be $24,000. Despite the risks, he refused to sell, letting the minimization of taxes drive his decision instead of the management of risk.

In January 2009, the stock fell below 300, and his investment was worth less than $60,000. If he had sold the stock at 700, the sale would have produced net cash of $116,000. Realizing how much the lost opportunity has cost him, he redoes the math and finds that if he sells at 300, the tax bill will be just $8,000 and he will still have a nice profit as he will realize a net of $52,000— not bad for his $20,000. So he decides to sell. Trying to avoid the $24,000 capital gains tax bill cost our investor $62,000.

Investors who have a low basis in a stock often let the tax situation drive their decisions, forgetting they are taking large risks.

Obviously, in hindsight, faced with the prospect of having to pay such large capital gains, the investor in our example would have been better off selling the stock and paying the tax. However, no hindsight is needed to prevent this type of mistake from occurring. Two things are required: The first is a written investment policy statement (IPS) with a rebalancing table. The second is the discipline to adhere to the plan. An IPS should have targets and limits on the allocation that any one stock or asset class is allowed within the portfolio. For example, our Google investor might have established a maximum buy limit for any one stock of 5 percent of the total portfolio. The maximum hold range might be set at 10 percent. If a stock exceeds 10 percent, the investor would sell enough shares to return the stock's position within the portfolio to the maximum 10 percent level or even to the target 5 percent (depending on what rules the investor establishes).

There is one other way you can avoid the mistake of being trapped by taxes, and it is implied in the following reminder: the only thing worse than having to pay taxes is not having to pay them.

MISTAKE 48

Do You Confuse Speculating with Investing?

R*isk* has four letters, but it is not a four-letter word, at least not in the colloquial sense. When it comes to investing, we need to distinguish between two very different types of risk: good risk and bad risk. Good risk is the type you are compensated for taking. Investors get *compensated* for taking *systematic* risks—risks that cannot be diversified away. The compensation is in the form of greater expected returns. Bad risk is the type for which there is no such compensation. Thus, it is called *uncompensated* or *unsystematic* risk.

With equity investing, there are these two forms of risk. Equities are more risky than fixed-income investments. Therefore, equities must *compensate* investors by providing greater *expected* returns to attract investors. Now let's turn to the "four-letter" type of risk, the *uncompensated* kind.

Diversification of Equity Portfolios

Equity investors face several types of risk. (This is true of any risky asset, be it stocks or bonds.) First, there is the systematic risk of investing in stocks. This risk cannot be diversified away, no matter how many stocks or different asset classes you own. Investors received an important reminder of this in 2008. Second, various asset classes carry different levels of risk. Large-cap stocks are less risky than small-cap stocks, and glamour (growth) stocks are less risky than distressed (value) stocks. These two risks also cannot be diversified away. Thus, investors must be compensated for taking them.

The third type of equity risk is that of the individual company. The risks of individual stock ownership can easily be diversified away by owning passive asset class or index funds that basically own all the stocks in an entire asset class or index. These vehicles eliminate the single-company risk in a low-cost and tax-efficient manner. Note that asset class risk can also be addressed by building a globally diversified portfolio, allocating funds across various asset classes: domestic and international, large cap and small cap, value and growth, and even real estate and emerging markets.

Since the risks of single-stock ownership can be diversified, the market does not compensate investors for taking that type of risk. This is why investing in individual companies is speculating, not investing. Investing means taking compensated risk. Speculating is taking uncompensated risk. Other examples of uncompensated risk are investing in sector funds (such as health care or technology) and individual country funds (other than a U.S. total stock market fund). Prudent investors recognize the difference between speculating and investing and, therefore, take only risks for which they are compensated.

The benefits of diversification are obvious and well known. Diversification reduces the risk of underperformance. It also reduces the volatility and dispersion of returns without reducing expected returns. Thus, a diversified portfolio is considered to be more *efficient* than a concentrated portfolio. The question is, why do investors take the bad kind of risk? They do so because they make the kinds of mistakes we have already discussed, mistakes such as being overconfident, confusing the familiar with the safe, and confusing information with knowledge.

Do You Try to Time the Market?

> It must be apparent to intelligent investors that if anyone
> possessed the ability to do so [forecast the immediate trend
> of stock prices] consistently and accurately he would become
> a billionaire so quickly he would not find it necessary
> to sell his stock market guesses to the general public.
>
> —Weekly staff letter, August 27, 1951,
> David L. Babson & Company
> Quoted in Charles Ellis, *The Investor's Anthology*

> Market timing is impossible to perfect.
>
> —Mark Rieppe
> Vice president, Charles Schwab Center for
> Investment Research, November 27, 1998

> Investors would do well to learn from deer hunters
> and fishermen who know the importance of
> "being there" and using patient persistence—so
> they are there when opportunity knocks.
>
> —Charles Ellis
> *Investment Policy*

In finance, a *black swan* refers to a large-impact, hard-to-predict, rare event beyond the realm of normal expectations. The stock market crash of October 19, 1987, when the Dow fell 23 percent in one day, would be an example. The flash crash of May 2010 is another one.

If investors could avoid the effects of black swans, the impact on investment returns would be enormous. Consider the following: A study by Javier Estrada, "Black Swans and Market Timing," on 15 stock markets in developed countries, including the United States, found that if investors could avoid the worst 10 days, their returns would be 150 percent more than the returns of buy-and-hold investors.[1] This makes market timing a tempting strategy. However, before being tempted, consider these words of wisdom from legendary investor Peter Lynch: "Far more money has been lost by investors in preparing for corrections, or anticipating corrections, than has been lost in the corrections themselves."[2]

Lynch's warning is supported by the evidence from a study by Benoit Mandelbrot and Richard Hudson that examined the daily index movement of the Dow Jones Industrial Average from 1916 to 2003. If daily returns were normally distributed, we should expect to see only 58 days during this period when the price changes of the index were more than 3.4 percent. In actuality, we saw a whopping 1,001 such days.

Even more eye-popping were the results of larger swings. We should expect a price change of more than 7 percent only once every 300,000 years. We actually saw 48 occurrences.[3]

Despite this evidence, market timing is embraced by a large percentage of individual and institutional investors. By examining the evidence from studies on market timing, we can see whether or not the belief in market timing efforts has been rewarded.

We begin by looking at the results of a study on market timing "experts." Mark Hulbert, publisher of *Hulbert's Financial Digest*, studied the performance of 32 of the portfolios of market timing newsletters for the 10 years ending in 1997.[4] During this period, the S&P 500 Index was up more than 18 percent per year. Here is what he found:

> The timers' annual average returns ranged from 5.8 to 16.9 percent.
> The average return was 10.1 percent.
> *None of the market timers beat the market.*

MoniResearch studied the performance of 85 managers with a total of $10 billion under management.[5] Here is what it found:

> The timers' annual average return ranged from 4.4 to 16.9 percent.
> The average return was 11.04 percent.
> *None of the market timers beat the market.*

Summary

Warren Buffett stated, "Our stay-put behavior reflects our view that the stock market serves as a relocation center at which money is moved from the active to the patient."[6] Buffett understood that investors do not earn returns smoothly over time. Instead, they earn them largely as a result of unpredictable bursts and crashes. Given that so much of the action happens on such a small number of days, the odds of successfully predicting the days to be in and out of the markets are close to zero. The real danger for investors is not being there when the big up moves occur.

Thus, the winning strategy is both to accept that markets cannot be timed and to build the expectation of black swans into an investment plan. In addition, broad global diversification, including an allocation to high-quality fixed-income assets sufficient to reduce overall portfolio risk to an acceptable level, helps mitigate the impact of the inevitable appearance of black swans. We agree with Javier Estrada's conclusion: "Market timing may be an entertaining pastime, but not a good way to make money."[7]

You can avoid the mistake of trying to time the market by developing an investment policy statement and having the discipline to ignore forecasts that have no value, other than possibly for entertainment. As Woody Allen said, "Most of success in life is in just showing up."[8]

Do You Rely on Market Gurus?

> For professional investors like myself, a sense of humor is
> essential. We are very aware that we are competing not
> only against the market averages but also against one
> another. It's an intense rivalry. We are each claiming, "The
> stocks in my fund today will perform better than what
> you own in your fund." That implies we think we can
> predict the future, which is the occupation of charlatans.
> If you believe you or anyone else has a system that can
> predict the future of the stock market, the joke is on you.
>
> —Ralph Wanger
> *A Zebra in Lion Country*

There is probably no arena for predictions where the payoff for being correct is more rewarding than the stock market. Therefore, it should not be surprising that a great amount of effort (and investor dollars) is expended in trying to predict the market's future direction. The question for investors is whether they should rely on the forecasts of industry professionals. The evidence suggests the answer is an emphatic no!

Despite all the innovations in information technology and all the academic research, forecasting stock market prices with any consistency or accuracy remains an elusive goal. William Sherden, author of *The Fortune Sellers*, was inspired by the following incident to write his book. In 1985, when preparing testimony as an expert witness, he analyzed the track records of inflation projections by different forecasting methods. He then compared those forecasts with what is called the "naïve" forecast—simply projecting today's inflation rate into the future. He was surprised to learn that the simple naive forecast proved to be the most accurate, beating the forecasts of the most prestigious economic forecasting firms equipped with their Ph.D.s from leading universities and thousand-equation computer models.

Sherden reviewed the leading research on forecasting accuracy from 1979 to 1995 and covering forecasts made from 1970 to 1995. He concluded that

> *Economists cannot predict the turning points in the economy.* He found that of the 48 predictions made by economists, 46 missed the turning points.
> *Economists' forecasting skill is about as good as guessing.* Even the economists who directly or indirectly influence the economy (the Federal Reserve, the Council of Economic Advisors, and the Congressional Budget Office) had forecasting records that were worse than pure chance.
> *There are no economic forecasters who consistently lead the pack in forecasting accuracy.*
> *There are no economic ideologies that produce superior forecasts.*
> *Increased sophistication provided no improvement in forecasting accuracy.*
> *Consensus forecasts do not improve accuracy.*
> *Forecasts may be affected by psychological bias.* Some economists are perpetually optimistic and others perpetually pessimistic.[1]

The year 2008 provided its share of evidence on the "wisdom" of paying attention to the so-called experts. It would seem that 2008 would be a year where the stock picks would have an easy time outperforming since the broad market was down sharply but some stocks like Wal-Mart actually rose. So let's see some of the forecasts the financial press provided us with:

> For its annual "Where to Invest" issue, *SmartMoney* scoured the globe for appealing opportunities and identified a dozen companies "likely to increase profits in a world filled with trouble spots."[2] *Outcome:* From the recommendation date of November 2, 2007, through December 31, 2008, the average share price decline of the 12 named stocks was 52.4 percent, compared with a drop of 40.2 percent for the S&P 500 Index and 35.4 percent for the Dow Jones Industrial Average.

> A money manager who successfully predicted the crash of 1987 was expecting a gain of 20 percent for the S&P 500 in 2008: "Our models show the S&P 500 is undervalued by 25 percent. . . . Our indicators are extremely bullish."[3] *Outcome:* Disappointment.
> A veteran market analyst favored "pockets of value," including stocks that had been "excessively punished" in the subprime-related meltdown: Nordstrom, Tiffany, J. Crew, and his favorite, American International Group.[4] *Outcome:* Prices fell on average 71 percent.

Unfortunately, for investors who rely on the forecasts of market analysts and strategists, such forecasts are likely to produce yachts only for the forecasters themselves, not for their clients. Steve Forbes, publisher of the magazine that bears his name, obviously agrees, quoting his grandfather, who founded the magazine 80 years ago: "You make more money selling the advice than following it."[5] We agree with Peter Lynch's conclusion: "To the rash and impetuous stockpicker who chases hot tips and rushes in and out of his equities, an 'investment' in stocks is no more reliable than throwing away paychecks on the horses with the prettiest names, or the jockey with the purple silks. . . . [But] when you lose [at the racetrack, at least], you'll be able to say, you had a great time doing it."[6]

In *The Fortune Sellers*, Sherden offers the following advice to investors:

> *Avoid market timers, for they promise something they cannot deliver. Cancel your subscription to market-timing newsletters. Tell the investment advisers selling the latest market-timing scheme to buzz off. Ignore news media predictions, since they haven't a clue. . . . Stop asking yourself, and everyone you know, What's the market going to do? It is an irrelevant question, because it cannot be answered.[7]*

Do You Use Leverage to Try to Enhance Investment Returns?

Many investors, often with encouragement from the brokerage community, use leverage in an attempt to generate increased investment returns. Leverage is the use of margin (borrowed funds) to increase the amount available to invest. When borrowing from a brokerage firm to increase equity exposure, the firm will typically lend individual investors up to an amount equal to their initial equity investment. Brokerage firms encourage the use of margin because it is almost riskless lending (as they hold the collateral, and the loan is overcollateralized) at high spreads. In addition, the firm will make incremental profits from the commissions or loads it is likely to earn from the incremental investments made. However, we hope to convince you that investors should not use margin.

If an investor owned $100,000 of stock, a brokerage firm would be willing to lend an additional $100,000, assuming the funds were used to buy more equities (with the total equity holdings used as collateral for the debt). The investor would have $200,000 of equity holdings and $100,000 (50 percent) margin. The firm will allow the investor to maintain that debt as long as the margin does not exceed 70 percent of the equity holdings. In our example, the value of the equity holdings would have to be maintained at a minimum of about $143,000 (since $100,000 is 70 percent of $143,000). If the value fell below that level, a *margin call* would be made. At that point, the investor would have to either pay down the debt to bring it back to the 70 percent level or put up more collateral.

Why would an investor use margin? The answer is simple, to enhance total returns. From 1926 through 2010, the S&P 500 Index returned 9.9 percent, outperforming riskless one-month Treasury bills by 6.3 percent per year. Now look at the incremental returns that margin can provide. It is important to note that investors cannot borrow at the risk-free rate. Margin costs are typically between 1.5 and 3 percent above the one-month London Interbank Offered Rate (LIBOR—the rate at which banks lend to each other). The size of the spread depends on the depth (profitability) of the relationship with the investor. For illustration purposes, we will assume a spread of 2 percent. Historically, the average spread between the LIBOR and one-month Treasury bills has been about 0.5 percent. (In the financial crisis of 2008, it widened to more than 4 percent and closed the year at around 1 percent.) Thus, an investor using margin to buy stocks would see the 6.3 percent premium over the riskless rate shrink (using our assumptions) by about 2.5 percent.

This means investors using margin were, on the portion earned with borrowed money, earning 2.5 percent less on the equity investment than those who did not use margin; and they were taking more risks because while nonleveraged investors can wait out bear markets (assuming they have the discipline to do so), margin investors have the risk of a margin call. If a fall in value causes the margin loan to exceed 70 percent of the collateral, the firm will call the loan. If the investor cannot come up with incremental collateral or pay down the debt to the required 70 percent level, the firm has the right to sell the collateral (and will in all likelihood do so) to pay the debt down to the required level. Thus, investors might be forced to sell their holdings. Forced margin calls are a frequent occurrence in severe bear markets—like the ones experienced in 2000 to 2002 and 2008. Investors who have their investments liquidated can never benefit from any future recovery in prices.

Rational investors only take incremental risk when they have an expectation of higher returns. Margin investors earn lower returns on the investment generated by the margin and take more risk. Thus, we can conclude that the use of margin for investing purposes is an inefficient use of one's capital. The rewards are simply not commensurate with the risk. We can see the evidence of how inefficient the use of margin is by examining the performance of the Rydex Nova Fund.

Nova is a leveraged, no-load fund designed to provide investment returns corresponding to 150 percent of the performance of the S&P 500. The fund achieves its target beta (exposure to the change in the S&P 500) of 1.5 through the purchase of shares of individual securities, stock index futures contracts, and options on securities and stock indexes. The key question for investors is whether the fund actually delivers this attractive 50 percent above the S&P 500's return. The year 1994 marked the Rydex Nova Fund's first full year of operation. For the 17-year period from the fund's launch in 1994 to 2010, the S&P 500 Index provided an annualized return of 8.3 percent. Unfortunately, Nova did not earn anything close to 150 percent of the return of the index. In fact, it earned just 6.1 percent. Additionally, the increase in beta caused the standard deviation of the fund to be 29.6 percent versus 20.7 percent for the S&P 500. As a result, Rydex Nova investors earned only 73 percent of the returns of the S&P 500—and yet experienced 43 percent greater volatility.

Summary

The use of margin is an inefficient way to enhance expected returns. If you wish to increase the expected return of your portfolio, the more prudent, as well as more efficient, approach is to increase your exposure to the riskier asset classes of small-cap and value stocks. In addition, you don't risk a margin call.

MISTAKE 52

Do You Understand That There Is Only One Way to Be a Buy-and-Hold Investor?

As we've seen, the historical record on efforts to time the market makes it clear that the buy-and-hold strategy is the winning one. Unfortunately, many investors make a mistake when implementing a buy-and-hold strategy. There is really only one way to truly be a buy-and-hold investor. The reason is that the only way to be sure your asset allocation remains what you want it to be is to hold only passively managed funds (index funds, exchange-traded funds, and passive asset class funds). Buy-and-hold investors who use active fund managers to implement their asset allocation can have their well-designed strategy undermined by the market timing efforts and the resulting style drifting that can accompany active management. Thus, while the investor is passive, the manager is active, undoing the buy-and-hold strategy.

The charters of most actively managed mutual funds give their portfolio managers great freedom to shift their allocations between asset classes at their discretion. Thus, not only do investors in such funds lose control of their asset allocation decisions, but they also end up taking unintended risks by unknowingly investing in markets, or types of instruments, they wanted to avoid. Perhaps the best example (but in no way unique) of this problem is the case of the legendary Fidelity Magellan Fund.

Over the years, many investors placed the equity portion of their portfolio in Fidelity Magellan. Unfortunately, in February 1996 Magellan's asset allocation was only 70 percent equity. The rest of the portfolio consisted of 20 percent bonds and 10 percent short-term marketable securities. Magellan's investment manager at the time, the highly regarded Jeffrey Vinik, was obviously making a big bet that long-term bonds and short-term marketable securities would outperform the equity markets.

How did Vinik's bet affect the investor's asset allocations? Let's assume that an investor with $100,000 to invest sought an 80 percent equity–20 percent fixed-income allocation. She invested her entire $80,000 equity allocation in Fidelity Magellan. Due to the strategy deployed by Mr. Vinik, she actually had only $56,000 ($80,000 × 70 percent) invested in equities.

	Desired Allocation		Actual Allocation	
Equity allocation	80%	$80,000	56%	$56,000
Fixed-income allocation	20%	$20,000	44%	$44,000
Total portfolio	100%	$100,000	100%	$100,000

Due to Fidelity Magellan's style drift, our investor's equity allocation was 56 percent, obviously less than the desired 80 percent. By placing funds with an active manager, she allowed someone else to modify her strategy. The key issue is not the outcome of Mr. Vinik's decision but the investor's loss of control of the asset allocation process. Incidentally, the market subsequently soared to new highs, bonds fell in value, and Mr. Vinik moved on. Notably, for the period February 1985 to June 1995, the composition of Fidelity's Magellan fund "varied over time to such a degree that it would have been virtually impossible for investors to determine the asset classes in which they were investing, or the risks to which they were being exposed."[1] This example was a very painful one for the buy-and-hold investors that lived through it. Unfortunately, it is by no means a unique one.

Summary

The case of Fidelity Magellan demonstrates why there is really only one way for investors to avoid this type of damage. They must use only passively managed funds. However, this is only a necessary condition for successful buy-and-hold investing. The sufficient condition is that investors need to rebalance their portfolio on a regular basis. Since asset classes change in price by varying percentages, it is necessary to rebalance the portfolio regularly to the desired asset allocation. Otherwise, the market will cause the same style drift that active managers cause! In other words, buy and hold doesn't mean buy and do nothing.

Do You Work with Commission-Based Advisors?

It has been a problem since the dawn of the retail brokerage business. Brokers have a strong incentive to get customers to trade when it might be in clients' interests to do nothing.
—*BusinessWeek*, July 14, 1997

Definition of a stockbroker: Someone whose objective it is to transfer assets from your account to their account.
—Anonymous

U nless you are a do-it-yourself investor, you are working with an investment advisor of some kind. That person or firm is typically either a stockbroker or a registered investment advisor. It is our strong advice that you should only work with investment advisors who are fee-only, not commission-based.

A fee-only relationship is the best way to ensure that the advisor's interests are aligned with yours. The only thing the advisors are selling is their advice. No one else is providing them with any compensation. Most fee-only advisors work on a fee that is based on a percentage of assets under management, in which case there is an alignment of interests. The more your portfolio is worth, the greater their compensation. Their incentive is to help you grow the value of your portfolio. If you work with an advisor who is paid on a commission basis, there is no guarantee the person selling you a product is not suggesting that particular product because he gets a large commission upon sale, even though there might be a better alternative for you. Remember, commission-based advisors are not just providing advice but also selling products.

The worst example of this conflict of interest is that investors in profit-sharing plans and other tax-deferred accounts have been sold expensive variable annuities. (It should be noted that, by law, under the "old" 403(b) plans, an individual could only hold variable annuities in a tax-deferred retirement plan. When the new 403(b)-7 was added, that changed.) Considering that the only valuable benefit of a variable annuity is the tax deferral, there is virtually no reason anyone should be paying the expensive charges of a variable annuity when the account structure already provides the benefit of the tax deferral. Of course, the salesperson will have received a commission of as much as 8 percent.

Commission-based advisors most likely will also push for expensive and tax-inefficient actively managed funds over index funds. The likely reason is not that they believe the actively managed funds will provide better performance but that they will be paid a load or receive a trailing fee as long as you hold the fund. Of course, it is possible they might actually believe, despite all evidence to the contrary, that somehow they can identify the few active managers who will beat their benchmarks in the future. But you could not be certain of their motives unless they were fee-only advisors whose interests were aligned with yours. Consider the following memo sent in response to requests from a brokerage firm's sales force for the firm to offer index funds. The sales force was simply responding to similar requests from clients who had heard about the superior performance of these passively managed funds:

> *Index funds are passively managed mutual funds. They simply buy and hold all the stocks of a popular index such as the Standard and Poor's 500. Because their turnover is low and they don't require large research staffs, most have low operating expenses. . . . The performance of an index fund is a function of two factors: the performance of the index itself, and the fees to operate and DISTRIBUTE the fund. For a fund to be successful in the brokerage community, it must adequately compensate brokers through either an upfront commission or an ongoing service fee. As a result, a broker-sold index fund would underperform no-load index funds. This is why most index funds are offered by no-load fund groups. (Emphasis ours)*

The reason that most brokers and commission-based advisors do not sell index funds is not because these funds do not perform well. They don't sell them because investors can buy them cheaper elsewhere. In addition, there is just not enough revenue available to compensate the broker, whose first priority is generating fees, not obtaining the best possible results for clients. Mutual fund sponsors avoid indexing because, though the record proves that it is the winning strategy for investors, it is not very profitable for fund sponsors. They see indexing as the losing *business* strategy. This is clearly a conflict of interest.

The same thing is true when it comes to individual stocks. Commission-driven compensation requires investors to trade to generate profits, from both commissions and market-making activities. (They can earn the bid-offer spread if they make a market in the particular stock being traded.) Thus, there is an incentive to have the investor actively trade an account, when doing nothing might be in the investor's best interests. The activity known as "churning" has been the cause of the filing of many investor lawsuits.

There is one other issue. A conflict of interest may arise when an investor wants to purchase bonds. A brokerage firm might be holding an inventory of bonds that it wants to dump. The firm will typically incent its brokers to dump these bonds on unsuspecting clients by offering the brokers larger commissions. An investor then might end up being sold a bond that might not be the most appropriate one for her based on her desired maturity and credit risk. In addition, although commissions will generally appear on a purchase statement, the firm may mark up its bond inventory so the investor ends up paying an above-market price, without the client's knowledge of this occurring. Investors are particularly vulnerable to this with municipal and corporate bonds, as prices are generally not as transparent as they are for stocks. Therefore, while you might see a commission charge, there typically will be a markup of 1 percent or even more. The investor will never see this cost, except through lower returns. This can be avoided by requiring the advisor to shop several wholesale market makers for the best price.

Do You Spend Too Much Time Managing Your Portfolio?

> You shouldn't spend time on your investments.
> That will just tempt you to pull up your plants and
> see how the roots are doing, and that's very bad
> for the roots. It's also very bad for your sleep.
> —Paul Samuelson
> Quoted in Jonathan Burton, *Investment Titans*

> Investors spend an absurd amount of time trying to
> control the one thing they can do the least about, which
> is their raw investment performance. They attempt to
> pick hot stocks, find star fund managers and guess the
> market's direction. Yet it is extraordinarily difficult,
> if not impossible, to do any of these things.
> —Jonathan Clements
> *Wall Street Journal*, July 2, 1999

> There's something in people, you might even call it a little
> bit of a gambling instinct. . . . I tell people [investing]
> should be dull. It shouldn't be exciting. Investing should
> be more like watching paint dry or watching grass grow.
> If you want excitement, take $800 and go to Las Vegas.
> —Paul Samuelson
> *Bloomberg*, September 1999

hortly after Larry's first book was published, he received a call from a doctor who related this story. He had been in practice only a few years and had a wife and a young child, with one more on the way. He had seen many of his friends generate large profits from trading stocks, and he had gotten caught up in the euphoria of day trading. After putting in his typical long day at the office, he would come home not to his wife, but to his computer. He spent hours studying charts and investment reports and following the chat boards. Within just a few months he had turned his small investment stake into about $100,000. Unfortunately, his wife no longer had a husband, and his child no longer had a father, the doctor now being married to his computer. As his wife began to seriously question their marriage, *luckily* for him, he lost all his profits within a few months.

Fortunately for the doctor, he recognized that his original gains were likely a matter of luck, similar to a hot hand at the craps table. He also recognized that he was not paying attention to the most important part of his life: his family. Someone suggested that he read Larry's book. After doing so, he called to thank Larry for helping him find not only the winner's game in investing but also the winner's game in life.

Indexing and passive investing may be boring, but they guarantee that you receive market returns in a low-cost and tax-efficient manner. They also free you from spending any time at all watching CNBC and reading financial publications that are basically not much more than what Jane Bryant Quinn called "investment pornography." Instead, you can spend your time with your family, doing community service, reading a good book, or pursuing your favorite hobby. Remember, investing was never meant to be exciting, despite what Wall Street and the financial press want you to believe. Investing is supposed to be about achieving your financial goals with the least amount of risk.

Ted Cadsby, president and CEO of CIBC Securities, put it this way: "Success in investing (as in much of life) is very much dependent upon putting probabilities in your favour—getting them working for you, not against you. And putting market odds in your favour couldn't be easier, because the best investment strategy is basically to do nothing!"[1]

The great tragedy in life is not that the vast majority of investors unnecessarily miss out on market returns that are available to anyone simply by adopting a passive investment strategy. The great tragedy in life is that they also miss out on the really important things in life in pursuit of the Holy Grail of outperformance. That is why this book is not just about helping you avoid the mistakes even smart investors make, but about helping you win the game of life.

MISTAKE 55

Do You Prepare Your Heirs?

Napoleon Bonaparte is widely regarded as one of the greatest commanders ever to have lived. His campaigns are studied at military academies all over the world. Yet he developed few military innovations. Perhaps the greatest contributor to his military success can be summed up in this quotation attributed to him: "Most battles are won or lost [in the preparation stage] long before the first shot is fired."

Each year Americans spend billions of dollars preparing their assets for transition to their heirs. They engage high-powered estate and tax planners who set up complex vehicles like family limited partnerships, life insurance trusts, charitable remainder trusts, charitable lead trusts, and various other kinds of trusts. Yet despite the best efforts of top-notch professional advisors, it is estimated that "70 percent of estates lose their assets and family harmony following the transition of the estate."[1] Given the talent engaged, it doesn't seem likely the failure is due to poor design. So why do the majority of plans fail?

According to Roy Williams and Vic Preisser, authors of *Estate Planning for the Post-transition Period*, "the major causes of post-transition failures were discovered to lie *within* the family."[2] The unsuccessful families failed mainly because the heirs were unprepared, they didn't trust each other, and communications broke down. In other words, while great attention is being paid by the family and its advisors to preparing the assets for transition to the heirs, very little, if any, attention is being paid to preparing the heirs for the assets they will inherit.

What Do Parents Worry about Most?

Consider the following list of the five things parents worry about most with respect to wealth and its effect on their children:

1. Too much emphasis on material things
2. Naïveté about the value of money
3. Spending beyond their means
4. Initiative being ruined by affluence
5. Will not do as well as parents would like[3]

Now consider the focus of these concerns. While the typical family worries about these issues, the focus on estate planning tends to be on issues of taxation, preservation of wealth, and governance, not on the transfer of family values. There is an obvious disconnect between the issues identified as the most important ones and the focus of the efforts being spent. Therefore, it should not come as a surprise when most plans fail.

Are Your Heirs Prepared for Their Assets?

The following are some questions that Williams and Preisser suggest you ask yourself to help determine if your heirs are prepared for their assets:

> Do your children (and their spouses, if any) know your estate plan?
> Have they read your will?
> Do they know the family's net worth, meaning both yours and theirs (if they have assets in their name)?
> Are they in communication with your team of advisors (your attorney, accountant, and financial or investment advisor)?

Two other important questions are: Have the children been involved in the formation of the investment policy statement? Are they familiar with the investment strategy, the goals, and the management of the assets?

Taboo Topic

Unfortunately, in the majority of cases, families treat money and the issues surrounding wealth as a taboo subject. And the "lessons" of noninvolvement get passed on from one generation to the next. Thus, in most cases the answers to the above questions are no—and that explains why the failure rate is so high. The solution to the problem is that while it is important to treat family wealth as a private matter, it should not be private *within* the family.

Those Who Fail to Plan, Plan to Fail

Williams and Preisser suggest that for a plan to be successful, heirs (including spouses) should have some influence in how the estate is structured. Among the issues that should be addressed is whether the estate plan matches the skills and interests of the heirs. And there should be a plan to prepare the heirs for their future responsibilities. Heirs should know the impact of their wealth on their family and the responsibilities of wealth.

Thus, a transition plan should include a family wealth mission statement (FWMS) that addresses the following issues:

1. The FWMS spells out the overall purpose of the family's wealth and a strategy to implement it, with roles well defined.
2. The *entire* family participates in the important decisions.
3. Family members have the option to participate in the management of assets.
4. Heirs understand and have bought into their roles.
5. Heirs have reviewed and understand all documents.
6. Asset distributions are based on readiness, not age of heirs.
7. The mission statement includes incentives and opportunities for heirs.
8. Younger children are encouraged to participate in philanthropic grant-making decisions.
9. Family unity is considered an important asset.
10. The family communicates well and regularly.[4]

Benefits of Creating an FWMS

> The document will articulate why you created an FWMS and why you are managing and distributing your estate in this manner. It should also articulate how the wealth was achieved, what life experiences shaped your financial philosophy, what the wealth

means to you (how it is important to you), and what values you wish to pass on.

> The process of creating an FWMS helps you to identify and examine the people and entities you hold in the highest esteem, leading you to make wealth transfer decisions that make the most sense to you. As a clear expression for heirs and others, the FWMS can be a tool to help pass on your personal values to future generations. It will identify the individuals for whom you feel responsible, it will specify the charities or organizations you feel passionate about and desire to support with social capital, and it will explain why you feel an obligation to give the charities a portion of your wealth.

> The FWMS succinctly informs your advisor of your intentions, saving both time and money as the advisor explores appropriate strategies to help you achieve your wishes. Thus, it should specifically identify how much money is needed during your lifetime and how much you wish to leave to your heirs. It should also identify why you feel this is an appropriate amount and what you want to achieve by giving them this money.

And finally, the FWMS document should be signed and dated to demonstrate that it is a valid document and accurately reflects your wishes.[5]

Summary

The moral of this tale is that just as most battles are won in the preparatory stage, the success of a family wealth transition plan depends on the effort and emphasis placed on transitioning not only the family's wealth, but the family's values as well.

Did You Begin Your Investment Journey without a Road Map?

No rational traveler would ever take a trip to a place she has never been without a road map and directions. Similarly, no rational businessperson would start a business without spending lots of time and energy thoroughly researching that business and then developing a well-designed plan. Investing is no different. It is not possible to make a rational decision about any investment without considering how the addition of that investment would impact the risk and return of the entire portfolio—and thus the odds of achieving the plan's objectives.

As we noted in the previous chapter, those who fail to plan, plan to fail (an old and wise saying!). Yet many investors begin their investment journey without a plan—an investment policy statement (IPS) laying out the plan's objectives and the road map to achieving them. The IPS includes a formal asset allocation identifying both the target allocation for each asset class in the portfolio and the rebalancing targets in the form of tolerance ranges. A written IPS serves as a guidepost and helps provide the discipline needed to adhere to a strategy over time.

Just as a business plan must be reviewed regularly to adapt to changing market conditions, an IPS must be a living document. If any of the plan's underlying assumptions change, the IPS should be altered to adapt to the change. Life-altering events (for example, a birth, a marriage, a large inheritance, or a new job) can impact the asset allocation decision in dramatic ways. Thus, the IPS and resulting asset allocation decisions should be reviewed whenever a major life event occurs.

Even market movements can lead to changes in the assumptions behind the IPS and the portfolio's asset allocations. For example, a major bull market like the one we experienced in the mid-2000s can lower the need to take risk for those investors who began the decade with a significant accumulation of capital. At the same time, the rise in prices lowered future expected returns, having the opposite effect on those with minimal amounts of capital (perhaps just beginning their investment careers). The lowering of expected returns to equities meant that to achieve the same expected return, investors would have to allocate more capital to equities than would have been the case had returns been lower in the past. The reverse is true of bear markets. They raise the need to take risk for those with significant capital accumulation while lowering it for those with little.

The Foundation of the Investment Plan

By outlining and prescribing a prudent and individualized investment strategy, the IPS is the foundation of the investment plan. Meir Statman, a behavioral finance professor at Santa Clara University, notes the importance of psyches in investment behavior, likening the situation to antilock brakes. "When at high speed, the car in front of us stops quickly, we instinctively hit the brake pedal hard and lock 'em up. It doesn't matter that all the studies show that when the brakes lock, we lose control." Statman suggests investors need antilock brakes for their investment portfolios as well:

> Instinctively we react to investment situations in ways that might have saved our lives fighting on distant battlefields long ago. But, today they are counterproductive, like locking up our brakes. When the market drops, our instinctive fear to flight is so strong, even the most rational investors find themselves caving in, to their own demise. And market tops can often be called soon after the staunchest of bears throws in the towel and turns bullish.[1]

An IPS can act as an investor's antilock braking system. Your own IPS will help provide the discipline to stick with your plan and reduce the risk that emotions (greed and envy in bull markets and fear and panic in bear markets) will impact the decision-making process.

Before writing an IPS, you should thoroughly review your financial and personal status. One's financial situation, job stability, investment horizon, tolerance for risk, and need for emergency reserves vary from another's. The IPS should not be developed in isolation. It should be integrated into an overall financial plan, one addressing investments and the entire spectrum of risk management issues (creditor protection and the need for life, health, disability, long-term care, liability, and even longevity insurance).

The written IPS should include a list of your specific goals such as

> The target net worth or financial goal
> The amount of assets you are planning on adding to your portfolio each year (assuming you are in the accumulation phase)
> The time at which you plan to begin withdrawals from the portfolio
> The dollar amount (or percentage) you plan on withdrawing each year

This will allow you to track progress toward the goal, making appropriate adjustments along the way.

The next step is to specify the asset allocation, first identifying how much will be allocated to equities and how much to fixed income. Within these two broad categories, you need to establish the appropriate percentage allocations for each of the individual asset classes, such as small cap, value, and emerging markets. Next list the ranges within which you will allow market movements to cause the designated allocation to drift before you will rebalance the portfolio.

It's important to view your broad categories and narrower categories as separate for rebalancing purposes. In the same table that follows, you'll notice that it's possible for each of the classes within domestic equity to be within the appropriate ranges, but for the overall domestic allocation to fall outside the boundaries. This would still mean that the portfolio needs rebalancing, even though the narrow classes are within the plan guidelines.

Sample Rebalancing Table

ASSET CLASS	MINIMUM ALLOCATION (%)	TARGET ALLOCATION (%)	MAXIMUM ALLOCATION (%)
U.S. large	7.5	10	12.5
U.S. large value	7.5	10	12.5
U.S. small	7.5	10	12.5
U.S. small value	7.5	10	12.5
Real estate	7.5	10	12.5
Total U.S.	**45**	**50**	**55**
International large value	3.75	5	6.25
International small	3.75	5	6.25
International small value	3.75	5	6.25
Emerging markets	3.75	5	6.25
Total international	**15**	**20**	**25**
Total equity	**65**	**70**	**75**
Nominal bonds	7.5	10	12.5
TIPS	15	20	25
Total fixed income	**25**	**30**	**35**

One last point. Creating a financial plan is not a one-time process. Your financial situation will change over time if for no other reason than your investment horizon changes as time marches on. Financial planning is a dynamic process that can be impacted by market conditions (altering your need to take risk), changes in employment (altering your risk tolerance), changes in marital status (altering your ability to take risk), inheritances, or any other life-altering event. A bear market may even test your assumptions about your own ability to absorb the stomach acid it can create. Once a year, you should revisit your financial plan to make sure the assumptions upon which you built the plan still hold true.

Do You Understand the Nature of Risk?

S ince we live in a world without crystal balls that allow us to clearly see the future, prudent investing is all about the management of risk and *expected* returns. A problem that both investors and investment advisors face is defining what exactly is risk. As you will see, risk can be many different things. And since risk can be many different things to different people, investors and advisors are faced with deciding which risks are the most important to manage.

The most commonly used academic definition of risk is *standard deviation*—a measure of volatility. Unfortunately, two investments with similar standard deviations can experience entirely different distributions of returns. While some investments exhibit normal distribution (the familiar bell curve), others may exhibit characteristics known as kurtosis and skewness. We will first define these terms and then explain why it is important to understand their implications.

Skewness measures asymmetry of a distribution. In other words, the historical pattern of returns does not resemble a normal distribution. Negative skewness occurs when the values to the left of (less than) the mean are fewer but *farther* from the mean than are values to the right of the mean. For example, the return series of –30 percent, 5 percent, 10 percent, and 15 percent has a mean of 0 percent. There is only one return less than 0 percent, and there are three higher; but the one that is negative is much *farther* from zero than the positive ones. Positive skewness occurs when the values to the right of (more than) the mean are fewer but farther from the mean than are values to the left of the mean.

Behavioral finance studies have found that, in general, people like assets with positive skewness. This is evidenced by their willingness to accept low, or even negative, expected returns when an asset exhibits positive skewness. The classic example is a lottery ticket. On the other hand, in general, they do not like assets with negative skewness. High-risk asset classes (e.g., junk bonds, emerging markets) typically exhibit negative skewness. And some investment vehicles, such as hedge funds, exhibit negative skewness.

Kurtosis measures the degree to which exceptional values, much larger or smaller than the average, occur more frequently (high kurtosis) or less frequently (low kurtosis) than in a normal distribution. High kurtosis results in exceptional values that are called *fat tails*. Fat tails indicate a higher percentage of very low and very high returns than would be expected with a normal distribution. Low kurtosis results in *thin tails*.

It is important for investors to understand that when skewness and kurtosis are present (the distribution of returns is not normal), investors looking *only* at the standard deviation of returns may receive a misleading picture of the riskiness of an investment—that is, the risks are understated.

Another risk measure that should be considered is the probability of a negative outcome. This is especially true of risk-averse investors who are more inclined to lose discipline and stray from a well-developed plan when risk actually shows up.

Along the same lines, risk can be defined as the probability of not achieving your financial objective. It is important to note that the future return of a portfolio should never be considered as a single point, but instead should be considered as a potential distribution of outcomes. The use of Monte Carlo simulation can help with estimating the risks (odds) of failure.

Another risk, one that is purely psychological, though real nonetheless, is what is known as *tracking error risk*. For example, U.S. investors who build globally diversified portfolios will experience investment results that are quite different from those experienced by the "market"—with the *market* defined as a broad major index such as the S&P 500 Index. Some years (e,g., 2000–2003) investors will like the divergence, as the tracking error is positive. Other years (say, 1998–1999) they may be unhappy with the divergence, as the tracking error is negative. Negative tracking error can lead to loss of discipline. Thus, investors that are sensitive to the risk of tracking error should consider either minimizing it or avoiding it altogether.

There is yet another risk that investors and advisors must deal with—maverick risk. As Robert Arnott points out:

> Practitioners "know" that the greatest peril is the risk of being wrong and alone—it is more acceptable to fail conventionally than to succeed unconventionally. Decisions that leave an investor alone carry the inherent risk of being wrong. If an investor is wrong and alone, a strong likelihood is that he will not have the patience to see the investment decision through.[1]

The decision, even if correct in the long run, will be reversed before it can succeed. We are all familiar with the expression "Misery loves company." Experiencing relatively low (but still positive) investment results may create more psychological risks to the investment plan being abandoned than experiencing losses if everyone around is having a similar experience.

While standard deviation is one important measure of risk, it is certainly not the only one investors should consider when developing a financial plan and investment policy statement. Prudent investors consider all the risks of investing (be they real or psychological) when developing their plans.

PART 4

Mistakes Made When Developing a Portfolio

MISTAKE 58

Do You Consider Investments in Isolation?

Steve Nash is the point guard for the Phoenix Suns of the NBA. Looking at some of his career statistics, in some ways they are ordinary. Through the end of the 2010–2011 season, he had averaged 14.6 points and 3.0 rebounds per game. Certainly there are those with far better statistics whom many would consider better players. Kobe Bryant of the Los Angeles Lakers is one example. Yet Steve Nash is a perennial all star and two-time Most Valuable Player—an award that Bryant finally won after the 2007–2008 season, his twelfth in the league. And at least as of the end of 2010, Nash has more MVP awards.

Nash won such accolades because his contributions go beyond his individual statistics, especially points and rebounds. Nash's main contribution is that he makes everyone around him better. Evidence of this is that he is always among the league leaders in assists, averaging 8.5 per game over his career. This attribute is why Nash is generally considered the greatest point guard of his era. It is also why it is important to not view a player's value to the team by viewing his statistics in isolation. One needs to consider how the player impacts the team's overall performance.

The same thing applies to investing. A common mistake made by investors, and even professional advisors, is to view an asset class's returns and risk in isolation. Just as the only right way to consider the value of Steve Nash is to consider how his play impacts the entire team, the only right way to view an asset is to consider how its addition impacts the risk and return of the portfolio.

In 1990, Harry Markowitz was awarded the Nobel Prize in Economics for his contributions to modern portfolio theory. Markowitz demonstrated that one could add risky, but low-correlating, assets to a portfolio and increase returns without increasing risk (or, alternatively, reduce risk without reducing returns). The following example will demonstrate just how important it is to consider investments in the whole.

From 1991 through 2007, the S&P 500 Index returned 11.4 percent per year and had a standard deviation of 17.0 percent per year. During the same period, the S&P Goldman Sachs Commodity Index (GSCI) returned just 6.8 percent and had a standard deviation of 25.6 percent. Why would anyone consider including in a portfolio an asset class that experienced 4.6 percent per year lower returns than the S&P 500 and also experienced much greater volatility? If you considered investments in isolation, such an addition would not happen.

However, a portfolio that consisted of 95 percent S&P 500 and 5 percent S&P GSCI would have provided the same return (11.4 percent) with a lower standard deviation (15.9 versus 17.0). This outcome was a result of the impact of the negative correlation (−0.20) of returns of the two asset classes. (Negative correlation is present when one asset produces higher-than-average returns and the other *tends to* experience lower-than-average returns.) Every investor should prefer the portfolio that included the lower-returning and more volatile S&P GSCI.

When considered in isolation, commodities appear to be a low-returning, risky asset. Yet their inclusion has historically improved portfolio performance.

As another example, consider the following. From 1970 through 2007, the MSCI EAFE Index returned 11.6 percent per year and had a standard deviation of 21.6 percent. During the same period, the S&P 500 returned 11.1 percent with a standard deviation of 16.6 percent. Now consider European investors. Should they have included the lower-returning S&P 500 as part of their portfolio? A portfolio that was allocated 50 percent to each of the two indexes would have still returned 11.6 percent, but would have lowered the standard deviation from 21.6 percent to 17.1 percent.

From a U.S. investor's viewpoint, the combined S&P 500–MSCI EAFE portfolio also produced superior results. The portfolio with both asset classes increased returns from 11.1 percent per year to 11.6 percent per year, a relative increase of 5 percent. And while the standard deviation did rise from 16.6 percent per year to 17.1 percent per year, that is a relative increase of less than

3 percent. Thus, the combined portfolio produced superior risk-adjusted returns.

Summary

John Ruskin was an author, poet, and artist best known for his work as an art and social critic. His essays on art and architecture were influential in the Victorian and Edwardian eras. He stated, "Not only is there but one way of doing things rightly, but there is only one way of seeing them, and that is seeing the whole of them."[1] Ruskin's advice applies to investing. There is only one right way to build a portfolio—by recognizing that the risk and return of any asset class by itself should be irrelevant. The only thing that should matter is considering how the addition of an asset class impacts the risk and return of the *entire portfolio*.

Do You Have Too Many Eggs in One Basket?

Every investor knows that putting too many eggs in one basket is a risky investment decision that can easily be avoided by building a diversified portfolio. Yet many executives and long-term corporate employees end up with a substantial portion of their assets in the stock of the company for which they work. We have seen numerous cases where employees have as much as 80 or even 90 percent of their entire net worth in their employer's stock. Typically, the unusually large share is the result of stock options and savings plans that encourage ownership of corporate stock.

Our experience has been that in the vast majority of cases, no actual decision was made to hold such a risky portfolio. The person just ended up with the portfolio without thinking about the risks incurred. In other cases, people believe that because they work for the company, they "know" just how good an investment they have. Let's examine why holding such an undiversified portfolio is really a poor decision, no matter how good the prospects for the company look. (Remember that the highly likely is not certain.) In fact, if an investor takes the time to think about the decision in a rational manner, he would likely never retain the vast majority of his assets in his own company's (or any other company's) stock.

Whenever we meet with a client who has a large percentage of her assets in her own company's stock, we ask her to put herself in the following situation. She is the single greatest blackjack player in the world, never making a mistake counting cards. A casino has offered her a challenge match in which only one deck of cards will be used. She can bet any amount she likes on any individual hand, from 1 cent to her entire net worth, let's say $2 million. She can also quit the game at any time. She accepts the challenge and proceeds to bet 1 cent on every hand. Finally, the perfect situation arises: The dealer has only four cards left, all of them kings. The dealer can only deal three cards (because the last one is face up) and then must shuffle and deal himself one more card. The client is then left with the following situation. She will have 20 points, and the dealer will have 10, with one more card to be dealt. With only 49 cards remaining, the client will have

> A 12.5 percent chance to lose (the four aces and other combinations which add to 21)
> A 30 percent chance to tie
> A 57.5 percent chance of winning

In all likelihood, this will be the best bet (investment) the client will ever have a chance to make. The odds of winning are 4.6 times (57.5/12.5) greater than the odds of losing, and there is only a 1 in 8 chance of losing. Now, with her spouse looking over her shoulder, she is asked, "How much of your $2 million net worth would you bet?" Very rarely does the answer even approach 10 percent of the client's net worth. Most people say something like $5,000 or $10,000. She is then asked if she believes the odds that her company's stock will outperform the market are as good as that blackjack bet. Like most people, she'll admit they're not.

What do we learn from the blackjack example? We learn that when the cost of losing (being wrong) is high, people become risk averse. Even with the odds greatly in their favor, they avoid risk.

We can apply the blackjack lesson to the example of investors with the vast majority of their assets in their own company's stock. First, investors who are also employees are actually making a double bet: if things go poorly, the company may lay off staff to reduce costs, and so their jobs may be in danger at the same time their investments may come under pressure.

Second, there is really no logical reason for investors to believe their company's stock will outperform. In his book *Behavioral Finance and Wealth Management*, Michael Pompian noted that at the end of 2000, 62 percent of Enron's 401(k) assets were invested in the company's stock.[1] Even though at the time it seemed to be a wise choice given how the stock had performed, it proved to be a disastrous decision.

However, such behavior isn't limited to just a previously high-flying company such as Enron. Pompian also noted that this can be seen at many other companies. For example, here are the percentages of 401(k) assets invested in company stock at the end of 2002 for selected companies:

> Procter & Gamble—94.7 percent
> Sherwin-Williams—91.6 percent
> Abbott Laboratories—90.2 percent
> Pfizer—85.5 percent[2]

Obviously not all investors' stocks can outperform the average. Some will do better, and some will do worse. However, since investors are risk averse when they might lose a large amount, it doesn't make sense to own only one stock, especially when higher returns are not expected. Even if it were logical to believe that an investor is likely to get higher returns, are the odds against being wrong as great as they are in the blackjack example? If investors wouldn't bet a large amount at the blackjack table with odds as stacked in their favor as they are in the hypothetical example, why should they make a large bet when the odds are far less favorable? Many employees of such once high flyers as Lehman Brothers, Bear Stearns, Fannie Mae, and Freddie Mac watched the vast majority of their net worth evaporate because they made the mistake of treating the highly unlikely as impossible.

It has been our experience that once people take the blackjack test, they become aware of just how risky a decision they have made. Ask yourself, If I currently didn't own any of this particular stock, how much would I buy? The risk of your portfolio can be substantially reduced by using the proceeds to build a globally diversified portfolio that reflects your unique appetite for risk, investment horizon, and financial goals. Finally, if you are ever tempted to put lots of eggs in one basket, remember that while this is the surest way to make a quick fortune, it is also the surest way to lose one.

Do You Underestimate the Number of Stocks Needed to Build a Diversified Portfolio?

In December 1968, a paper titled "Diversification and the Reduction of Dispersion" concluded that an investor needed to construct a portfolio containing as little as 15 randomly selected stocks before the benefits of diversification were basically exhausted.[1] A similar 1970 study by Lawrence Fisher and James Lorie found that 90 percent of the diversification benefit came from just 16, and 95 percent of the benefit could be captured by just 30 stocks.[2] Some individual investors might feel comfortable managing a portfolio of such limited size on their own. Alternatively they might choose to have their portfolio managed by what is known as a *separate account manager*. If a much larger number of stocks were needed to achieve effective diversification, it could only likely be achieved in a cost-effective way through the use of mutual funds.

A more recent study—coauthored by John Campbell, Martin Lettau, Burton Malkiel, and Yexiao Xu—argues that a dramatic increase in the volatility of individual stocks and a declining correlation of stocks within the S&P 500 Index have led to a significant increase in the number of securities needed to achieve the same level of portfolio risk. Their study—titled "Have Individual Stocks Become More Volatile?"—found that for the two decades prior to 1985, a portfolio would have had to consist of at least 20 stocks to reduce excess standard deviation (a measure of diversifiable portfolio risk) to 10 percent. From 1986 to 1997 that figure increased to 50. Whereas the study found there was a large increase in the volatility of individual stocks, the authors found no increase in overall market volatility or even industry volatility. The implication of increased volatility of individual stocks and unchanged volatility of the S&P 500 taken together is that correlations between stocks have declined. Reduced correlation between stocks implies that the benefits of, and the need for, portfolio diversification have increased over time. [3]

The authors offer three explanations for the increased volatility of individual stocks, the first of which is the increased influence of institutional investors over the past 40 years. Institutional investors have exhibited a herd mentality; thus, when hundreds of funds and pension plans rush to buy or sell at roughly the same time, price changes are now more exaggerated. A second explanation is the advent of retail day traders. The third explanation is the tendency for companies to go public at a much earlier stage, when they are likely to be more volatile.

Consider now an investor who wants to achieve broad global asset class diversification. He would need to hold several hundred small-cap and large-cap stocks. And then he would probably have to add a similar number of small-cap and large-cap value stocks, real estate stocks, foreign large-cap stocks, emerging market stocks, and so on. There is simply no way to achieve this type of diversification by building your own portfolio of individual stocks.

Perhaps the following is the most dramatic example of the need for and logic of broad diversification as the winning strategy. Although the 1990s witnessed one of the greatest bull markets of all time, 22 percent of the 2,397 U.S. stocks in existence throughout the decade had negative returns. Not negative real returns, but negative absolute returns.[4] The implication for individual investors is that broad-based index or passively managed asset class mutual funds (or their equivalent ETFs) provide the most effective diversification, and do so at a very low cost. And the evidence is clear that there is a great need for diversification.

MISTAKE 61

Do You Believe Diversification Is Determined by the Number of Securities Held?

Most investors understand the need to diversify their portfolios. They understand that diversification reduces the risk of having all your eggs in one basket. Unfortunately, many, if not most, investors still do not understand how to construct a portfolio that *effectively* diversifies risk.

Far too many investors fail to understand that diversification is not based solely on the number of securities held. The result is that they invest in many different stocks and many different mutual funds. To understand why this idea leads to poor investment decisions, we need to understand the factors that determine returns. Professors Eugene Fama and Kenneth French provided us with the answer when they published their famous paper "The Cross-Section of Expected Stock Returns," in the June 1992 issue of the *Journal of Finance*. Their study demonstrated that the vast majority of equity returns are explained by the exposure to the risk factors of size (determined by market capitalization) and value (determined by book-to-market). The study showed that portfolios of stocks in the same asset class, such as large-cap growth stocks or small-cap value stocks, have returns that are well explained by the returns of their respective asset class. Thus, the return on a stock or group of stocks is determined primarily by whether the stock is categorized as small cap or large cap, value or growth, and domestic or international.[1]

Let's look at two portfolios that potential clients presented to our firm, Buckingham Asset Management, for analysis in 2000. In each case, the investors believed their portfolios were highly diversified, based on owning a large number of different assets. By putting their portfolios under the microscope of the Fama-French model, it was easy to see that in fact they had minimal diversification: almost all their assets fell into just one asset class. Thus, the portfolios held assets that had high correlation to each other.

In examining the portfolios, we used the CRSP definitions for size and value. Stocks that are ranked in deciles 1 through 5 by market capitalization are considered large-cap stocks. Stocks that are in deciles 6 through 10 are considered small-cap stocks. Stocks ranked in deciles 1 through 3 by book-to-market are considered growth stocks. Stocks that are in deciles 8 through 10 are considered value stocks. Stocks in deciles 4 through 7 are considered core stocks.

The first example involves an investor who held a portfolio of 14 stocks and 11 mutual funds (Portfolio A). Of the 14 stocks, 12 were ranked in the top decile of stocks by market capitalization, while the other 2 were in the second and third deciles, respectively. Thus, they were all large-cap stocks. Of the 14 stocks, 9 would be considered growth stocks, and only 1 would be considered a value stock. Three of the remaining stocks fell in the fourth decile, just barely missing being classified as a growth stock.

Let's now look at the mutual funds. Of the 11 mutual funds, 10 were in the first decile by size. The remaining fund fell in the fifth decile, still a large-cap holding. The median market cap was above $1 billion, meaning the weighted-average market cap was probably much higher. When ranking by BtM, 7 of the 11 fell in the first decile, while the other 4 fell in the second decile. Once again, the portfolio was heavily concentrated in the asset class of large-cap growth stocks.

It is worth noting that the portfolio did have some diversification, as 15 percent of the assets were international. Also noteworthy is that the investor was holding more than 8 percent cash, even though he believed he held no cash in this portfolio. The actively managed funds had built up cash positions, thereby reducing the investor's equity exposure to well below the desired level. (As we have seen, style drift is one of the risks of using actively managed funds as the building blocks of a portfolio.)

The bottom line was that Portfolio A, despite its diversity in terms of number of holdings, was not diversified at all by asset class. (It was virtually an all large-cap growth portfolio.) In fact, because the mutual funds were all investing in the same asset class, it was highly likely that the funds held shares in many of the very same stocks the client owned independently.

The second client, who had Portfolio B, was even more diversified in terms of number of holdings, with 22 stocks and 19 mutual funds. The BtM data are only presented for 17 funds, as Morningstar's database, upon which the analysis is based, did not have complete information. Of the 22 stocks, 20 were first decile by size, 1 was second decile, and 1 was third decile.

When looking at BtM, 15 were first decile, and a total of 20 would be considered growth stocks. As the remaining stocks were in deciles 4 and 7, not a single holding could be considered a value stock. Thus, the stock holdings were basically all large-cap growth stocks.

Looking at the mutual funds, we find a similar picture. Of the 19 mutual funds, 18 were first decile by size, and 1 was second decile. Looking at BtM, of the funds for which data were available, there were 16 that were first decile and 1 second decile. Looking at the weighted averages, we found that 95 percent of the portfolio was first decile by size (5 percent was fifth decile) and that 77 percent was first decile and 21 percent second decile by BtM.

The bottom line was that despite 41 different holdings, Portfolio B had virtually no diversification (except for diversifying away the single-stock and the single-industry risk). Like the first portfolio, it was essentially an all large-cap growth portfolio, with no exposure to small-cap and value stocks. The only true diversification was from the 16 percent allocation to international stocks, though here too it was all large-cap growth—which has a fairly high correlation to U.S. large growth, and so it is not as effective a diversifier as one might think. To gain more genuinely effective diversification internationally, one must use the asset classes of international small-cap and emerging markets.

The two portfolios probably performed very well in 1998 and 1999 when large-cap growth stocks exhibited strong performance. Our two investors were probably very happy. When their holdings are all in a well-performing asset class, investors seem to forget the principles of and reasons for diversification—no one can predict when an asset class will perform relatively well or relatively poorly.

Both these investors met with our firm in the summer of 2000, when large-cap growth stocks had already entered what would prove to be a severe bear market (especially for NASDAQ-listed stocks)—and when value stocks experienced one of their greatest periods of outperformance relative to growth stocks. All of a sudden, these same investors became concerned about the performance of their portfolios, as all their assets seemed to be doing poorly at the same time. These two portfolios are not unique in their lack of diversification. In fact, they are quite typical in that they hold many stocks and funds but are very heavily concentrated in the asset class of U.S. large-growth stocks.

Professors Fama and French showed us the way to achieve effective diversification. To do so, one must diversify across the asset classes of small cap and large cap, growth and value, and domestic and international. And the best building blocks are index or passive asset class funds, since they are low cost and tax efficient and do not style-drift.

MISTAKE 62

Do You Believe Focused Funds Outperform?

An often-heard excuse for the persistence with which active managers fail to outperform their benchmarks is that the typical fund is "overdiversified." By owning so many stocks, the value of the manager's best ideas is diluted. The solution (or sales pitch) is to create "focused" funds: funds that concentrate holdings in the manager's 10, 20, or perhaps 40 best ideas. By owning just the best ideas, focused funds should be able to easily trounce both the competition and appropriate passive benchmarks. Based on this premise, there are even funds that hire several submanagers for just their single best idea.

Fact or Fantasy?

To test the hypothesis about focused funds, Travis Sapp and Xuemin Yan compared their performance with that of more diversified portfolios. Using the Center for Research in Security Prices and Thompson Financial databases, they examined the performance of all domestic equity funds, excluding funds that held fewer than 12 stocks. The following is a summary of the findings from their study "Security Concentration and Active Fund Management: Do Focused Funds Offer Superior Performance?"

› Controlling for various fund characteristics, fund performance is *positively* related to the fund's number of holdings both before and after expenses.
› The quintile of funds with the fewest holdings (an average of 29) produced an annual three-factor alpha of –1.44 percent.
› Focused funds had higher volatility than diversified funds.

> › Compared with diversified funds, focused funds had higher expenses, explaining some, but not all, of their underperformance.
> › At the one-year level, the buys of focused funds *underperformed* their sells by 0.3 percent.
> › The attrition rate of focused funds is higher than that of diversified funds.[1]

The authors noted that the underperformance of focused funds is not solely related to their higher expenses but also to liquidity problems:

As the ownership stake in a firm becomes relatively large, the focused fund is unable to quickly react to new information without their trading having a substantial price impact that would diminish the performance of the fund. Also, since the investment flows from routine purchases and redemptions must be spread over a relatively small number of securities, even liquidity-motivated trades can have a relatively large price impact.

The authors also found another drag on returns related to liquidity. The average cash balance for diversified funds was 7.8 percent versus 12.8 percent for focused funds. Higher cash balances are generally detrimental to fund performance since cash generally underperforms equities.

The liquidity issues combine to create a drag on the returns of focused funds so that even if the managers have better stock-picking ability, the fund's returns may underperform. The authors concluded that there is no evidence that focus translates into value for investors and that there are good reasons for viewing an investment in these funds with caution.

Supporting Evidence

In the September 2001 issue of its *FundInvestor* publication, Morningstar sought the answer to the question: Do a fund's largest holdings (which logically should reflect its best ideas) outperform the rest of its holdings? Morningstar compared the returns of a fund's top 10 holdings with the overall returns of the portfolio. The study, which covered a five-year period, found that just 48 percent of funds produced returns higher than their top 10 picks—about what randomness would suggest. Interestingly, on average, the top 10 picks underperformed the returns of the entire portfolios by 0.16 percent per year.[2]

Summary

While Wall Street and the financial press might continue to hype concentrated funds, the evidence suggests that these funds are just another example of products that are the triumph of hope (and hype) over wisdom and experience. In other words, they are products designed to be sold, not bought. The prudent strategy does not involve buying focused funds. Instead, the prudent strategy, the one most likely to provide the highest risk-adjusted returns, is to own passively managed funds that are broadly diversified across the entire asset class to which the investor is seeking exposure.

Do You Understand That in Times of Crisis the Correlations of All Risky Assets Rise?

A common refrain during the recent financial crisis was, "I am as diversified as it gets. My portfolio has every asset class imaginable. I have substantial exposure to small-cap value and international stocks. Yet every single asset class dropped pretty much the same during this downturn. What went wrong?" Absolutely nothing. The problem comes from not fully understanding the concept of correlation of returns.

Correlation of Returns

Prudent investors build portfolios that include asset classes that have low correlation—the measure of the strength of the linear relationship between two variables. Values can range from +1.00 (perfect positive correlation) to –1.00 (perfect negative correlation). Positive correlation means that when one asset produces above-average returns, the other *tends* to also produce above-average returns. Conversely, negative correlation means that when one asset produces below-average returns, the other *tends* to produce below-average returns. Thus, the lower the correlation of returns, the more effective the asset class is as a diversifier of portfolio risk. Note the relatively low annual correlations of some of the various asset classes to the S&P 500 Index for the period 1988 to 2010.

Based on these historical relationships, investors expect that while all asset classes will do poorly from time to time, the non-perfect correlations of the various asset classes will prevent them from all doing poorly at the *same* time. Unfortunately, investors make the mistake of not putting enough emphasis on the key words *tends to*.

ASSET CLASS	ANNUAL CORRELATION TO THE S&P 500 INDEX
Fama-French Large Value	.91
Fama-French Small	.78
Fama-French Small Value	.60
Dow Jones US Select REIT Index	.44
MSCI EAFE Index	.73
MSCI Emerging Market Index	.52

Some investors fail to understand that correlations are not stable. They drift. And while international stocks and emerging market stocks are exposed to some different economic and political risks than are U.S. stocks, they are also exposed to some of the same risks that can impact the global economy. And when those risks show up (typically during times of financial and political crises), correlations among all risky asset classes tend to turn high. Just when the benefits of diversification are needed most, they go AWOL.

One of Larry's favorite expressions is that "the only thing you don't know about investing is the investment history you don't know." Knowing the history of returns would have prevented investors from misunderstanding the benefits of equity diversification. The latest financial crisis revealed nothing new about correlations. For example, all major equity asset classes produced negative returns during the global recession of 1973 to 1974 as the S&P 500 Index, large-cap value stocks, small-cap stocks, small-cap value stocks, and international large stocks fell 37, 20, 53, 46, and 34 percent, respectively. And the systemic risk of equities showed up again when the financial crisis that began with U.S. housing prices falling sharply spread around the world in the summer of 2008. Every major equity class experienced a dramatic bear market. In some cases, it was the worst since the Great Depression.

The following table shows the *total return* for various indexes during three recent crises. Note that in each crisis, the correlations of returns rose dramatically. The only difference in the crisis of 2008 is the depth of the bear market.

	JULY–AUGUST 1998	SEPTEMBER 2001	JANUARY–NOVEMBER 2008
S&P 500	−8.1	−15.4	−37.7
Russell 1000 Value	−7.0	−16.4	−37.7
Russell 2000	−13.5	−26.0	−37.4
Russell 2000 Value	−11.0	−22.3	−33.0
MSCI EAFE	−10.1	−11.5	−46.6
MSCI Emerging Markets	−15.5	−26.7	−56.6

The Lesson

Most of the time, risky asset classes do not exhibit very high correlation. And many have low correlations. Among the asset classes that tend to have low correlation with U.S. equities are real estate, international small-cap stocks, and emerging market stocks. The reason for the low correlations is that economic and political conditions impact the various asset classes in different ways most of the time. That explains the low long-term correlations. However, in times of global crisis, all risky assets tend to correlate highly. And that leads us to the important lesson the markets teach us.

In times of crisis, the only effective diversifiers of equity risk are high-quality fixed-income investments—the safest of which are obligations that carry the full faith and credit of the U.S. government. During this crisis, while all equity asset classes were experiencing severe bear markets, U.S. Treasury instruments were providing positive returns.

MISTAKE 64

Do You Fail to Consider Your Labor Capital When Constructing Your Portfolio?

The most important decision investors generally will make is the asset allocation decision. This is because the allocation of assets is the main determinant of the risk and expected reward of a portfolio. Discipline to stay the course is the other dominant factor in the outcome of a strategy, with stock picking and market timing having little if any impact. No investors should begin their financial journey without thoroughly considering the issues we will discuss below. And after careful consideration, they should then put their asset allocation plan into writing in the form of an investment policy statement.

The asset allocation decision should address an investor's willingness, need, and ability to take risk. The willingness to take risk is defined by how much of a loss an investor can stomach and not only avoid panicking, but also be able to rebalance (buy more of an asset class that has performed poorly) and, most importantly, sleep well enough at night to enjoy her life. The lower your tolerance for risk, the lower your equity allocation should be. This will help you avoid panicking when an inevitable bear market arrives.

The need to take risk is defined by the rate of return needed to meet the minimum financial goals set by the investor. A high required rate of return results in a need to maintain a high exposure to risky assets. A low required rate of return allows an investor to achieve her goals without taking much risk.

Finally, we turn to the ability to take risk. This ability is defined by two issues. The first is the length of the investment horizon. The longer the horizon, the greater the ability to take equity risk, as the investor has a greater ability to wait out a bear market. The other issue is how highly an investor's "intellectual capital" is correlated with the risk of owning equities. Let's address this important but often overlooked issue.

Let's define *intellectual capital* as the ability to earn income. Some businesses and professions are highly cyclical and are thus highly correlated to the economic cycle and the risks of owning stocks. Good examples of professions that might fall into the high-correlation category are automobile workers, construction workers, and upscale retailers. Other professions have very stable incomes, as their ability to generate income has little or no correlation to the economic cycle. Good examples of occupations that might fall into the low-correlation category are health-care professionals and tenured professors.

Since one of the keys to properly constructing a portfolio is to own assets with low correlation, all other things being equal, investors whose intellectual capital is highly correlated to the economic cycle should consider taking less equity risk than those whose intellectual capital has low correlation to equity risks. The reason is that an investor would not want the following situation to occur: A weak economy causes the market to drop and the investor to lose his job. In turn, this causes him to have to sell financial assets to meet expenses.

Of course, one should consider the relative size of the intellectual capital to the size of the financial assets as well. The less dependent one is on current earned income, the less of an issue intellectual capital becomes. Consider that for most retirees, they no longer have any correlation of their intellectual capital to the economy, as they are no longer employed. Of course, the more dependent one is on earned income, the more of an issue intellectual capital and its correlation to the economy and equity risk become.

Also keep in mind what we learned in Chapter 13 about how owning international assets can help hedge against having your intellectual capital tied up in the domestic market.

Summary

It is extremely important for investors to consider all their assets, including their intellectual capital, as well as their unique ability, willingness, and need to take risk, when constructing the portfolio that is right for them. As always, a good financial advisor can help you sort through these important issues.

Do You Believe the Investment World Is Flat?

The World Is Flat is a national bestseller book by Thomas L. Friedman. Friedman makes the case that regional and geographical divisions are becoming increasingly irrelevant. From an investment standpoint, this trend to "globalization" supposedly lessens the need for global diversification. However, before we allow this idea to guide our investment decisions, we can check the historical evidence.

To test the hypothesis that globalization has led to a reduction in the benefits of global diversification, we will examine the historical correlations of returns between the S&P 500 Index and the MSCI EAFE Index for the period from 1970 to 2007. We will split the 38-year period into two equal 19-year periods to see if there is a trend toward rising correlations:

› For the first period, 1970 to 1988, the annual correlation of the S&P 500 to the MSCI EAFE was 0.623.
› For the following period, 1989 to 2007, the annual correlation actually fell slightly to 0.614.

We can also examine the correlation data for international small caps. Historically, international small-cap stocks have had lower correlations to U.S. stocks, making them superior diversifiers of the risks of domestic equities:

› For the first period, 1970 to 1988, the annual correlation of the S&P 500 to international small-cap stocks was just 0.459—significantly lower than the 0.623 correlation of the MSCI EAFE for the same period.
› For the following period, 1989 to 2007, the annual correlation actually fell to 0.374—again, significantly lower than the 0.614 of the MSCI EAFE for the same period.

As you can clearly see, there was no trend toward rising correlations. Apparently the benefits of global diversification are as strong as ever.

Given the data, what explains all the noise about a new paradigm where the benefits of global diversification have disappeared? The answer can be explained in one simple word—*recency*. Recency is the tendency to give too much weight to recent experience, while ignoring the lessons of long-term historical evidence. Before getting into the most recent data, we need to cover two important points.

The first important point is that correlations are not static. As we discussed in Chapter 63, correlations tend to drift in a random manner. For investors, what should matter is the long-term historical evidence. And the longer the time frame, the more confident we can be about the data. Sometimes events occur that impact both domestic and international equity markets in very similar ways. This is particularly true during periods of crisis like 1973 to 1974, 2000 to 2002, and 2008. Then there are other periods when equity markets perform quite differently.

The second important point is that equity markets do experience periods of high correlation. This occurred during the global financial crisis of 2008. That is why it is important that investors recognize the need to hold a sufficient amount of high-quality fixed-income assets to keep the risk of the overall portfolio at a level that is consistent with their ability, willingness, and need to take risk. This is the most important of the asset allocation decisions.

Recent Data Driving Expectations

From 2003 to 2008, we experienced a relatively short period of very high correlation of U.S. and international stock returns. During that time, the annual correlation of the S&P 500 to the MSCI EAFE rose to 0.998. And even for the period from 2000 through 2008, the annual correlation was 0.978. These high correlations led to a lot of noise from the press and Wall Street about rising correlations. However, this is a very short period. And we have seen similar episodes of very high correlations. For example, for the five-year period from 1972 through 1976, the annual correlation of the S&P 500 to the MSCI EAFE rose to 0.874. That period probably produced similar cries about how global diversification was no longer needed. However, over the following five years, the annual correlation fell all the way to 0.258.

Unfortunately, we cannot know what the next five years will bring. We don't have clear crystal balls. However, there is nothing new in the data to suggest that over the long term the benefits of international diversification are any lower than they have been.

Lessons Learned

There are two important lessons to be learned from the above data. First, you should be skeptical of cries that "this time it's different." Second, you should ignore the noise of the market. Noise sells for two reasons—the media need you to tune in so they can make profits, and the people on Wall Street need you to believe that you should pay them big fees to manage assets in these "changing times." Unfortunately, what is in the best interests of the financial media and Wall Street is usually not in the best interests of investors.

Finally, consider this: Let us suppose that for whatever reason global equity markets do in fact become more closely correlated. Would that make global diversification unappealing? It is hard to see why that would be the case. Would it make sense for U.S. citizens to restrict their ownership of auto industry stocks to Ford and GM and eliminate firms such as Toyota or Porsche from consideration?

Summary

The bottom line is that international diversification is as important as ever. In fact, it has been said that diversification is the closest thing there is to a free lunch—so you might as well eat a lot of it. And remember, the greatest diversification benefits are still in international small-cap stocks and emerging market stocks.

Do You Confuse Indexing with the Exclusive Use of an S&P 500 Fund?

Investors often confuse indexing with the exclusive use of the most popular indexing vehicles, such as S&P 500 Index funds or equivalent ETFs. They may also make the mistake of believing that by purchasing an S&P 500 Index fund, they will own a highly diversified asset with holdings in 500 different companies. Therefore, investors may be content with holding an S&P 500 Index fund as the sole asset in their portfolio. However, investors building such a portfolio are not really getting effective diversification. The lack of diversification arises both from the way Standard & Poor's selects stocks for inclusion in the index and also from the market-capitalization weighting mechanism used to calculate the index.

Not only are most investors surprised that an S&P 500 Index fund does *not* own an equal amount of 500 different companies, but they are also surprised at just how skewed the index is toward the largest-cap stocks in the index. A great example of how skewed the index can be to a small number of stocks was the weightings of the S&P 500 as of year-end 1999 (near the peak of the bubble in growth stocks):

> The largest 50 stocks: 60 percent
> The largest 100 stocks: 75 percent
> The largest 200 stocks: 88 percent
> The largest 300 stocks: 95 percent[1]

Here is another interesting statistic: at the start of the second quarter of 2000 (when the bubble had begun to burst), the weighted average market cap of the S&P 500 stocks was $143 billion, and yet only 16 stocks were larger than the average! It is important to note that if the 500 stocks in the index were equally weighted (instead of market-cap weighted), the average market cap would have been just $24 billion, or one-sixth of the actual weighted average of the S&P 500.[2]

If you invest in the S&P 500, even though you own 500 stocks, you haven't achieved effective diversification across asset classes. That should not be construed to mean either that it is a poor investment or that you shouldn't own this type of fund. It does mean, however, that if you want to diversify your portfolio beyond the asset class of large-cap growth stocks, you need to broaden your portfolio's holdings.

Total stock market funds were created to help investors achieve greater diversification than they would achieve in just an S&P 500 Index fund. The appeal of owning the entire market is intuitively attractive from a diversification perspective. However, once again the market-cap weighting mechanism used to make index funds easy to manage provides a far different outcome from what one would expect. Market-cap weighting means that a stock's weighting in an index is based on the total market cap of the individual stock as a percentage of the total market cap of all the stocks contained in the index.

Most investors would be surprised how little exposure a total market fund has to the asset classes of small-cap and value stocks. Using CRSP data, at the end of 2008 small-cap stocks (deciles 6–10 by market cap) were 8.2 percent of the total, and value stocks (deciles 8–10 by BtM) were just 5.4 percent. Again, a total market fund is not inherently bad. However, you should only want to own a total market fund if that is the asset allocation you seek.

Summary

Indexing is a wonderful strategy. However, indexing does not mean that an investor should hold only an S&P 500 Index fund or a total stock market fund. Instead, investors should determine the amount of exposure they want to each of the five major U.S. asset classes (large cap, large-cap value, small cap, small-cap value, and real estate). They also need to determine the amount of exposure they want to the major international asset classes (large cap, large-cap value, small cap, small-cap value, real estate, and emerging markets). Only after having made those decisions can investors decide how to construct a portfolio that will meet their objectives. (If you're interested in learning more about constructing a portfolio based on your unique risk profile, read *The Only Guide You'll Ever Need for the Right Financial Plan*.)

Do You Consider Your Home as Your Exposure to Real Estate?

Diversification across asset classes is an important component of any investment plan. Put simply, diversification reduces risk by not putting all your eggs in one basket. It is also important to diversify across asset classes that have low correlation. Real estate is an asset class that not only has its own risk and reward characteristics, but also has a relatively low correlation to other U.S. equity asset classes. It is therefore a good diversifier of risk and should be considered when constructing an asset allocation plan. A problem arises, however, when investors consider their own home as their real estate allocation.

A home is clearly real estate. However, it is very undiversified real estate. First, it is undiversified by type. There are many types of real estate: office, warehouse, industrial, multifamily residential, hotel, and so on. Owning a home gives an investor exposure to just the residential component of the larger asset class of real estate. Even then, by excluding multifamily residences, it is only exposure to the single-family component.

A second problem is that a home is undiversified geographically. Home prices might be rising in one part of the country and falling in another.

A third problem is that home prices may be more related to exposure to an industry than to real estate in general. For example, in the late 1990s, home prices in Silicon Valley skyrocketed, riding the technology boom. Homes in other areas of the same state experienced a totally different pricing environment. This creates another problem in that often your employment prospects are highly correlated to the value of your home. This problem would be further compounded if your investment portfolio were loaded with assets with exposure to the same industry to which your home is exposed. This is often true of executives who own stock in their company or have stock options. The following situation is a good example of the problem.

Seattle used to be considered a one-company (Boeing) town. A senior executive at Boeing owned an expensive home in Seattle. She had the vast percentage of her financial assets invested in Boeing stock. She thought she had some diversification of assets because her home was considered real estate exposure—not Seattle, nor Boeing, nor airline, nor even oil price exposure.

Boeing was impacted by a recession in the airline industry. The company's stock, reflecting those troubles, fell sharply. Strike one for our investor. Boeing reacted by laying off employees, including our investor. Strike two. With unemployment rising, Seattle home prices collapsed. Strike three for our unlucky investor. The problem was that all the risks—employment, equity, and home—to which our investor was exposed were highly correlated.

The bottom line is that owning a home and considering it exposure to real estate is like being a senior executive with lots of stock and options in Microsoft and thinking you have exposure to large growth stocks. The correlation of any one stock to the overall asset class of equities, or large growth stocks, might turn out to be very low. Stocks might be up overall, but your stock might be down. Similarly, real estate might be up, but the price of your home might be down. Therefore, as a general rule, you should not consider your home as your exposure to real estate. About the only real protection a home provides is against inflation in construction costs. And since land is typically a more important component of home prices than the cost of construction, it may not be much protection at all (besides providing a roof protecting your head).

Let's now turn to how a home is financed. If a home is financed with a mortgage, that mortgage effectively is a short (negative) bond position and should be considered so when looking at your overall portfolio. Thus, if you have $100,000 invested in a bond fund and also have a mortgage of $100,000, your net fixed-income exposure is zero.

However, whether the mortgage is a fixed- or variable-rate loan does impact your exposure to interest rate (and inflation) risk. For example, a fixed-rate mortgage does provide inflation protection. (A floating-rate mortgage does provide some inflation protection, as there is typically a maximum rate.) A fixed-rate mortgage also has a "put" feature. If interest rates decline, the put (putting the mortgage back to the lender by paying it off) allows the borrower to refinance the mortgage at the then current rate. This provides protection against falling interest rates (for those on fixed incomes) and deflation. If a home were financed with an adjustable-rate mortgage, the risk picture would be considerably different, as the rate on the mortgage would move up or down as interest rates changed. Therefore, it is very important that you consider how a home is financed in developing an asset allocation strategy.

The best way to gain exposure to the broad equity real estate asset class is to own an index or passively managed real estate investment trust (REIT) fund that invests in all equity REITs. For the period 1978 to 2010, the Dow Jones Wilshire REIT Index provided a rate of return of 12.5 percent. This compares with a return of 11.4 percent for the S&P 500 Index. It is also worth noting that REITs were up 6.1 percent in 1981 when the S&P 500 fell by 4.9 percent. In 1984 and 1992, when the S&P 500 rose just 6.3 percent and 7.7 percent, respectively, REITs returned 21.8 percent and 28.3 percent, respectively. And from 2000 through 2002, while the S&P 500 lost 14.6 percent per year, REITs returned 15.1 percent per year. Of course, there are also periods when the S&P 500 outperformed REITs. For example, from 1998 to 1999 the S&P 500 outperformed REITs by 24.7 percent per year to –8.9 percent per year.

The combination of the lack of predictability of returns, the low correlation, and their inflation hedge makes a strong case for including REITs as an asset class in an investment portfolio.

Summary

While a home is clearly an asset that has value, and should be considered such when preparing your balance sheet (and any mortgage should be on the liability side of the balance sheet), there are several reasons why it really should be treated as more of a consumption item than an investment item.

First, as we discussed, it should not be considered as exposure to the broad asset class of real estate. Second, you cannot manage it as you can financial assets—you cannot set an asset allocation to your home and regularly rebalance, and you cannot tax-manage it on a regular basis either.

Do You Fail to See the Risk in High-Yield Investments?

When a sophisticated provider of financial services stands
toe to toe with a naïve consumer, the all-too-predictable
conclusion resembles the results of a heavyweight
champion and a ninety-eight-pound weakling. The
individual investor loses in a first-round knockout.

—David Swensen
Unconventional Success, p. 341

Whenever interest rates fall to historically low levels, Wall Street's product machines crank out securities that entice investors with extravagant yields, but come accompanied by great risks. These products come under the broad category known as *structured products*. The category includes products with alluring names such as *accumulators*, *super track notes*, *principal protection notes*, and *reverse convertibles*. However, you would do well to realize that whenever Wall Street has invented a better mousetrap, you can be sure that you're the mouse.

The common denominator among these products is they are complex securities. And the one thing you can be 100 percent sure of is that the complexity is designed to favor the issuer. Financial institutions are clever at designing complex securities with high coupons that attract investors, but have lots of risk that is hard to quantify without a Ph.D. in mathematics. What are the odds an individual investor can properly value these securities? The issuers know that the answer is slim to none. On the other hand, the issuers know exactly what the value is.

Consider this tale about reverse convertibles from Meir Statman's book *What Investors Really Want*. Banks sold $7 billion of these instruments in 2008. The idea is simple: The note is linked to specific stock. If the stock goes up, you receive your principal back plus a high interest payment once the note matures. If the stock goes down, you receive the underlying shares instead of your principal.

Statman wrote that an 85-year-old radiologist invested $400,000 in these instruments, not understanding the risks. He lost $75,000 when the underlying shares dropped. "I had no idea this could happen," he said. "I have no desire to own Yahoo! stock or the others."[1]

Financial institutions typically design these products so that they carry a high coupon. That's the attraction. What you can be sure of is that if an investment carries a high yield, there is risk, even when you cannot see it. The good news is that you don't have to know how to analyze these complex instruments. All you have to know is that the objective of the chief financial officers of the issuers is to raise funds at the lowest cost of capital. Since the flip side of a high expected return to investors is a high cost of capital to the issuer, a security that provides investors with a high expected return defeats that purpose. Because it is likely that the sophisticated issuer will know how to value it, you can be sure that the instrument has a low expected return, despite the high coupon. In other words, the instrument contains poison pills, typically in the form of options the investor is selling at below-market rates. For example, studies on the category of reverse convertibles have found their coupons are from 3 to 12 percent below their fair market values, which is exactly why financial institutions love them. They are raising capital at very low costs.

Summary

There is an old adage about something being too good to be true. The wisdom of the adage is really a matter of perspective. Certainly if something appears to be too good to be true, it almost certainly will be from the buyer's perspective. When the buyer learns all the details, buyer's remorse will set in. This is not the case, however, for the seller, for whom the transaction was highly rewarding. Remember, if you cannot identify the sucker at the poker table, you're the sucker.

MISTAKE 69

Do You Purchase Products Meant to Be Sold, Not Bought?

When the capital gains tax rates were lowered to 15 percent in 2003, the sales of variable annuities (VAs) should have come to a screeching halt. Unfortunately for investors, they continued to be aggressively (and successfully) marketed. For example, in 2004, sales exceeded $50 billion, and the total amount of VAs outstanding exceeded $1 trillion.[1] And by year-end 2008, it was estimated that $1.4 trillion of VA policies were in force.[2] The reasons: investors are not fully informed, and they are being exploited by aggressive salespeople whose only interest is in collecting the large commissions these products offer.

A VA is a mutual fund–type account wrapped inside an insurance policy. The insurance component allows the investment earnings to be tax deferred. Unfortunately, the tax deferral is just about the only good thing you can say about these investment products. Virtually everything else about them is not only bad; it is really bad. The negatives include

> The generally high cost of the insurance wrapper
> The high operating expenses of the investment account component
> The lack of passive, low-cost investment choices inside most annuity wrappers
> The lack of liquidity
> The loss of the potential for a step-up in basis for the estate of the investor, when a holding's cost basis becomes the current market value rather than the original purchase price, typically resulting in much lower capital gains taxes when the holding is eventually sold by the beneficiary
> Perhaps worst of all, the conversion of low-taxed capital gains into highly taxed ordinary income

Perhaps the most amazing fact about annuities is how many are sold to people holding them inside an account that is already tax deferred. Since the only real benefit of this high-cost product is the tax efficiency, selling this product to an investor to hold inside an account that is already tax deferred borders on the criminal.

The bottom line is that the tax deferral comes at a very high price. The 1997 Tax Act cut capital gains tax rates while leaving ordinary income tax rates high. Thus, the benefit of wrapping an annuity around an equity portfolio virtually vanished for almost all asset classes. As a *Forbes* column stated, "That should have stopped annuity sales cold."[3]

To demonstrate how large a drawback the conversion of capital gains into ordinary income creates, Jeffrey Brown and James Poterba performed a comparative analysis. They assumed a federal tax rate on capital gains and dividends of 15 percent and a federal tax on ordinary income of 33 percent. They also assumed a total return on stocks of 8 percent, 2 percent of which comes from dividends. The result was that even if we assume that VAs cost only 0.25 percent per year more than an equivalent investment in a mutual or exchange-traded fund (while the average VA has total expenses of about 1.65 percent), the investment horizon would have to be at least 40 years to break even.[4] This 40-year breakeven point becomes even more important when you consider that the average age of a nonqualified VA buyer is 60 (making the breakeven point age 100) and that only 4 percent of nonqualified annuities are sold to investors under age 35.[5] The case is even more compelling because this analysis did not consider the other aforementioned tax issues.

And if that didn't do the trick, the introduction of ETFs and tax-managed mutual funds by such fund families as DFA and Vanguard should have. Tax-managed funds take the tax efficiency benefit of passive investing to an even higher level. These new funds have basically eliminated any financial argument for purchasing a VA as a vehicle for equity investing. (The one exception to this would be the asset class of real estate. Because of the requirement that REITs have to distribute virtually all their income, which is taxed at the higher ordinary income tax rates, real estate is a tax-inefficient asset class.) Of course, most investors don't need an annuity, as they can simply hold their real estate assets inside an IRA, SEP, or tax-deferred plan. Unfortunately for investors, there does not appear to be any slowdown in annuity sales, thanks to the self-interest of salespeople.

In addition to the benefit of tax deferral, there is a second benefit that VAs provide—life insurance. There are many different versions of insurance. One of the most common forms stipulates that if the policyholder dies before annuitization begins, the heirs will receive at least the nominal value of the premiums paid.

A 2001 study on the value of this benefit, "The Titanic Option: Valuation of the Guaranteed Minimum Death Benefit in Variable Annuities and Mutual Funds," by Moshe Milevsky and Steven Posner found that a simple return of the premium death benefit was worth between 0.01 and 0.10 percent of the policy, depending on the investor's gender and purchase age and the underlying asset volatility. In contrast, the authors found that the median mortality and expense-risk charge for a return-of-premium VA was 1.15 percent.[6] In addition, only 5 percent of contracts have insurance charges of less than even 0.75 percent, and 12 percent of contracts charge more than 1.40 percent.[7] Clearly, the insurance benefit is far exceeded by its cost. As further evidence of these excessive costs, consider that in any given year only 0.4 percent of VA contracts are surrendered on account of death or disability.[8] And only a small fraction of those have losses that trigger a death benefit.

The bottom line is that annuities are costly to own. Expenses (such as insurance expenses, portfolio management fees, and "mortality" charges) average in excess of 2 percent a year, but can range as high as 3 percent or more. Surrender charges are common, starting out typically at 7 percent, reaching as high as 9 percent if you cash out in the first year and declining to zero in the seventh year or even as long as the tenth year. Also, if you cash out before you reach the age of 59½, you have to pay a tax penalty, except under certain narrow circumstances.

Consider the experience that the no-load fund giant T. Rowe Price had when it sent potential customers software to help them determine whether VAs were right for them.[9] The program factored in the investor's age, income, tax bracket, and investment horizon, and it regularly told potential buyers that they would be better off in a plain old fund, let alone a low-cost, tax-efficient, passively and tax-managed fund. An educated consumer, as it turned out, was not a good prospect for annuities.

There are a handful of exceptions to the high-cost rule, which include AEGON, Schwab, TIAA-CREF, and Vanguard. They are mostly sold to people with existing VAs through Section 1035 *tax-free* exchanges. Existing holders of VAs are looking to escape from their current high costs and poor investment choices. Unfortunately, the surrender charges often keep investors trapped for an extended period. The analysis to find out when and if a 1035 exchange makes sense is fairly straightforward.

If the terms of VAs are so bad, why do so many people buy them? The answer is that the tax-deferral sales pitch mesmerizes them. Fortunately, the tax deferral comes much cheaper and more effectively through low-cost, tax-efficient mutual funds that are both passively managed and tax-managed. A tax-managed mutual fund has another advantage over the supposedly tax-favored annuity. With mutual funds, you may escape the capital gains tax altogether by either donating the fund shares to charity or leaving them in your estate. (You receive a step-up in basis upon death.) No such option is available to an annuity holder. Transfer or bequeath an annuity to anyone but your spouse, and you trigger recognition of the full appreciation as income.

About the only legitimate remaining use of a VA is for creditor protection. Many states (e.g., New York, Florida, and Texas) protect assets in VAs from creditors to one degree or another. The laws, however, are complex. Therefore, before you purchase (or get talked into) an annuity for this specific purpose, you should consult your attorney. Doctors worried about malpractice suits, for example, might want to consider VAs. If this is the case, then you shouldn't pay a penny more than you have to in expenses.

If you are currently holding a high-cost annuity, you should check out one of the low-cost, no-surrender-charge annuities. If the applicable surrender-charge period is over or even nearly over, the decision to make the tax-free Section 1035 exchange will be easy. Section 1035 of the tax code allows investors to swap one similar annuity for another without triggering a tax, as would be the case if an investor sold one annuity and then bought another. Whatever you do, do not succumb to the sales pitch for the new "bonus" annuities. This is a new and aggressive tactic of the industry, to keep investors imprisoned in a high-cost product and generate new and even larger commissions for the sales force. Annuity holders with a few years left in their surrender-charge period are approached with the following "typical" story:

> *I understand that you are unhappy with your current VA because of poor performance of the investment choices. I also understand that you have a 3 percent surrender charge left. We are going to "help" by giving you an up-front "bonus" of 3 percent to cover the surrender charge. It will not cost you anything to switch.*

Unfortunately, the only "bonus" is to the salesperson. The new sale starts the surrender period all over again, and the surrender period of the new product is often even longer and more expensive than on the original annuity. The surrender-charge period may now be extended to as many as 10 years, and the prepayment penalty increased from 7 percent to as much as 9 percent. Given that the annuity holder will now be locked into another high-cost (or even higher-cost) product for a much longer time, you might ask, Where's the bonus? It is likely to be in the form of higher commissions to the sales force.

In June 2000, the SEC finally issued an "investor alert" and placed a brochure on its Web site to help investors understand the benefits, costs, and risks of variable annuities.

Equity-Indexed Annuities

Equity-indexed annuities (EIAs) are a particular type of variable annuity. They are described by those selling them as providing "the best of both worlds"—the potential rewards of equity investing without the downside risks (because of the presence of a guaranteed minimum return). The typical EIA offering has the following characteristics:

> A link to a *portion* of the positive changes in an index (typically the S&P 500). The percentage of the index's gain is called the *participation rate*. Participation rates vary but are typically between 50 and 100 percent.
> Principal protection.
> A minimum guarantee, regardless of the performance of the index.
> Tax-deferred growth potential.

> Income options to meet your specific needs.
> A death benefit guaranteeing beneficiaries 100 percent of the annuity's indexed value.

There is an adage that the devil is in the details. As is the case with the category of structured notes, the devil is in the fine print—the insurance companies that issue them structure EIAs so that the terms favor them. "Insurance companies add trivial insurance benefits, disadvantageous tax treatment and exorbitant costs to mutual funds and sell them as equity-indexed annuities." This was the conclusion of a study by Craig McCann and Dengpan Luo, two Ph.D.s in financial economics from leading graduate schools. The researchers also concluded that an astounding 15 to 20 percent of the premium paid by investors in EIAs is a transfer of wealth from unsophisticated investors to insurance companies and their sales forces.[10] Our conclusion: EIAs are the poster children for products that are too good to be true. They are sold because they provide the seller with far greater commissions than does the sale of mutual funds. It appears that the National Association of Securities Dealers agrees. In June 2005, the NASD issued an investor alert, describing the complexities of EIAs and their potential pitfalls.[11]

Again, you don't even have to read the fine print. And you don't have to know how to analyze the costs embedded in the product. All you have to understand is the basic principle that the insurance company is in the business of selling products that make them the most money, not deliver high returns to you.

Do You Chase the IPO Dream?

O ne of the more costly mistakes investors make is to buy initial public offerings. Like the variable annuities just discussed, IPOs are products meant to be sold, not bought. Wall Street loves IPOs because they generate great fee income. Desperately searching for the next Microsoft or Google, investors seem to buy IPOs with the same frenzy with which they buy lottery tickets. Unfortunately, all too often they end up with the next E-Loan, Priceline, or Mortgage.com. Let's look at the reality of actual performance.

A study covering the period 1970 to 1990 examined the returns from a strategy of buying every IPO at the end of the first day's closing price and then holding each investment for five years. The average return provided by this strategy was just 5 percent per year. It was also 7 percent per year *less* than a benchmark of companies of similar market capitalization.[1]

A U.S. Bancorp Piper Jaffray study of 4,900 IPOs, covering the period May 1988 to July 1998, found that less than one-third of new issues were above their IPO price by July 1998. In addition, almost a third weren't even trading any longer (they had gone bankrupt, been acquired, or were no longer trading in an active market).[2]

University of Florida finance professor Jay Ritter looked at 1,006 IPOs that raised at least $20 million from 1988 to 1993. He found that the median IPO underperformed the Russell 3000 by 30 percent in the three years after going public. He also found that 46 percent of IPOs produced negative returns.[3]

Here is one more bit of anecdotal evidence against the wisdom of investing in IPOs, unless you are lucky enough to get them at the preopening price. The academic studies usually measure returns on an investable strategy. They therefore typically use the price at the close of the first day of trading. Unfortunately, many investors may not be so lucky to buy at the close. Let's look at the case of one of the hottest of all IPOs. VA Linux Systems set a new record for the single greatest one-day appreciation for an IPO with its offering on December 9, 1999. The headline of the following day's *Wall Street Journal* screamed "VA Linux Registers Pop." The IPO price was 30, and the stock closed at 239.25, a pop of almost 700 percent. However, the stock opened at 299 and rose to 320 before falling about 81 points to its final closing price. Trading volume was 7.6 million shares, which was enormous especially considering that the number of outstanding shares was 4.4 million. It is obvious that there was a great deal of money lost by investors who bought the stock after the initial offering. The one-day loss for a buyer at the opening price was 20 percent, and the loss grew to 40 percent after just five days of trading. The *Journal*, however, focused on the gains from the IPO price, not the huge losses experienced by most retail investors.[4]

Another amusing tale about the VA Linux offering: One of our coworkers, Vladimir Masek, received a cold call from a broker at Edward Jones. The broker offered him the "opportunity" to get in at 280 on the first day of trading. Vladimir asked him, "Who is VA Linux?" The broker replied that it was a wonderful new company with an operating system that would put Microsoft out of business, etc. Vladimir then told the broker that he knew very well what Linux was. In fact, he was probably one of the first one hundred or so people in this country ever to install the system on his computer and use it. Yet he had never heard of VA Linux. The broker had absolutely no idea that Linux is freely distributable, is a wonderful technology, and is good for users, but that there did not appear to be any way for VA Linux to profit from the technology. The broker never called Vladimir again.

In the face of this poor performance, why do investors continue to chase the latest IPO? There are two explanations for this seemingly irrational behavior. First, unless investors happen to read scholarly publications such as the *Journal of Finance*, they are unlikely to be aware of the facts. Second, even when informed, investors often act in what appear to be irrational ways. In this case, it is another example of the *triumph of hope over experience*. Investors seem to be willing to accept the high probability of low returns in exchange for the small chance of a home run or, possibly even more important, a great story to tell at the next cocktail party.

Summary

There is an old saying in sports that sometimes the best trades are the ones you don't make. You can avoid the mistake of investing in IPOs by remembering that while IPOs have provided huge profits for the Wall Street firms that market them, they have generated very poor returns for investors. IPOs are investments best avoided. Yes, it is possible that by investing in an IPO you might be buying the next Microsoft, but it is more likely that you will end up owning an asset that delivers poor returns.

MISTAKE 71

Do You Understand That You Can Be Too Conservative?

Larry is an avid tennis player but, unfortunately, heavy amounts of his favorite game left him facing tendonectomy surgery for tennis elbow. Fortunately, his surgeon believed in aggressive postsurgery therapy. He was out of a cast and began physical therapy within one week. Within several months, he was free of pain and back on the tennis court.

On the other hand, Larry has friends who have undergone the same surgery, but their doctors prescribed more conservative treatment. They were in casts for significantly longer periods, and their physical therapy regimen was less aggressive. As a result, their recovery periods were much longer. The most conservative strategies are not always the most appropriate. This is certainly true when it comes to investing.

As we approach and enter retirement, our ability to take financial risks decreases. One reason is that with a shorter investment horizon, we have less ability to wait out the inevitable bear markets. Another is that if we are no longer working, we don't have the same ability to replace or recover from financial losses. And a third is that our willingness to take risk, and suffer the psychological strains that bear markets can produce, is likely reduced. Thus, it is logical for investors to lower their equity allocations when they reach, or even approach, the retirement stage of their lives. However, as you will see, it is possible to become too conservative. Let's look at the historical evidence.

We begin by considering the cases of Portfolios A, B, C, and D. Portfolio A is invested in long-term government bonds. Portfolio B allocates a small portion (10 percent) to stocks in the form of an investment in the S&P 500 Index. Portfolios C and D are a bit more aggressive, allocating, respectively, 20 and 30 percent of their portfolios to the S&P 500. The time frame is 1926 to 2010.

The following table shows the returns and standard deviations of their portfolios:

	PORTFOLIO A ALL BONDS	PORTFOLIO B 90% BONDS	PORTFOLIO C 80% BONDS	PORTFOLIO D 70% BONDS
Annualized return	5.5%	6.1%	6.8%	7.3%
Annual standard deviation	9.5%	8.9%	8.8%	9.2%
Worst year	−14.1% (2009)	−10.8% (2009)	−12.9% (1931)	−16.7% (1931)

Adding a small allocation to stocks increased returns while actually reducing the volatility of the portfolio. And while the risks in terms of the worst one-year losses were greater when the equity allocation was 30 percent, the portfolios with a 10 percent and 20 percent allocation to stocks produced better worst cases.

The conclusion we can draw from the evidence is that adding a small amount of equities to an all-bond portfolio raises returns while actually reducing volatility. The reason is that while stocks are more volatile than bonds, stocks have a low correlation to bonds. The annual correlation of the S&P 500 to long-term government bonds was just 0.07. And there are many periods when bonds produce negative returns while stocks are producing great returns. Consider the evidence in the following table:

YEAR	S&P 500 INDEX (%)	LONG-TERM GOVERNMENT BONDS (%)
1933	54.0	−0.1
1951	24.0	−4.0
1958	43.4	−6.1
1967	24.0	−9.2
1980	32.4	−4.0
1999	21.0	−9.0
2009	26.5	−14.9

Of course, as you can see in this next table, there are also periods when bonds provided a safe haven from the storms that hit equities:

YEAR	S&P 500 (%)	LONG-TERM GOVERNMENT BONDS (%)
1930	−24.9	4.7
1937	−35.0	0.2
1957	−10.8	7.5
1962	−8.7	6.9
1974	−26.5	4.4
2000	−9.1	21.5
2002	−22.1	17.9
2008	−37.0	25.8

More Effective Diversification

There are other ways investors can improve the efficiency of their portfolios. Let's look at two of them. The first relates to another mistake investors make when they become very conservative. As we discussed in Chapter 13, many investors believe that international equities are riskier than domestic stocks, and so they limit their equity holdings to only U.S. stocks. The evidence presented in the following table makes the case for why international equities should be included in portfolios.

Let's consider three portfolios. Portfolio A holds only bonds. Portfolio B adds a 20 percent allocation to the S&P 500. Portfolio C adds a 10 percent allocation to both the S&P 500 and the MSCI EAFE Index. The data cover the period 1970 to 2010.

	PORTFOLIO A 100% BONDS	PORTFOLIO B 80% BONDS, 20% S&P 500	PORTFOLIO C 80% BONDS, 10% S&P 500, 10% EAFE
Annualized return	8.7%	9.3%	9.4%
Standard deviation	11.7%	10.3%	10.3%

Portfolio C not only produced the highest return but also produced the lowest standard deviation. Note that the historical evidence also suggests that including some allocation to small-cap and value stocks would further increase the efficiency of these portfolios. This is especially true on the international side, where the greatest diversification benefits come from adding the stocks of smaller companies. (International small-cap stocks have significantly lower correlation to U.S. stocks than do international large caps.)

Let's now look at another way to improve the efficiency of a portfolio, while still maintaining its conservative nature. This time we will shift the maturity of our bond holdings from long-term Treasury bonds to five-year Treasury notes, reducing term (price) risk. As you will see, the reduction in risk will allow us to increase our equity holdings without increasing the volatility of the portfolio. Portfolio A is 80 percent long-term Treasury bonds and 20 percent S&P 500. Portfolio B is 70 percent five-year notes and 30 percent S&P 500. Portfolio C is 65 percent five-year notes and 35 percent S&P 500. The period is 1926 to 2010.

	PORTFOLIO A 80% LONG-TERM TREASURY BONDS, 20% S&P 500	PORTFOLIO B 70% FIVE-YEAR TREASURY NOTES, 30% S&P 500	PORTFOLIO C 65% FIVE-YEAR TREASURY NOTES, 35% S&P 500
Annualized return	6.8%	7.2%	7.4%
Standard deviation	8.8%	7.3%	8.0%

As you can see, Portfolios B and C were both more efficient than A.

Summary

While it is appropriate for investors to become more conservative as they approach and enter the retirement phase of their lives, the evidence suggests that you can actually become too conservative. Doing so might cause portfolios to "fail," leaving investors alive without the financial assets needed to provide the lifestyle they had worked so hard to achieve.

Fortunately, it is not necessary to become so conservative that equities are actually excluded from a portfolio. The evidence suggests that portfolios with globally diversified equity allocations of as much as 30 to 35 percent, when combined with shorter-term fixed-income assets, are likely to produce greater returns with volatility that is similar to or even lower than that produced by a portfolio of "safe" longer-term government bonds.

MISTAKE 72

Is Your Withdrawal Assumption Rate in Retirement Too Aggressive?

Unfortunately, this is not only a very common mistake, but one with the potential for a devastating impact: running out of assets to support your expected lifestyle. Let's see why this is true.

From an investment perspective, the key question when approaching retirement is: What should my portfolio value be to provide a high level of confidence that the assets will not be exhausted during my life? A retiree must address the following issues:

> What is my (and my spouse's) life expectancy?
> What will the level of inflation be?
> What will the portfolio's investment returns be?
> How much will I need to maintain my desired lifestyle?

Time, inflation, volatility, and expected returns take on greater significance in retirement. During your working life, a few bad years of high inflation or negative investment returns can be overcome. You can add savings or work longer to make up for any portfolio shortfall. In retirement, however, money is being withdrawn all the time, in both good and bad years.

Let's first address the issue of life expectancy. Most individuals underestimate their life expectancy. For example, the average couple, when both individuals are 65, has a second-to-die life expectancy of well over 20 years. In addition, when determining how long you'll need your assets to last in retirement, you should not simply take average life expectancies as your guide. An average results in approximately a 50 percent chance of living longer. The following table, a safer benchmark, is based on a probability of only a 20 percent chance of outliving the expected time frame. For example, a 60-year-old male has only a 20 percent chance of living beyond 27 more years.

Investment Horizon to Plan on When Developing a Retirement Plan

AT AGE	FEMALE	MALE
55	36	32
60	31	27
65	27	22
70	22	18

Source: National Center for Health Statistics.

It is important to understand that a married couple's second-to-die life expectancy is greater than the longer of the two individual life expectancies.

Turning to the issue of investment returns and inflation, a common investor mistake is the singular use of averages when projecting returns. Let's see how that might happen.

Say it is the start of 1998. You determine that for the period 1926 to 1997, a portfolio consisting of 75 percent S&P 500 Index and 25 percent U.S. government bonds returned an average of 10 percent. During the same time period, the inflation rate was 3 percent. Therefore, the real (inflation-adjusted) rate of return for this 75-25 portfolio was 7 percent. You might conclude that you could withdraw $70,000 per year from a $1 million portfolio and maintain the same real income in the long term, increasing the $70,000 by the future rate of inflation. The problem with this approach is that inflation rates and investment returns vary each year, and using averages may cause unexpected and unpleasant surprises. If you retire before the start of a bull market, it is likely that you could withdraw 7 percent per year and maintain a portfolio in excess of $1 million. Retiring at the beginning of a bear market, however, can produce very different results. For example, had you retired at the end of 1972, withdrawn 7 percent of your original principal every year, and adjusted that for inflation, you would have run out of funds within 10 years, by the end of 1982! This is because the S&P 500 declined by almost 40 percent in the 1973 to 1974 bear market.

Systematic withdrawals during bear markets exacerbate the effects of the market's decline, causing portfolio values to fall to levels from which they may never recover. For instance, if an investor withdraws 7 percent in a year when the portfolio declines by 20 percent, the result is a decline in the portfolio of 27 percent in that year. A 37 percent increase is now required in the next year just to get even, plus another 7 percent for the annual withdrawal (a total of 44 percent) to make up for the prior year's decline. But that is not the end because you also have to take into account the inflation that occurred during the year.

Given the possibility of a market decline occurring at the very early stages of retirement, investors need to determine how much money they can withdraw annually and still have only a minimal risk they might outlive their assets. On the basis of historical evidence, as a general rule investors with a 30-year or longer investment horizon should not withdraw more than 4 percent of the starting value of a portfolio. This amount can be increased every year by the previous year's inflation rate, thereby maintaining the same level of real purchasing power. With at least a 50 percent allocation to equities, the historical evidence suggests that you will have less than a 5 percent chance of outliving your assets with this strategy. Note that even a 75-year-old investor has an investment horizon of about 15 years. At 15 years the maximum suggested withdrawal rate is still just 6 percent.

Using a 4 percent withdrawal rate, it is easy to calculate the portfolio size needed to feel comfortable about retirement. Investors can estimate the amount of pretax income desired (after subtracting any social security and pension income) and then multiply that figure by 25 (inverse of 4 percent). For example, investors needing $50,000 a year in pretax income after taking into account social security (and so on) must achieve a portfolio of $1.25 million ($50,000 × 25). Using the 6 percent withdrawal rate, the multiplier would be about 17.

You can avoid the mistake of being too aggressive in your assumptions by using the following tables as a guideline. The numbers under the percent withdrawal columns represent the likelihood of not running out of money while you are still alive. The tables are for various investment horizons and life expectancies. As your horizon shortens, you can begin to withdraw, with a high degree of safety, slightly larger percentages, but probably far less than most investors would assume.

Odds (%) of Not Running Out of Money
(30-Year Time Periods between 1926 and 1996)

ASSET ALLOCATION	WITHDRAWAL % INITIAL YEAR*			
	4%	5%	6%	7%
100% stocks	95	85	68	59
75% stocks and 25% bonds	98	83	68	49
50% stocks and 50% bonds	95	76	51	17
25% stocks and 75% bonds	71	27	20	12
100% bonds	20	17	12	0

Odds (%) of Not Running Out of Money
(20-Year Time Periods between 1926 and 1996)

ASSET ALLOCATION	WITHDRAWAL % INITIAL YEAR*			
	4%	5%	6%	7%
100% stocks	100	88	75	63
75% stocks and 25% bonds	100	90	75	61
50% stocks and 50% bonds	100	90	75	55
25% stocks and 75% bonds	100	82	47	31
100% bonds	90	47	20	14

Odds (%) of Not Running Out of Money
(15-Year Time Periods between 1926 and 1996)

ASSET ALLOCATION	WITHDRAWAL % INITIAL YEAR*			
	4%	5%	6%	7%
100% stocks	100	100	91	63
75% stocks and 25% bonds	100	100	95	82
50% stocks and 50% bonds	100	100	93	79
25% stocks and 75% bonds	100	100	89	70
100% bonds	100	100	71	39

*Initial dollar amount inflated in subsequent years, based on actual inflation to maintain the same standard of living.

Source: Study by Phillip L. Cooley, Carl M. Hubbard, and Daniel T. Walz, using data from Ibbotson Associates. Stocks are represented by the S&P 500 Index, and bonds are represented by long-term, high-grade corporate.

Using these tables, we can see that in order to have a likelihood of success of 90 percent or greater, an investor with a 30-year horizon would need to limit withdrawals to just 4 percent per year, a 20-year horizon would require limiting withdrawals to 5 percent per year, and a 15-year horizon would require limiting withdrawals to 6 percent per year. Note that in each case to achieve that 90 percent likelihood of success requires an equity allocation of at least 50 percent or so. Note also that if you plan on having a higher withdrawal rate, then you really need to have a high allocation to equities to maintain even a reasonable chance of not running out of funds.

Remember that it is wise to plan your retirement with conservative assumptions about the withdrawal percentage because being wrong and running out of assets is too painful an outcome to contemplate.

MISTAKE 73

Do You Hold Assets in the Wrong Location?

When faced with a choice of locating assets in either taxable or tax-advantaged accounts, taxable investors should have a *preference* for holding equities (versus fixed-income investments) in taxable accounts. However, regardless of whether the investor will hold stocks or fixed-income investments, investors should always prefer to first fund their deductible retirement account [i.e., IRA, 401(k), or 403(b)] or Roth IRA before investing any taxable dollars. The exception is the need to provide for liquidity for unanticipated funding requirements. Because tax-advantaged accounts are the most tax-efficient investment accounts, investors should always take the maximum advantage of their ability to fund them.

There are six advantages to holding equities rather than fixed income in a taxable account:

1. Equities receive capital gains treatment, while fixed-income investments (with the exception of municipal bonds) are taxed at ordinary income tax rates.
2. Securities in taxable accounts receive a step-up in basis for the heirs at death, eliminating capital gains (but not the estate tax). However, on the downside, securities with unrealized losses in taxable accounts receive a step-down in basis at death.
3. Capital gains taxes are due only when realized. Investors do have at least some ability to time the realization of gains. In addition, the advent of core funds, tax-managed funds, and ETFs has greatly improved the tax efficiency of equity investing.
4. When there are losses in taxable accounts, the losses can be "harvested" for tax purposes. The more volatile the asset, the more valuable the option to harvest losses becomes. Equities are more volatile than fixed-income assets.

5. Assets held in taxable accounts can be donated to charities. By donating the appreciated shares (preferably those with the largest long-term capital gain), capital gains taxes can be avoided. Because equities have higher expected returns than fixed-income assets, this option is more valuable for equities.

6. Foreign stock holdings often entail taxes on dividends being withheld at the source. Investors can, however, claim a foreign tax credit that can then be used as a credit against U.S. taxes. However, this credit does no good unless the asset is held in a taxable account. Currently, if the foreign asset is held in a tax-advantaged account, the loss of the foreign tax credit leads to a reduction of returns of about 9 percent of the amount of the dividend. It is important to remember that if the investment in international assets is a "fund of funds," then any foreign tax credit cannot be passed on to the investor by the fund of funds.

Exceptions

The exceptions to the strategy of preferring to hold equities in taxable accounts and fixed-income investments in tax-advantaged accounts include

› **REITs.** Because their dividends are considered nonqualified and are taxed at ordinary income tax rates, REITs are a tax-inefficient equity asset class. Since investors can hold tax-efficient municipal bonds, those investors who value the diversification benefits of REITs should locate the REIT holdings in a tax-advantaged account, even before they locate bonds in that account. Again, municipal bonds can be held in taxable accounts.

› **Commodities.** As with REITs, those investors who value the diversification benefits of commodities should locate these assets in tax-advantaged accounts, even if that means having to hold fixed-income investments in taxable accounts.

› **Liquidity needs.** Investors with anticipated, or the potential for unanticipated, liquidity and cash flow needs from their taxable holdings should consider holding some fixed-income investments (generally municipal bonds) in their taxable accounts. One widely used rule of thumb is to have six months of spending needs in highly liquid assets of the highest investment grades.

Order of Preference

There will be investors whose asset allocation will require them to hold equities in both taxable and tax-advantaged accounts. The following is the order of preferences for holding assets in a tax-advantaged account:

1. REITS and commodities
2. Nominal bonds
3. TIPS
4. Domestic and international equities for which no tax-managed funds are available
5. Domestic equities—value
6. Domestic equities—small cap
7. Emerging markets—value
8. Emerging markets—small cap
9. Emerging markets—core
10. Domestic equities—core
11. Domestic equities—large
12. International equities—small cap
13. International equities—value
14. International equities—core

Additional Information

As you analyze your options, you will want to keep these things in mind:

> The more tax-efficient funds should be placed in the taxable accounts.
> Tax-managed funds will generally be more tax efficient than funds that are not managed for tax efficiency.
> The broader definition of the asset class, the more tax efficient the fund is likely to be. For example, a total market fund will be more tax efficient than a narrow (e.g., small-cap) asset class fund, and a small-cap fund (that holds both value and growth) will be more tax efficient than a small-cap value fund.
> Large-cap funds are more tax efficient than small-cap funds.

> Marketwide and growth funds are more tax efficient than value funds.
> Multiasset class funds (e.g., core funds) are more tax efficient than single asset class funds due to lower turnover as stocks migrate from one asset class to another. For example, holding an international core fund that has both developed and emerging markets will be more tax efficient than holding two separate funds. In addition to the reduction in forced turnover, rebalancing costs (among individual asset classes) will be reduced, and the core funds will not have to trade if a country changes classifications from an emerging market to a developed market.
> The more volatile the asset class, the more valuable the tax option. Thus, all else being equal, the more volatile asset classes (e.g., emerging markets) should be held in taxable accounts.

Do You Believe That All Passively Managed Funds Are Created Equal?

Prudent investors begin their investment journey by creating an investment plan in the form of an investment policy statement. IPSs define the investors' goals and the specific asset allocations they will use to achieve those goals. Once asset allocations are determined, the next decision is the choice of investment vehicles that will be used to gain exposure to each of the respective asset classes. The choice is much simpler for passive investors than it is for active investors because the universe of funds from which to choose is much smaller. However, even for passive investors, the choice is not as simple as just looking at the expense ratios of the various alternatives and choosing the cheapest alternative. The reason is that not all "index" funds are created equal.

While the expense ratio is important, it should not be the only consideration. A fund manager can add value in several ways that have nothing to do with active investing. Let's explore some of the ways a fund can add value in terms of portfolio construction, tax management, and trading strategies.

1. Choice of Benchmark Index, or How a Fund Defines Its Asset Class

This impacts returns in several ways:

> It impacts turnover, which impacts trading costs and tax efficiency. Some indexes have a higher turnover than others. And some indexes have buy-and-hold ranges designed to reduce the negative impact of turnover (on both transaction costs and tax efficiency).

> It impacts exposure to the risk factors of size and value: the greater the exposure, the higher the risk and expected return of the fund.
> The correlation of the fund to the other portfolio assets is affected: the lower the correlation, the more effective the diversification.
> Some indexes are more opaque than others, preventing actively managed funds from exploiting the "forced turnover" that is created when indexes are reconstructed (typically annually). The lack of opaqueness has historically created problems for index funds that replicate the Russell 2000 Index.
> A fund can add value by incorporating the momentum effect by temporarily delaying the purchase of stocks that are exhibiting negative momentum and by temporarily delaying the sale of stocks that are exhibiting positive momentum.
> A fund can screen certain securities for poor risk and return characteristics (e.g., stocks in bankruptcy, very low priced stocks, IPOs). For example, while utilities and real estate stocks typically have high book-to-market ratios (and, therefore, are found in most value indexes), they have very low betas (exposure to equity risk). The result is their inclusion in value indexes that use book-to-market as the screen creates a drag on returns.
> How often an index reconstitutes can impact returns. Most indexes reconstitute annually. The lack of frequent reconstitution can create significant style drift. For example, from 1990 through 2006, 20 percent of stocks in the Russell 2000 would leave the index when it was reconstituted at the end of June. The result is that a small-cap index fund based on the Russell 2000 would have seen its exposure to the small-cap risk factor drift lower over the course of the year. The drift toward lower exposure to the risks factors results in lower expected returns.

2. Patient Trading

If a fund's goal is to replicate an index, it must trade when stocks enter or exit the index, and it must also hold the exact weighting of each security in the index. A fund whose goal is to earn the return of the asset class can be more patient in its trading strategy (if it can withstand tracking error), using market orders and block trading that can take advantage of discounts offered by active managers who desire to sell large blocks of stock quickly. Patient trading reduces transaction costs, and block trading can even create negative trading costs in some cases.

3. Tax Management

While indexing is a relatively tax-efficient strategy (due to relatively low turnover), there are ways to improve the tax efficiency of a fund. The first is to harvest losses whenever they are significant. The second is to minimize the realization of short-term capital gains. The third is to create wider hold ranges to reduce turnover.

4. Securities Lending

Securities lending refers to the lending of securities by one party to another. Securities are often borrowed with the intent to sell them short. In the international markets, there is another reason for securities lending to occur that has to do with the different tax treatment of dividends to domestic versus foreign investors. Thus, the opportunities to add value are greater in foreign markets.

As payment for the loan of the security, the parties negotiate a fee. Some fund families are more aggressive than others in generating security lending fees. Unfortunately, you have to dig deep into the annual reports to find the data. However, it is worth the effort, as the differences can be large, especially in the case of small-cap (both domestic and international) and emerging market funds.

Summary

There is only one way to see things right, and that is in the whole. While ETFs and the index funds of Vanguard are often the cheapest in terms of expense ratios, when evaluating similar passively managed mutual funds, it is important to consider not only the operating expense ratio, but also all the ways that a fund can add value. A little bit of extra homework can pay significant dividends.

MISTAKE 75

Do You Trust but Fail to Verify?

What do the Royal Bank of Scotland, Nomura Holdings (Japan), the Elie Wiesel Foundation for Humanity, Steven Spielberg's Wunderkinder Foundation, and the New York Mets all have in common? They are all victims of the Bernie Madoff scandal that might have a cumulative cost to investors of as much as $50 billion.

This loss is a tragedy of epic proportions. However, the real tragedy is that had investors followed some basic rules of prudent investing, the investments would never have been made.

There Is Nothing New in Investing

Many aspects of the Madoff affair are depressingly familiar to the story behind failed hedge funds:

> The exclusive nature of the "club" creates an aura that seems to attract investors the way swim-up bars attract guests at all-inclusive resorts. Investors seem to value the sense of membership in an exclusive club. They yearn to be members of the "in crowd."
> In addition to their "sex appeal," such investment opportunities lure investors with the ever-present hope of market-beating returns.
> Trust in the promoter due to some social affiliation encourages investment.
> The investors did not know where their money was placed.
> Returns seemed too good to be true.
> Investors received no audited financial statements.
> The speed of the ultimate collapse was incredible.

Investors should also have been aware that the returns reported by Madoff were inconsistent with his particular strategy of buying puts and selling covered call options on stocks in the portfolio. During bear markets, the strategy likely would have resulted in losses, though less than that of the overall market. Yet Madoff was reporting consistent profits. That alone should have alerted investors. But if that were not enough, the number of trades that would have been required to execute the strategy far exceeded the number of trades reported on the entire exchange!

Pay No Attention to the Man behind the Curtain

Madoff was able to execute his massive fraud because he operated behind a "curtain." In contrast, publicly traded mutual funds operate with a high degree of transparency. Among the advantages of investing in publicly traded investment vehicles are these:

1. Publicly held mutual funds are a highly regulated industry (the SEC).
2. Mutual funds are required to have audited financial statements. The audits verify the financial statements of the mutual funds including correspondence with the custodians, brokers, and transfer agent of the funds that confirms the securities held.
3. Mutual funds do not act as custodian of the assets.
4. Mutual funds do not perform the fund's accounting themselves.

Summary

Among those who experienced the greatest losses from the fraud perpetrated by Madoff are some of the largest banks and some of the largest hedge funds. Each of them touted their ability to identify the money managers who would deliver market-beating returns on a risk-adjusted basis. They proudly discussed their superior due diligence efforts that serve to protect investors. As the academic evidence has demonstrated, such claims are without merit. There is no better example of the triumph of hope and hype over wisdom and experience than this episode.

The saddest part of this great tragedy is that if investors had known the historical evidence and followed the basic rules of prudent investing, this tragedy would have been avoided. Based on those experiences, it is hard to understand why you would give your hard-earned assets to someone who invests those assets in a way that is not completely transparent, where you take 100 percent of the risks but the person takes 22 percent of the returns, you earn those returns in a tax-inefficient manner, and there is no evidence of any persistence of performance beyond the randomly expected. To repeat, it is the triumph of hype and hope over wisdom and experience. And hope is not an investment strategy.

MISTAKE 76

Do You Have a Plan B?

As we've previously discussed, no traveler would begin a drive to a place she had never been without a road map. Yet only a small percentage of investors have a written investment policy statement. Prudent investors should not make any investments until they have answered at least these four important questions:

1. How long is my investment horizon?
2. Is there a high correlation of my labor income to equity returns?
3. What is my risk tolerance?
4. What is my financial objective?

However, these may still not be enough. Investment plans should consider not only the expected returns on equities and bonds, but also the possibility that returns will be well below those expectations. For example, it is likely that in January 1990, very few Japanese investors expected Japanese large-cap stocks to produce negative returns over the next 20 years. As a domestic example, the S&P 500 Index produced negative returns for the 10 years from 1999 through 2008—the first time this had occurred since 1930.

Since we know that severe bear markets will likely occur from time to time, and we cannot know how long they will last, a critical part of the financial planning process is to consider a "Plan B." This consists of the actions that might have to be taken if financial assets fall to such a great degree that the investor may run out of assets. Or it might be that an investor has a bequeathing goal (might have children to whom he would like, or need, to leave a significant estate), and he does not wish to put that objective at risk.

Plan B should list the actions that would need to be taken if financial assets were to drop to a predetermined level. Those actions might include remaining in the workforce longer (or returning to the workforce if that is possible), reducing current spending, reducing the financial goal (the need to spend), selling a home (or second home), or moving to a location with a lower cost of living. Consider the following example.

It is 2003, and Mr. and Mrs. Brown are each 50 years old. Mrs. Brown is a successful doctor, and Mr. Brown is a college professor. They plan to retire at 60. Working with their advisor, they decided their risk tolerance allowed them to hold a portfolio that built in a "worst-case" cumulative loss of 25 percent. Using that figure, they decided that an equity allocation of 60 percent was appropriate. Based on the historical evidence, the Browns knew that while there was a reasonably high probability their portfolio would not experience a total loss of more than 25 percent, there was still the possibility that a greater loss would occur. Not making contingency plans for that seemingly remote possibility is the same mistake as not buying life insurance because the odds of dying in the near future are very low.

The Browns did not make that mistake. They recognized that the possibility of failure existed. However, while they recognized that possibility existed, they did not want to plan on that scenario as the "base case."

The Worst Case Should Not Be the Base Case

Using the worst case as the base case means that the ability to take risk is very low and, therefore, that returns are going to be very low. It also results in investors' spending far less than they would have been able to if the worst case never occurred. The Browns had worked hard, saved well, and wanted to enjoy the rewards of their efforts. On the other hand, they did not ignore the possibility of failure. With that in mind, they decided on the following steps should the need arise:

> They would sell their second home.
> They would reduce their daily spending requirements by 10 percent.
> They would reduce their travel budget by 50 percent.
> They would continue working until at least age 65.

They then also discussed the potential for having to take further steps, such as the possibility of having to downsize their current home or of moving to a part of the country with a lower cost of living. While hoping they would never have to execute any of these steps, they were prepared to do so.

Although having a formal written plan is not necessary, putting the plan in writing helped the Browns to face the fact that the risks they were taking were real and that they needed to be prepared to take these steps if they wanted to live their current lifestyle, something they desired to do.

For the next five years, the Browns lived well and enjoyed their lifestyle. When the financial crisis of 2008 arrived, they were prepared and began to implement some of the alternatives they had discussed in 2003. Others were not so well prepared.

Summary

Having a well-developed investment plan is certainly important. However, it is not sufficient unless that plan is integrated into an overall estate, tax, and risk management plan and anticipates the potential for having to adopt Plan B if the markets "don't cooperate" with the base plan. Those who both anticipate and prepare for the possibility of negative outcomes are far more likely to be successful in dealing with them.

Do You Keep Repeating the Same Mistakes?

Like many people, one of my (RC's) constant goals was to get in better shape. Each time the bug hit me, I'd make the same push: dust off one of my old workout routines, clean out the fridge, and tell myself this time would be different. And each time, the movement would be short-lived, as something would always come up:

> Work and other activities would get busy, leaving me less time to exercise (or at least giving me the excuse to skip the gym).
> A few dinners out with friends would get me off my diet.
> A few sales at the grocery store would fill up my fridge with foods grown in a processing plant, rather than on a farm.

For whatever reason, I kept trying the same routine and expected different results. People who are much smarter than I am would call that insanity. In reality, I had no logical reason to think this time would be different; yet without having the right knowledge about what would work best for me, I kept making the same mistakes.

The same can be true of investing. Without the knowledge necessary to make prudent decisions about your investments, it can be easy to continue making the same mistakes, even while telling yourself this time will be different.

In some cases, you may have made some investing mistakes without even knowing it. In other cases, you may have known you were making a mistake, but simply didn't realize how much it was costing you. Our goal with this book is to help give you the knowledge you need to overcome biases and behavioral tendencies to make smart investing decisions. You no longer have ignorance as a defense for making the mistakes covered in this book. As Carol Tavris and Elliot Aronson noted in their book

Mistakes Were Made (But Not by Me), "If you can admit a mistake when it is the size of an acorn, it is easier to repair than when it has become the size of a tree, with deep, wide-ranging roots."[1]

However, you may discover that overcoming these obstacles is a tall task and that you need help in achieving your financial goals. The same was true of me for my fitness goals. My big change happened when a friend recommended his trainer. I checked him out and decided it was time to do something different.

We went over some of the changes I needed to make. Some of the changes the trainer recommended—such as cutting out caffeine—were difficult and ones I frequently struggled (and still struggle) with. Others—such as cutting out bagels—seemed to fly in the face of conventional wisdom.

Still, I was determined to give myself the best chance of achieving my goals, and so I committed to the program. In 2009, I ran my first half marathon and finished three more that year. In 2010, I notched eight races across four states.

Perhaps you're in a similar boat with your investments: the behavioral biases you face are too challenging, and you need a little help in developing and adhering to a plan. Finding a trusted advisor to help you on your financial journey may end up being one of the best investments you make.

Whether you find an advisor to help or go at it alone, our suggestion is to come up with an investment plan that is tailored to your ability, willingness, and need to take risk. In your plan, clearly identify your goals and include an appropriate asset allocation and rebalancing table that give you the best chance of achieving those goals. Your plan should also address issues of taxes and outside risks that could cause the plan to fall short (such as death or disability). (For more on how to create an investment plan, read Larry's *The Only Guide You'll Ever Need for the Right Financial Plan*.)

CONCLUSION

I have personally tried to invest money, my clients' and
my own, in every single anomaly and predictive result
that academics have dreamed up. And I have yet to make
a nickel on any of these supposed market inefficiencies.
An inefficiency ought to be an exploitable opportunity.
If there's nothing investors can exploit in a systematic
way, time in and time out, then it's very hard to say that
information is not being properly incorporated into stock
prices. Real money investment strategies don't produce
the results that academic papers say they should.

—Richard Roll
Financial economist and principal of the portfolio management
firm Roll and Ross Asset Management
Wall Street Journal, December 28, 2000

As I traipse around the country speaking to investing groups,
or just stay in my cage writing my articles, I'm often accused of
"disempowering" people because I refuse to give any credence
to anyone's hope of beating the market. The knowledge that
I don't need to know anything is an incredibly profound
form of knowledge. Personally, I think it's the ultimate form
of empowerment. You can't tune out the massive industry
of investment prediction unless you want to: otherwise,
you'll never have the fortitude to stop listening. But if you
can plug your ears to every attempt (by anyone) to predict
what the markets will do, you will outperform nearly every
other investor alive over the long run. Only the mantra
of "I don't know, and I don't care" will get you there.

—Jason Zweig

"This time it's different." Those are the four most dangerous words in the English language for investors. Yes, the world is changing at a very rapid pace, probably faster than ever. The Internet, telecommunications, and biotechnology are all contributing to the incredible pace of change. The investment world is also changing rapidly. Not only do individual investors now have access to the same timely information as do institutional investors, but they also now have far more investment options than they used to, including such new instruments as ETFs, TIPS, and I bonds. The financial world is a far different place than it was just a few years ago. However, none of this in any way changes the basic principles of investing. Passive investors outperform active investors with about the same predictability that one expects from spawning salmon, migrating whales, and the swallows of Capistrano. If you follow the 12 simple steps that follow, you will avoid making the mistakes that even smart investors make. As Ted Cadsby stated, "While investors can be irrational, and markets move in exaggerated ways in the short term, a long-term and disciplined approach to investing can overcome both of these problems."[1]

1. Listen carefully to the words of Gary Belsky and Thomas Gilovich:
   a. Any individual who is not professionally occupied in the financial services industry (and even most of those who are) and who in any way attempts to actively manage an investment portfolio is probably suffering from overconfidence. That is, anyone who has confidence enough in his or her abilities and knowledge to invest in a particular stock or bond (or actively managed mutual fund or real estate investment trust or limited partnership) is most likely fooling himself.
   b. Most such people—probably you—have no business at all trying to pick investments, except perhaps as sport. Such people—again, probably you—should probably divide their money among several index funds and turn off CNBC.[2]
2. Unless it is for entertainment value, turn off CNBC, cancel your subscriptions to financial trade publications, and don't visit Internet chat boards that tout great funds, great stocks, or new and interesting investment strategies. If you need or enjoy the excitement of active investing, set up an entertainment account with 5 to 10

percent of your assets and go ahead and play the market. The odds are you will underperform, but you won't go broke.

3. Determine your unique risk tolerance, need to take risk, investment horizon, and cash flow needs.

4. Build a globally diversified portfolio of passive investment vehicles such as passive asset class funds, index funds, and ETFs consisting of multiple asset classes. For the equity portion, you should strongly consider including such risky asset classes as small-cap and value stocks, real estate, international stocks, and emerging markets. Too many investors confuse indexing with the exclusive use of an S&P 500 Index fund or a total stock market fund. As Peter Bernstein stated: "If I am going to own an S&P 500 index fund, which I used to think was the answer to all maidens' prayers, I'm buying a very undiversified portfolio in which the greatest weights are the stocks that have gone up the most. Is that really how I want to invest?"[3]

5. Write and sign an investment policy statement. Review it annually to remind yourself why you adopted your strategy and to see if personal circumstances have caused changes to your original assumptions.

6. Using guidelines established in your IPS, regularly rebalance your portfolio to its targeted asset allocation. Checking your portfolio on a quarterly basis is more than sufficient.

7. Place your most tax-efficient asset classes in your taxable accounts and your least tax-efficient asset classes in your tax-deferred accounts. Whenever possible, use tax-managed funds for taxable accounts.

8. Tax-manage your portfolio throughout the year.

9. Save as much as you can as early as you can.

10. Understand the true cost of major expenditures.

11. Don't turn desires into needs.

12. Enjoy your life.

By following the advice in this book, you can avoid the investment mistakes that even the smartest people make. Your tuition will have been only the cost of this book. On the other hand, you could choose to play the game of picking stocks, timing the market, and investing in actively managed funds. If you follow that path, consider the following caution: every few years the market hands out tuition bills that are much more expensive than the cost of this book.

For those interested in learning more about modern portfolio theory and the efficient market hypothesis, we recommend reading *The Only Guide to a Winning Investment Strategy You'll Ever Need*, *The Quest for Alpha*, and *Wise Investing Made Simple*. We hope the knowledge you gain from them will help you avoid what Richard Thaler cautions us against, and what we will conclude with: "If you are prepared to do something stupid repeatedly, there are many professionals happy to take your money."[4]

ENDNOTES

PART 1

Mistake 1

1. Meir Statman, *What Investors Really Want*, New York: McGraw-Hill, 2011.
2. Robert McGough, "Aging Bull Scores Again," *The Wall Street Journal*, Apr. 6, 1998.
3. Jonathan Fuerbringer, "Why Both Bulls and Bears Can Act So Bird-Brained," *The New York Times*, Mar. 30, 1997.
4. Peter Bernstein as quoted in Jonathan Burton, *Investment Titans*, New York: McGraw-Hill, 2000.
5. Brad Barber and Terrance Odean, "Trading Is Hazardous to Your Wealth," *The Journal of Finance*, April 2000.
6. Brad Barber and Terrance Odean, "Boys Will Be Boys," *Quarterly Journal of Economics*, February 2001.
7. Brad Barber and Terrance Odean, "Do Investors Trade Too Much?" *American Economic Review*, December 1999.
8. John Liscio, "The U.S.: Love It, Don't Leave It," *Dow Jones Asset Management*, November–December 1999.
9. Eleanor Laise, "If We're So Smart, Why Aren't We Rich?" *SmartMoney*, June 2001.
10. Jonathan Clements, *25 Myths You've Got to Avoid*, New York: Fireside, 1999.
11. James H. Smalhout, "Too Close to Your Money?" *Bloomberg Personal Finance*, November 1997.
12. Meir Statman as quoted in Jonathan Clements, "To Sell or Not? It Depends on Your Needs," *The Wall Street Journal*, Aug. 6, 1998.

Mistake 2

1. Gabriel Presler, "Buying Unloved Funds Could Yield Lovable Results," *Morningstar FundInvestor*, January 2001.

2. Lee Barney, "Chasing Hot Funds Translates to Diminished Returns, Study Finds," *TheStreet.com*, Jan. 17, 2001.
3. Russel Kinnel, "Mind the Gap," *Morningstar FundInvestor*, July 2005.
4. John Bogle, "The Yawning Gap between Fund Returns and Shareholder Returns," *Journal of Indexes*, May/June 2008.
5. Don Phillips, "Indexing Goes Hollywood," 2005 *Morningstar Indexes Yearbook*, 2006.

Mistake 3

1. Akio Morita as quoted in Gene Bylinsky, "Where Japan Will Strike Next," *Fortune*, Sept. 25, 1989.
2. Meir Statman as quoted in Victoria Collins, *Invest Beyond.com*, p. 35.
3. Jason Zweig, "The Trouble with Humans," *Money*, November 2000.

Mistake 4

1. Amos Tversky as quoted in Gary Belsky and Thomas Gilovich, *Why Smart People Make Big Money Mistakes*, New York: Simon & Schuster.

Mistake 5

1. Jonathan Clements, *25 Myths You've Got to Avoid*, New York: Fireside, 1999.
2. Edward C. Johnson III as quoted in Ben Warwick, *Searching for Alpha*, New York: Wiley, 2000.
3. Clements.
4. John Bogle, "Investing with Simplicity," *Bogle Financial Markets Research Center*, Oct. 3, 1998.
5. John Bogle as quoted in Dean LeBaron and Romesh Vaitilingam, *The Ultimate Investor*, Dover, NH: Capstone, 2001, p. 201.

Mistake 6

1. Henry Fielding, *The True Patriot*.
2. Edward Chancellor, *Devil Take the Hindmost*, New York: Farrar, Straus and Giroux, 1999.
3. Robert Shiller, *Irrational Exuberance*, Princeton, NJ: Princeton University Press.
4. Burton Malkiel, "Where Logic Ends and Speculation Begins," *The Wall Street Journal*, Apr. 4, 2000.

Mistake 7

1. Toddi Gutner, "Chicks' Picks Come Home to Roost," *BusinessWeek*, Oct. 8, 2001.

Mistake 12

1. Thomas Gilovich, R. P. Vallone, and Amos Tversky, "The Hot Hand in Basketball: On the Misperception of Random Sequences," *Cognitive Psychology*, vol. 17, pp. 295–314.
2. Burton Malkiel, *A Random Walk Down Wall Street*, London: Norton.
3. Mark Hulbert, "Why Top Returns Are Not in the Stars," *The New York Times*, Apr. 4, 1999.
4. Jonathan Clements, *25 Myths You've Got to Avoid*, New York: Fireside, 1999, p. 86.
5. Marty Whitman as quoted in Steven Goldberg, "Out of Step," *Kiplinger's*, January 2000.

Mistake 13

1. Gur Huberman, *Familiarity Breeds Investment*, September 1999.
2. Kenneth R. French and James M. Poterba, "Investor Diversification and International Equity Markets," *American Economic Review*, vol. 81, no. 2, pp. 222–226.
3. Debra Glassman and Leigh Riddick, "What Causes Home Asset Bias and How Should It Be Measured?" *Journal of Empirical Finance*, March 2001.
4. Hersh Shefrin and Meir Statman, "Behavioral Portfolio Theory," 1997 paper.
5. David Laster, "Measuring Gains from International Equity Diversification," *Journal of Investing*, Fall 1998.

Mistake 14

1. Gary Belsky and Thomas Gilovich, *Why Smart People Make Big Money Mistakes*, New York: Simon & Schuster.

PART 2

Mistake 16

1. Lynn Hume, "Judge Dismisses SEC Case against Former Broker, Rules Markups Not Excessive," *Bond Buyer*, May 1, 2002.

Mistake 17

1. Marty Whitman as quoted in Raymond Fazzi, "Going Their Own Way," *Financial Advisor*, March 2001.
2. Brad Barber and Terrance Odean, "All That Glitters: The Effect of Attention and News on the Buying Behavior of Individual and Institutional Investors," *Review of Financial Studies*, 2008, vol. 21, no. 2, pp. 785–818.
3. Jason Greene and Susan Watts, "Price Discovery on the NYSE and the NASDAQ," *Financial Management*, Spring 1996.

Mistake 18

1. Christopher R. Blake and Matthew R. Morey, "Morningstar Ratings and Mutual Fund Performance," *Journal of Financial and Quantitative Analysis*, September 2000.
2. John Bogle, "The Stock Market Universe—Stars, Comets, and the Sun," speech before the Financial Analysts of Philadelphia, Feb. 15, 2001.
3. Warren Buffett, "Berkshire Hathaway Letter to Shareholders," Berkshire Hathaway, 1996.
4. Russel Kinnel, "How Expense Ratios and Star Ratings Predict Success," *Morningstar Advisor*, Aug. 10, 2010.

Mistake 19

1. Karen Damato, "Quarterly Mutual Funds Review: Ghosts of Dead Funds May Haunt Results," *The Wall Street Journal*, Apr. 4, 1997.
2. Karen Damato, "Quarterly Mutual Funds Review: Coming of Age: Newborn Funds Can Fade after Fast Starts," *The Wall Street Journal*, Oct. 9, 2000.
3. Ibid.

Mistake 20

1. Russ Wermers, "Mutual Fund Performance: An Empirical Decomposition into Stock-Picking Talent, Style, Transactions Costs, and Expenses," *The Journal of Finance*, vol. 55, no. 4, August 2000.
2. "Low-Turnover Funds Outperform Their Active Trading Rivals," *St. Louis Post-Dispatch*, Aug. 12, 1997.
3. Dimensional Fund Advisors.
4. Carole Gould, "It's Gnawing at Your Fund and Now It Has a Gauge," *The New York Times*, July 11, 1999.
5. John Bogle, *Common Sense on Mutual Funds*, New York: Wiley, 1999.

6. Scott West and Mitch Anthony, *Storyselling for Financial Advisors*, Chicago: Kaplan Business, 2000.

Mistake 21

1. Larry Putnam, "Magical Run or a Bunch of Hype?" *Indexfunds.com*, July 29, 2000.
2. Russ Wermers, "Mutual Fund Performance: An Empirical Decomposition into Stock-Picking Talent, Style, Transactions Costs, and Expenses," *The Journal of Finance*, vol. 55, no. 4, August 2000.
3. Deb Bortner as quoted in David Evans, "Stock Educator Wade Cook Loses Big with Own Money," *Seattle Times*, May 5, 2001.

Mistake 23

1. Walter Updegrave, "Why 100% Stocks Is 80% Wrong," *Fortune*, Aug. 16, 1999.

Mistake 24

1. Brad Barber and Terrance Odean, "Too Many Cooks Spoil the Profits: The Performance of Investment Clubs," *Financial Analysts Journal*, January/February 2000.
2. John Nofsinger, *Investment Madness*, Upper Saddle River, NJ: Pearson Education, 2001.

Mistake 25

1. John Bogle, *John Bogle on Investing*, New York: McGraw-Hill, 2000.
2. Temma Ehrenfeld, "Indexing Works," *Financial Advisor*, May 1, 2011.
3. William Sherden, *The Fortune Sellers*, New York: Wiley, 1997.
4. Christopher Philips, "Do Active Managers Outperform in Bear Markets?" *Vanguard Investment Perspectives*, Spring/Summer 2009.

Mistake 26

1. John Bogle, *Common Sense on Mutual Funds*, New York: Wiley, 1999.
2. Lipper Analytical Service.
3. Mark M. Carhart, "*On Persistence in Mutual Fund Performance*," doctoral dissertation, University of Chicago, December 1994.
4. *The Index Insider*, January 2001.

Mistake 27

1. Joel Dickson and John Shoven, "Ranking Mutual Funds on an After-Tax Basis," National Bureau of Economic Research, July 1993.
2. Richard Evans, *The Index Fund Solution*, New York: Simon & Schuster, 2000.
3. James Garland, "The Tax Attraction of Tax-Managed Index Funds," *Journal of Investing*, Spring 1997.
4. Robert D. Arnott and Robert H. Jeffrey, "Is Your Alpha Big Enough to Cover Your Taxes?" *Journal of Portfolio Management*, Spring 1993.
5. Jonathan Clements, "As Stock Funds Rack Up the Big Gains, Uncle Sam's Tax Register Is Ringing," *The Wall Street Journal*, June 10, 1997.

Mistake 28

1. Gary P. Brinson, L. Randolph Hood, and Gilbert L. Beebower, "Determinants of Portfolio Performance," *Financial Analysts Journal*, July/August 1986.
2. Eugene Fama, Jr., "Parsimony," *Dimensional Fund Advisors*, March 2001.
3. Roger G. Ibbotson and Paul D. Kaplan, "Does Asset Allocation Policy Explain 40%, 90%, or 100% of Performance?" *Financial Analysts Journal*, January/February 2000.

Mistake 30

1. Colby Wright, Prithviraj Banerjee, and Vaneesha Boney, "Behavioral Finance: Are the Disciples Profiting from the Discipline?" *Journal of Investing*, Winter 2008.

Mistake 31

1. Ken Brown, "New Study Snips Away at Hedge Funds," *The Wall Street Journal*, Feb. 22, 2001.
2. Roger G. Ibbotson and Peng Chen, "The A, B, Cs of Hedge Funds: Alphas, Betas, and Costs," working paper, September 2006.
3. Stephen T. Brown as quoted in Mara Der Hovanesian, "Hedge Fund Follies," *BusinessWeek*, Sept. 17, 2001.

Mistake 32

1. Andrew Lo as quoted in Peter Coy, "He Who Mines Data May Strike Fool's Gold," *BusinessWeek*, June 16, 1997.

2. Laura Washington, "What's the Stock Market Got to Do with Butter Production in Bangladesh?" *Money*, Mar. 1, 1998.
3. *Humphrey-Hawkins Report*, Section 2: Economic and Financial Developments in 1997, Alan Greenspan, July 22, 1997.
4. William Bernstein, "The Efficient Frontier," Summer 2002.
5. Clifford S. Asness, "Fight the Fed Model: The Relationship between Stock Market Yields, Bond Yields, and Future Returns," *Journal of Portfolio Management*, Fall 2003.

PART 3

Mistake 35

1. William Sharpe, "The Arithmetic of Active Management," *Financial Analysts Journal*, January/February 1991.
2. Amy Barrett and Brent Brodeski, "Survivor Bias and Improper Measurement," *Zero Alpha Group*, March 2006.

Mistake 37

1. Peter Bernstein, "Wimps and Consequences," *Journal of Portfolio Management*, Fall 1999.

Mistake 39

1. Nassim Nicholas Taleb, *Fooled by Randomness*, New York: Random House, 2008.
2. John Bogle, *Common Sense on Mutual Funds*, New York: Wiley, 1999.
3. Ibid.
4. James Gipson as quoted in Karen Damato, "Old Style Fund Ideas Turn Timely," *The Wall Street Journal*, Apr. 23, 1999.

Mistake 40

1. Nassim Nicholas Taleb, *Fooled by Randomness*, New York: Random House, 2008.

Mistake 41

1. Rob Bauer, Rik Frehen, Hurber Lum, and Roger Otten, "The Performance of U.S. Pension Plans," Apr. 3, 2007.
2. Amit Goyal and Sunil Wahal, "The Selection and Termination of Investment Management Firms by Plan Sponsors," May 2005.

Mistake 45

1. John Bogle, *Bogle on Investing*, New York: McGraw-Hill, 2000.
2. Jeremy Siegel, "Big-Cap Tech Stocks Are a Sucker's Bet," *The Wall Street Journal*, Mar. 14, 2000.
3. "Excerpts from the Senate Testimony by Greenspan," *The New York Times*, Feb. 27, 1997.

Mistake 49

1. Javier Estrada, "Black Swans and Market Timing: How Not to Generate Alpha," November 2007.
2. Peter Lynch, "Fear of Crashing," *Worth*, September 1995.
3. Benoit Mandelbrot and Richard Hudson, *The (Mis)Behavior of Markets*, New York: Basic Books, 2004.
4. Jeffrey Laderman, "Market Timing: A Perilous Ploy," *BusinessWeek*, Mar. 9, 1998.
5. Ibid.
6. Warren Buffett, "Berkshire Hathaway Letter to Shareholders," *Berkshire Hathaway*, 1992.
7. Estrada.
8. Woody Allen as quoted in Jonathan Burton, *Investment Titans*, New York: McGraw-Hill, 2000.

Mistake 50

1. William Sherden, *The Fortune Sellers*, New York: Wiley, 1999.
2. Russell Pearlman, "Where to Invest 2008," *SmartMoney*, January 2008.
3. Anne Tergesen, "What the Pros Are Saying," *BusinessWeek*, Dec. 31, 2007.
4. Brian Caulfield, "Shoot to Kill," *Forbes*, Jan. 7, 2008.
5. Steve Forbes as quoted in Virginia Baldwin Hick, "Defying Physics Experts: Economy Will Keep on Rolling," *St. Louis Post-Dispatch*, Oct. 4, 1997.
6. Peter Lynch, *One Up on Wall Street*, New York: Simon & Schuster, 2000.
7. Sherden.

Mistake 52

1. Peter Bernstein, *Against the Gods*, New York: Wiley, 1998.

Mistake 54

1. Ted Cadsby, *The 10 Biggest Investment Mistakes Canadians Make*, Toronto: Stoddart Publishing, 2000.

Mistake 55

1. Roy Williams and Vic Preisser, *Estate Planning for the Post-transition Period*, preview copy, May 2007.
2. Ibid.
3. Ibid.
4. Ibid.
5. Ibid.

Mistake 56

1. Meir Statman as quoted in Nick Murray, *Investment Advisor*, April 1996.

Mistake 57

1. Robert D. Arnott, "What Risk Matters? A Call for Papers!" *Financial Analysts Journal*, May/June 2003.

PART 4

Mistake 58

1. John Ruskin as quoted in Richard M. Titmuss, *Commitment to Welfare*, London: George Allen and Unwin, 1976.

Mistake 59

1. Michael Pompian, *Behavioral Finance and Wealth Management*, Hoboken, NJ: Wiley, 2006.
2. Ibid.

Mistake 60

1. J. Evans and S. H. Archer, "Diversification and the Reduction of Dispersion: An Empirical Analysis," *The Journal of Finance*, December 1968.

2. Lawrence Fisher and James Lorie, "Some Studies of Variability of Returns on Investments in Common Stocks," *Journal of Business*, April 1970.
3. John Campbell, Martin Lettau, Burton Malkiel, and Yexiao Xu, "Have Individual Stocks Become More Volatile? An Empirical Exploration of Idiosyncratic Risk," *The Journal of Finance*, February 2001.
4. "To Sleep Well, Diversify," *In the Vanguard*, Winter 2001.

Mistake 61

1. Eugene Fama and Kenneth French, "The Cross-Section of Expected Returns," *The Journal of Finance*, June 1992.

Mistake 62

1. Travis Sapp and Xuemin (Sterling) Yan, "Security Concentration and Active Fund Management: Do Focused Funds Offer Superior Performance?" *The Financial Review*, February 2008.
2. "Do a Fund's Top 10 Holdings Equal Its Best Ideas?" *Morningstar FundInvestor*, September 2001.

Mistake 66

1. Ken Fisher, "Passive Is Active," *Bloomberg Personal Finance*, April 2000.
2. Ibid.

Mistake 68

1. Meir Statman, *What Investors Really Want*, New York: McGraw-Hill, 2011.

Mistake 69

1. Jeffrey Brown and James Poterba, "The Household Ownership of Variable Annuities," working paper, October 2005.
2. Leslie Scism, "Added Value—and Anxiety—for Variable-Annuity Owners," *The Wall Street Journal*, Feb. 2, 2009.
3. Carolyn T. Geer, "The Great Annuity Rip-Off," *Forbes*, February 1998.
4. Brown and Poterba.
5. William Reichenstein, "Claim That Variable Annuities Usually Beat Mutual Funds Proves Lame: Critique of Huggard's Analysis in

March 1999 Issue of *Financial Planning*," Baylor University, July 24, 2002.

6. Moshe A. Milevsky and Steven E. Posner, "The Titanic Option: Valuation of the Guaranteed Minimum Death Benefit in Variable Annuities and Mutual Funds," *The Journal of Risk and Insurance*, March 2001.
7. Brown and Poterba.
8. Geer.
9. Ibid.
10. Craig McCann and Dengpan Luo, "An Overview of Equity-Indexed Annuities," February 2006.
11. Joan Warner, "EIAs: Behind the Hype," *Financial Planning*, October 2005.

Mistake 70

1. Tim Loughran and Jay Ritter, "The New Issue Puzzle," *Journal of Finance*, March 1995.
2. "Dow Jones Industrial Average Closes above 10,000," *The Wall Street Journal*, Mar. 30, 1999.
3. Ruth Simon, "IPOs over the Internet? Tread Carefully," *The Wall Street Journal*, Feb. 24, 1999.
4. Floyd Norris, "Market Place: A Return to Earth for the Stock Class of 2000," *The New York Times*, Mar. 8, 2001.

Mistake 77

1. Carol Tavris and Elliot Aronson, *Mistakes Were Made (but Not by Me)*, London: Pinter & Martin, 2007, p. 221.

CONCLUSION

1. Ted Cadsby, *The 10 Biggest Investment Mistakes Canadians Make*, Toronto: Stoddart Publishing, 2000.
2. Gary Belsky and Thomas Gilovich, *Why Smart People Make Big Money Mistakes*, New York: Simon & Schuster, 2010.
3. Peter Bernstein as quoted in Jonathan Burton, *Investment Titans*, New York: McGraw-Hill, 2000).
4. Richard Thaler, *The Winner's Curse*, Princeton, NJ: Princeton University Press, 1994.

GLOSSARY

401(k) A defined contribution plan offered by a corporation to its employees that allows employees to set aside tax-deferred income for retirement purposes.

403(b) A retirement plan offered by nonprofit organizations, such as universities and charitable organizations, rather than corporations. Similar to a 401(k) plan.

5 percent/25 percent rule Numerical formula used to determine the need to rebalance a portfolio.

Active management The attempt to uncover securities the market has either undervalued or overvalued; also the attempt to time investment decisions in order to be more heavily invested when the market is rising and less so when the market is falling.

Alpha A measure of performance against a predetermined benchmark. Positive alpha represents outperformance; negative alpha represents underperformance.

Arbitrage The process by which investors exploit the price difference between two exactly alike securities by simultaneously buying one at a lower price and selling the other at a higher price (thereby avoiding risk). This action locks in a risk-free profit for the arbitrageur (person engaging in the arbitrage) and, in an efficient market, eventually brings the prices back into equilibrium.

Asset allocation The process of determining what percentage of assets should be dedicated to which specific asset classes.

Asset class A group of assets with similar risk and reward characteristics. Cash, debt instruments, real estate, and equities are examples of asset classes. Within a general asset class, such as equities, there are more specific classes such as large and small companies and domestic and international companies.

Barra indexes Indexes that divide the three major S&P indexes (400 for mid cap, 500 for large cap, and 600 for small cap) into growth and value categories. The top 50 percent of stocks as ranked by book-to-market value are considered value stocks, and the bottom 50 percent are considered growth stocks. This creates both value and growth indexes for all three S&P indexes.

Basis point The smallest unit of measure used to quote yields. It is equal to 1/100 of 1 percent, or 0.0001.

Benchmark An appropriate standard against which actively managed funds can be judged. Actively managed large-cap growth funds should be judged against a large-cap growth index such as the S&P 500, while small-cap managers should be judged against a small-cap index such as the S&P 600.

Bid-offer spread The difference between the bid and the offer. The bid is the price at which you can sell a security, and the offer is the price you must pay to buy a security. The spread is the difference between the two prices and represents the cost of a round-trip trade (purchase and sale) excluding commissions.

Book-to-market (BtM) ratio The ratio of the book value per share to the market price per share, or book value divided by market capitalization.

Book value An accounting term for the equity of a company. Equity is equal to assets less liabilities; it is often expressed in per-share terms. Book value per share is equal to equity divided by the number of shares.

Call An option contract that gives the holder the right, but not the obligation, to buy a security at a predetermined price on a specific date (European call) or during a specific period (American call).

Center for Research in Security Prices (CRSP) A financial research center at the University of Chicago Graduate School of Business. The CRSP creates and maintains premier historical U.S. databases for stocks (NASDAQ, AMEX, NYSE), indexes, bonds, and mutual funds. These databases are used by leaders in academic and corporate communities for financial, economic, and accounting research.

Churning Excessive trading in a client's account by a broker seeking to maximize commissions, regardless of the client's best interests. Churning is a violation of NASD rules and is illegal.

Closet index fund An actively managed fund whose holdings so closely resemble the holdings of an index fund that investors are unknowingly paying very large fees for minimal differentiation.

Coefficient of correlation A statistical term describing how closely related the price movement of different securities or asset classes is; the higher the coefficient, the more prices move in the same direction.

Compensated risk Risk that cannot be diversified away (e.g., the risk of owning stocks). The market rewards investors for accepting compensated risk with a risk premium (greater expected return) commensurate with the amount of risk accepted.

Concave investing Specifically, the opposite of convex investing. Investors follow a strategy of purchasing yesterday's underperformers (buying low) and selling yesterday's outperformers (selling high).

Convex investing The tendency for individual investors to buy yesterday's top-performing stocks and mutual funds (buying high) and sell yesterday's underperformers (selling low).

Correlation In mathematics, the measure of the linear relationship between two variables. Values can range from +1.00 (perfect positive correlation) to −1.00 (perfect negative correlation). An example of a strong positive correlation would be stocks of two oil companies. A strong negative correlation might exist between an oil company (that benefits from rising oil prices) and an airline company (that benefits from a fall in oil prices).

CPI Consumer price index.

CRSP See *Center for Research in Security Prices.*

Data mining A technique for building predictive models of the real world by discerning patterns in masses of data.

Diamond An exchange-traded fund that replicates the Dow Jones Industrial Index.

Distressed stocks Stocks with high book-to-market values and/or low price-to-earnings ratios. Distressed stocks are generally considered to be value stocks.

DJIA Dow Jones Industrial Average.

EAFE (Europe, Australasia, and Far East) Index Index similar to the S&P 500 Index in that it consists of the stocks of the large companies from the EAFE countries. The stocks within the index are weighted by market capitalization. The index is maintained by Morgan Stanley Capital International. Also known as the *MSCI EAFE Index*.

Efficient market hypothesis (EMH) A hypothesis that markets are "informationally efficient." Prices on traded assets (e.g., stocks, bonds) already reflect all known information and are unbiased in the sense that they reflect the collective beliefs of all investors about future prospects. The EMH states that it is not possible to consistently outperform the market by using any information the market already knows, except through luck.

Emerging markets The capital markets of less developed countries that are beginning to develop characteristics of developed countries, such as higher per capita income. Countries typically included in this category would be Brazil, Mexico, Thailand, and South Korea.

Ex ante Before the fact.

Exchange-traded fund (ETF) A cross between an exchange-listed stock and an open-ended, no-load mutual fund. For practical purposes, ETFs act like open-ended, no-load mutual funds. Like mutual funds, they can be created to represent virtually any index or asset class. Like stocks (but unlike mutual funds), they trade throughout the day.

Expense ratio The operating expenses of a fund expressed as a percentage of total assets. These expenses are subtracted from the investment performance of a fund in order to determine the net return to shareholders.

Ex post After the fact.

Foreign tax credit A credit against U.S. tax for tax due in a foreign country on foreign source income.

Four-factor model Model used to determine differences in the performance between diversified equity portfolios. The differences are best explained by the amount of exposure to the risk of the overall stock market (beta), company size (market capitalization), price (book-to-market ratio) characteristics, and momentum.

Fundamental security analysis The attempt to uncover mispriced securities by focusing on predicting future earnings.

Futures contract An agreement to purchase or sell a specific collection of securities or a physical commodity at a specified price and time in the future. For example, an S&P 500 futures contract represents ownership interest in the S&P 500 Index at a specified price for delivery on a specific date on a particular exchange.

Growth stock A stock trading, relative to the overall market, at a high price-to-earnings ratio (or at a relatively low book-to-market ratio) because the market anticipates rapid earnings growth, relative to the overall market.

Hedge fund A fund that generally has the ability to invest in a wide variety of asset classes. Hedge funds often use leverage in an attempt to increase returns.

I bond A bond that provides both a fixed rate of return and an inflation protection component. The principal value of the bond increases by the total of the fixed rate and the inflation component. The income is deferred for tax purposes until funds are withdrawn from the account holding the bond.

Index fund A passively managed fund that seeks to replicate the performance of a particular index (such as the Wilshire 5000, the S&P 500, or the Russell 2000) by buying all the securities in that index in direct proportion to their weight within that index (by market capitalization).

Initial public offering (IPO) The first offering of a company's stock to the public.

Institutional fund A mutual fund that is not available to individual investors. Typical clients are pension and profit-sharing plans and endowment funds.

Institutional-style fund A mutual fund that is available to individual investors, under certain conditions, such as through registered investment advisors. These advisors require their clients to commit to the same type of disciplined, long-term, buy-and-hold strategy that is characteristic of institutional investors.

Investment pandering Advice on market or securities values that is designed to titillate, stimulate, and excite you into action but has no basis in reality.

Investment policy statement (IPS) Statement that provides the investor's financial goals and the strategies that will be employed to achieve them. Specific information on matters such as asset allocation, risk tolerance, and liquidity requirements should be included in the IPS.

Investment pornography Extreme examples of investment pandering.

Kurtosis The degree to which exceptional values, much larger or smaller than the average, occur more frequently (high kurtosis) or less frequently (low kurtosis) than in a normal (bell-shaped) distribution. High kurtosis results in exceptional values that are called *fat tails*. Low kurtosis results in *thin tails*.

Leverage The use of debt to increase the amount of assets that can be acquired, for example, to buy stock. Leverage increases the riskiness of a portfolio.

Loser's game A game in which, while it is not impossible to win, the odds of winning are so low that it does not pay to play.

Market-cap weighting Determining the ownership of individual stocks by their percentage of market capitalization relative to all market capitalization of all stocks within an index or other benchmark. An index fund's holdings are market-cap weighted, not equally weighted.

Market capitalization The market price per share times the number of shares.

Mean-variance analysis The process of identifying optimal mean-variance portfolios, that is, portfolios with the highest expected return among all portfolios with the same variance (or standard deviation), or equivalently, portfolios with the lowest variance (or standard deviation) among all portfolios with the same expected return.

Microcaps The smallest stocks by market capitalization: the ninth and tenth CRSP deciles. Other definitions used are the smallest 5 percent of stocks and stocks with a market capitalization of less than about $200 million.

Modern portfolio theory (MPT) A body of academic work founded on the following concepts. First, markets are too efficient to allow returns in excess of the market's overall rate of return to be achieved through trading systems. Active management is therefore counterproductive. Second, asset classes can be expected to achieve, over sustained periods, returns that are commensurate with their level of risk. Riskier asset classes, such as small companies and value companies, will produce higher returns as compensation for their higher risk. Third, diversification across asset classes can increase returns and reduce risk. For any given level of risk, a portfolio can be constructed that will produce the highest expected return. Finally, there is no right portfolio for every investor. Each investor must choose an asset allocation that results in a portfolio with an acceptable level of risk.

Mortgage-backed security (MBS) A financial instrument representing an interest in assets that are mortgage related (either commercial or residential).

MPT See *modern portfolio theory.*

MSCI EAFE Index See *EAFE Index.*

NAIC National Association of Investment Clubs.

NASD National Association of Securities Dealers.

NASDQ or NASDAQ The National Association of Securities (Automated) Quotations. A computerized marketplace in which securities are traded; frequently called the *over-the-counter market.*

NASDAQ 100 Index The 100 largest capitalization stocks on that exchange.

NAV Net asset value.

Negative correlation Relationship between assets where one tends to experience above-average returns when the other tends to experience below-average returns, and vice versa.

No-load fund A mutual fund that does not impose any charge for purchases or sales.

Nominal returns Returns that have not been adjusted for the negative impact of inflation.

NYSE New York Stock Exchange.

Out of sample Data from a study covering different time periods or different geographical regions from the original study.

Passive asset class funds Funds that buy and hold all securities within a particular asset class. The weighting of each security within the fund is typically equal to its weighting, by market capitalization, within the asset class. Each security is then typically held until it no longer fits the definition of the asset class to which the fund is seeking exposure. For example, a small company might grow into a large company and then no longer fit within the small company asset class. Fund managers may also use common sense and research to implement screens to eliminate certain securities from consideration (in an attempt to improve risk-adjusted returns). To be considered a passive fund, however, those screens cannot be based on any technical or fundamental security analysis. Examples of passive screens would be minimum market capitalization, minimum number of years of operating history, and minimum number of market makers in the company stock.

Passive management A buy-and-hold investment strategy, specifically contrary to active management. Characteristics of the passive management approach include lower portfolio turnover, lower operating expenses and transaction costs, greater tax efficiency, full investment at all times, and a long-term perspective.

Price-to-earnings (P/E) ratio The ratio of stock price to earnings. Stocks with high P/E ratios (relative to the overall market) are considered growth stocks. Stocks with low P/E ratios (relative to the overall market) are considered value stocks.

Prudent investor rule A doctrine embedded within the American legal code stating that a person responsible for the management of someone else's assets must manage those assets in a manner appropriate to the financial circumstance and tolerance for risk of the investor.

Put An option contract that gives the holder the right, but not the obligation, to sell a security at a predetermined price on a specific date (European put) or during a specific period (American put).

Qubes (QQQ) An exchange-traded fund that tracks the NASDAQ 100 Index.

Real estate investment trust (REIT) A security that sells like stock on the major exchanges and invests in real estate directly, through either properties or mortgages. Equity REITs invest in and own properties. Mortgage REITs loan money for mortgages to owners of real estate or purchase existing mortgages or mortgage-backed securities. Their revenues are generated primarily by the interest they earn on the mortgage loans.

Real returns Returns that reflect purchasing power because they are adjusted for the effect of inflation.

Rebalancing The process of restoring a portfolio to its original asset allocation. Rebalancing can be accomplished either through adding newly investable funds or by selling portions of the best-performing asset classes and using the proceeds to purchase additional amounts of the underperforming asset classes.

Registered investment advisor (RIA) A firm registered with the appropriate national (SEC) or state regulators with advisors who have passed the required exams. RIA is not an accredited professional designation.

Retail funds Mutual funds that are sold to the general public, as opposed to institutional investors.

Risk premium The higher expected, not guaranteed, return for accepting the possibility of a negative outcome.

ROA Return on assets.

Russell 2000 The smallest 2,000 of the largest 3,000 stocks within the Russell Index. Generally used as a benchmark for small-cap stocks.

S&P 400 Index A market-cap weighted index of 400 mid-cap stocks.

S&P 500 Index A market-cap weighted index of 500 of the largest U.S. stocks designed to cover a broad and representative sampling of industries.

S&P 600 Index A market-cap weighted index of 600 small-cap stocks.

SEC Securities and Exchange Commission.

Sharpe ratio A measure of the return earned above the rate of return earned on riskless short-term U.S. Treasury bills relative to the risk taken, with risk being defined as the standard deviation of returns. *Example:* The return earned on an asset was 10 percent. The rate of 1-month Treasury bills was 4 percent. The standard deviation was 20 percent. The Sharpe ratio would be equal to 10 percent minus 4 percent (6 percent) divided by 20 percent, or 0.3.

Short selling Borrowing a security for the purpose of immediately selling it, with the expectation that the investor will be able to buy the security back at a later date at a lower price.

Skewness A measure of the asymmetry of a distribution. Negative skewness occurs when the values to the left of (less than) the mean are fewer but *farther* from the mean than are the values to the right of the mean. For example, the return series of –30 percent, 5 percent, 10 percent, and 15 percent has a mean of 0 percent. There is only one return less than zero percent, and three higher; but the one that is negative is much farther from zero than the positive ones. Positive skewness occurs when the values to the right of (more than) the mean are fewer but *farther* from the mean than are the values to the left of the mean.

Spiders (SPDRs) Exchange-traded funds that replicate the various Standard & Poor's indexes.

Standard deviation A measure of volatility, or risk. For example, given a portfolio with a 12 percent annualized return and an 11 percent standard deviation, an investor can expect that in 13 out of 20 annual periods (about two-thirds of the time) the return on that portfolio will fall within one standard deviation, or between 1 percent (12 percent – 11 percent) and 23 percent (12 percent + 11 percent). The remaining one-third of the time an investor should expect the annual return will fall outside the 1 to 23 percent range. Two standard deviations (11 percent × 2) would account for 95 percent (19 out of 20) of the periods. The range of expected returns would be between –10 percent (12 percent – 22 percent) and 34 percent (12 percent + 22 percent). The greater the standard deviation, the greater the volatility of a portfolio. Standard deviation can be measured for varying time periods—e.g., you can have a monthly standard deviation or an annualized standard deviation measuring the volatility for a given time frame.

Style drift Movement away from the original asset allocation of a portfolio, either by purchasing securities outside the particular asset class a fund represents or by not rebalancing to adjust for significant differences in performance of the various asset classes within a portfolio.

Systematic risk Risk that cannot be diversified away. The market must reward investors for taking systematic risk, or they would not take it. That reward is in the form of a risk premium, a higher *expected* return than could be earned by investing in a less risky instrument.

Tactical asset allocation (TAA) The attempt to outperform a benchmark by actively shifting the portfolio's exposure to various asset classes (the portfolio's asset allocation).

TIPS See *Treasury inflation-protected security.*

Tracking error The amount by which the performance of a fund differs from the appropriate index or benchmark. More generally, when referring to a whole portfolio, the amount by which the performance of the portfolio differs from a widely accepted benchmark, such as the S&P 500 Index or the Wilshire 5000 Index.

Transparency The extent to which pricing information for a security is readily available to the general public.

Treasury inflation-protected security (TIPS) A bond that receives a fixed stated rate of return, but also increases its principal by the changes in the consumer price index. Its fixed-interest payment is calculated on the inflated principal, which is eventually repaid at maturity.

Turnover The trading activity of a fund as it sells securities from a portfolio and replaces them with new ones. Assume that a fund began the year with a portfolio of $100 million in various securities. If the fund sold $50 million of the original securities and replaced them with $50 million of new securities, it would have a turnover rate of 50 percent.

Uncompensated risk Risk that can be diversified away (e.g., the risk of owning a single stock or sector of the market). Since the risk can be diversified away, investors are not rewarded with a risk premium (higher expected return) for accepting this type of risk. Also called *unsystematic risk.*

Value stocks Stocks of companies that have relatively low price-to-earnings ratios or relatively high book-to-market ratios. These are considered the opposite of growth stocks.

Variable annuity An investment product with an insurance component. Taxes are deferred until funds are withdrawn.

Volatility The standard deviation of the change in value of a financial instrument within a specific time horizon. It is often used to quantify the risk of the instrument over that time period. Volatility is typically expressed in annualized terms.

Winner's game A game in which the odds of winning are reasonably high and the prize of winning is commensurate with the risk of playing.

ACKNOWLEDGMENTS

No book is ever the work of one person or in this case two. This book is no exception. We both would like to thank the principals at Buckingham Asset Management and BAM Advisor Services: Adam Birenbaum, Ernest Clark, Madaline Creehan, Bob Gellman, Ed Goldberg, Joe Goldberg, Mont Levy, Steve Lourie, Vladimir Masek, Al Sears, Bert Schweizer III, and Brenda Witt for their support and encouragement.

We also thank Sam Fleischman, our agent, for all his efforts.

And finally, Larry would like to thank the love of his life, his wife, Mona, for her tremendous support and understanding for the lost weekends and many nights that he sat at the computer well into the early morning hours. She has always provided whatever support was needed, and then some. Walking through life with her has truly been a gracious experience.

RC would like to thank his wonderful family for providing all their love and encouragement over the years and for putting up with him even on vacations as he still spent hours working away at his computer.

Index

ABOUT THE AUTHORS

Larry Swedroe is the bestselling author of The Only Guide series and other successful investment guides. He writes the blog "Wise Investing" for CBS MoneyWatch.com and speaks frequently at financial conferences. He is also a principal and Director of Research for The Buckingham Family of Financial Services, which includes Buckingham Asset Management and BAM Advisor Services. In addition, he has held executive-level positions at Prudential Home Mortgage, Citicorp, and CBS.

RC Balaban is a former journalist and currently the media specialist for The Buckingham Family of Financial Services, which includes Buckingham Asset Management and BAM Advisor Services.